Build your business drawing skills for effective communication at work

VISUAL WORKING

Buro BRAND
Den Haag, The Netherlands
info@burobrand.nl
www.burobrand.nl

Author Willemien Brand
with essential input from:
Georgette Pars
Mahana Tuimaka

BIS Publishers
Borneostraat 80 A, 1094 CP Amsterdam, The Netherlands
T +31 (0)20 515 02 30
bis@bispublishers.com
www.bispublishers.com

ISBN 978 90 636 9677 1

1st printing

Build your business drawing skills for effective communication at work

VISUAL WORKING

Willemien Brand

BIS PUBLISHERS

TABLE OF CONTENTS

PART 2

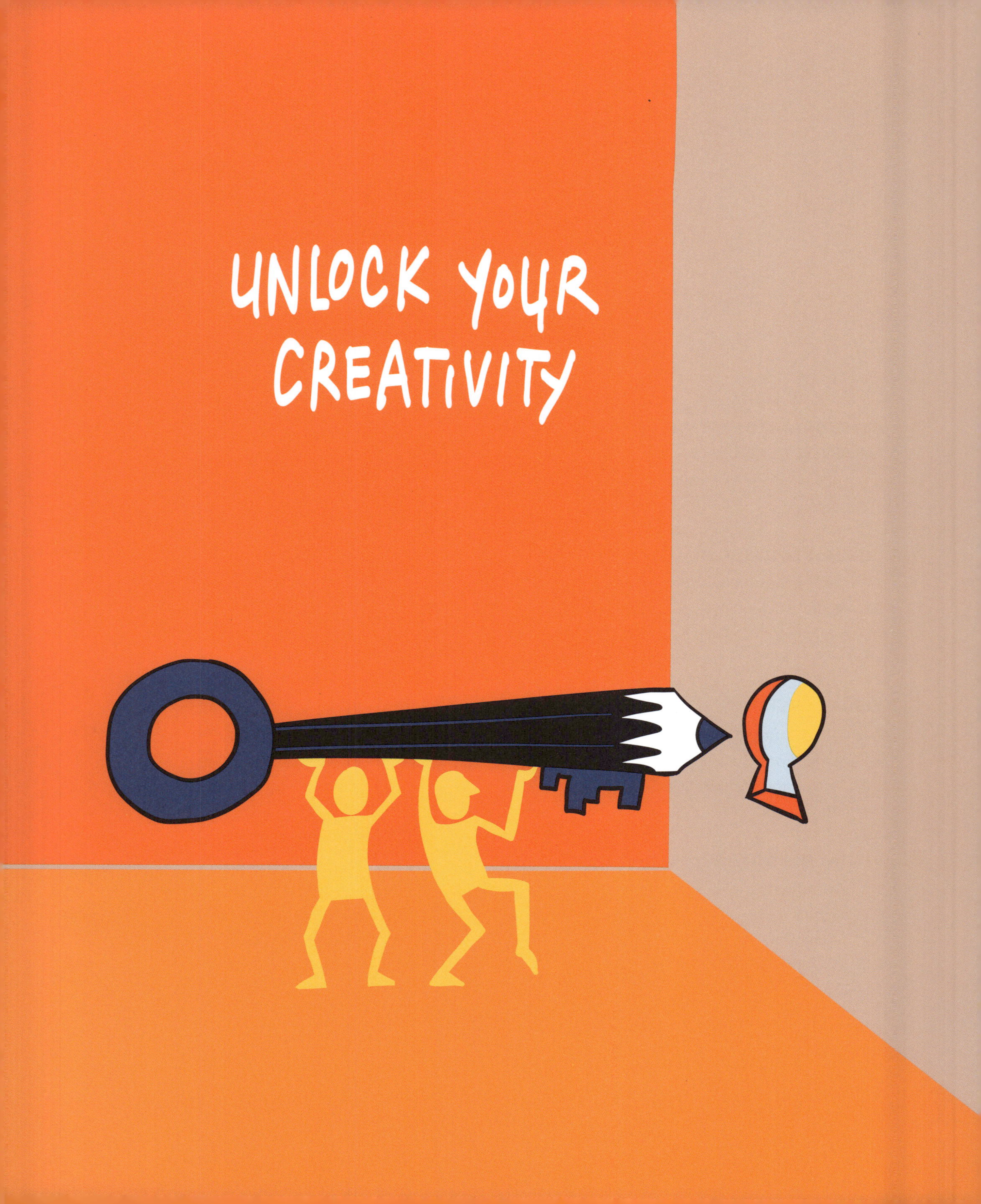
UNLOCK YOUR
CREATIVITY

1. INTRODUCTION

If you have this book in your hands (and obviously you do), that means you want to start (or continue) drawing and see how Visual Working can enhance your work.

When I founded Buro BRAND, Visual Thinking was almost unheard of. But we've come a long way since then. In this book, we will not only focus on setting out and practicing the basics of Visual Thinking, we will also bridge the gap between being able to draw and being able to put those skills to work in business settings.

Our previous books, Visual Thinking and Visual Doing, focus more on the implementation of Visual Thinking. They give you tips, tools and inspiration to use it personally, in teams, or for organizations. This book can be seen as a prequel, where we take a step back and help you with the actual drawing skills you need to conquer the world visually.

What do you need to start this book?
A positive frame of mind, a nice place to work and your favorite drawing materials. Anything will do! We still use our favorite tools of the trade; chisel points, black and gray markers and beautiful pencils with bright colors. (See chapter 2.1 for more about materials.)

We also challenge you to share your work with your colleagues/clients/co-workers. Ask if it resonates or if they get completely different ideas from it. That's when it really gets interesting! Do try it!

We believe there is a Visual Thinker in everyone! We would love to see your work, so feel free to share it with us on Instagram or LinkedIn!

Have fun & enjoy your skills!
Willemien Brand

WHAT YOU WILL LEARN

1.1 The power of Visual Thinking
1.2 The Visual Thinking fundamentals
1.3 How to use this book

1.1 THE POWER OF VISUAL THINKING

Drawing is used for a number of reasons: to present a technical product design, artistic purposes, to convey an idea. Or you can use drawings to communicate more effectively.

In this book we focus on exactly that: how do you use drawing to effectively communicate in a business environment?

What makes drawing such an important skill to have?
So why is drawing such an important skill? We distinguish three major reasons:

---

1 The first reason is our visual brain.

Our brains are wired visually. Visual information has been essential for our survival as a species and the parts of the brain that process it have been evolving longer than we have been using spoken or written language. That's why drawing is still an essential tool in communicating ideas and driving change.

2 Second: it's underused.

Though we are all by nature 'Visual Thinkers', it is a skill that rarely gets the attention it deserves. Our education system focuses mainly on developing spoken and written language skills. These are obviously very important, but schools generally neglect a large and incredibly rich area of communication: Visual Communication.

3 Third and last, it stands out.

Closely related to the previous point is that we live in an "information-heavy age" where attention spans are extremely short. Nowadays, you have to do ever more to stand out from the crowd. You have to surprise people and stimulate their imagination. And using visuals in your communication is a great way of doing exactly that. It is time to unleash our visual power. Not only in a passive, but in an active way, together with speaking and writing. So you can reach your goals, communicate better and work more effectively.

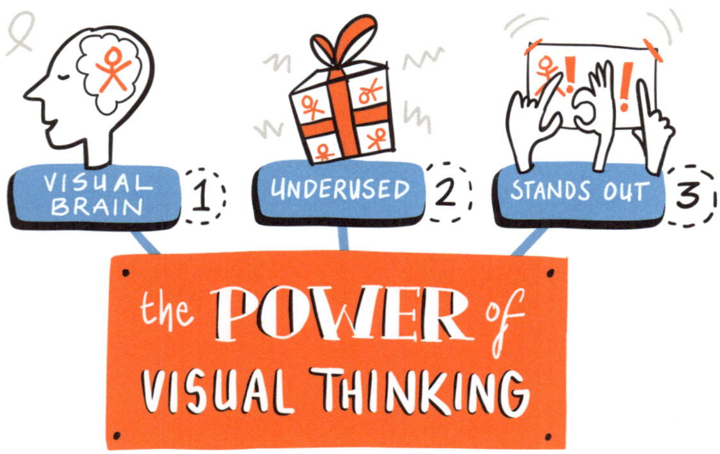

the IMPACT of VISUAL THINKING

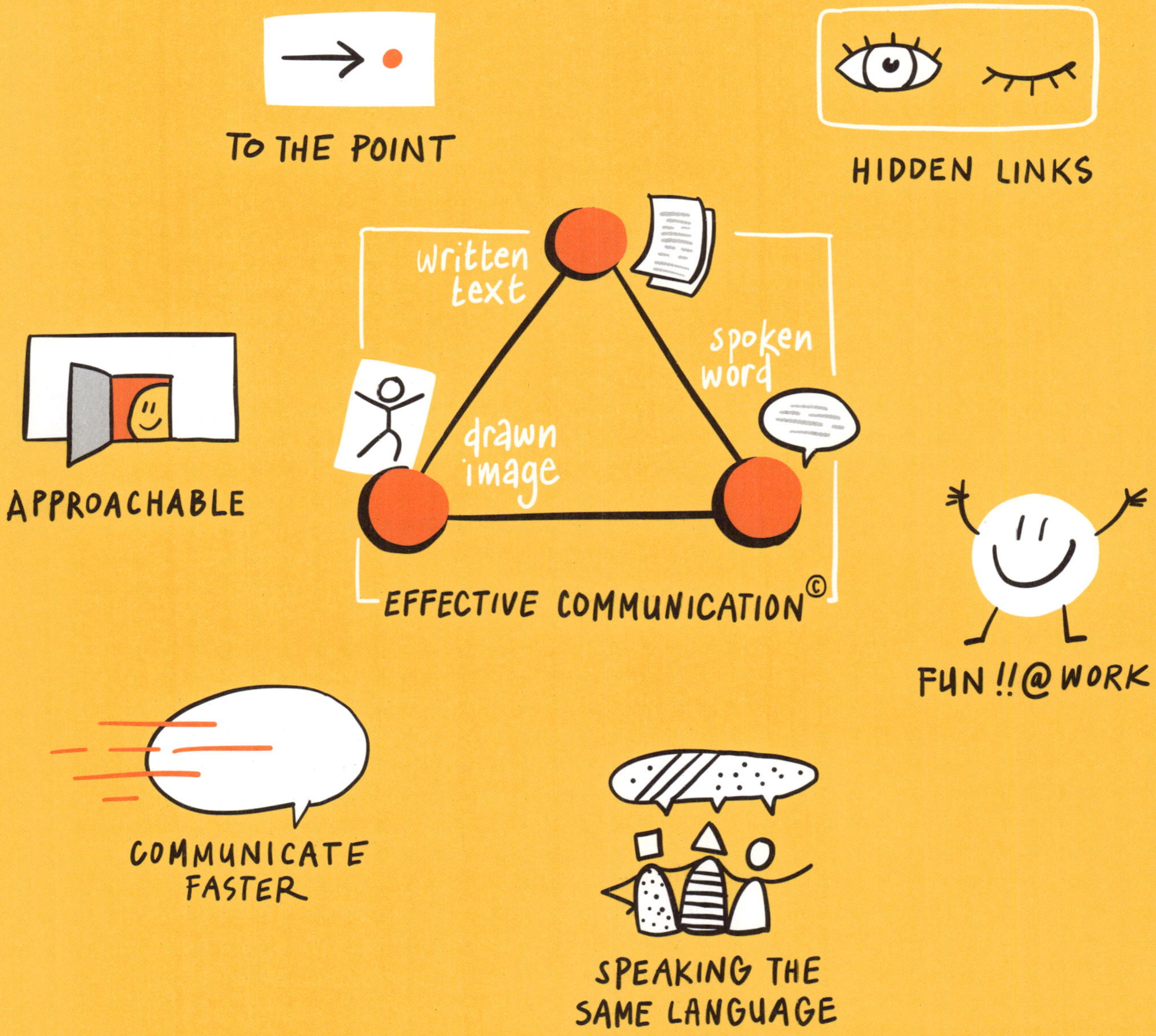

1.2 THE VISUAL THINKING FUNDAMENTALS

Using Visual Thinking in your work is about more than just drawing. We found that you need to develop four key skills in order to use Visual Thinking successfully.

They are: courage, creativity, drawing skills and a sense of understanding of the possibilities and power of Visual Thinking.

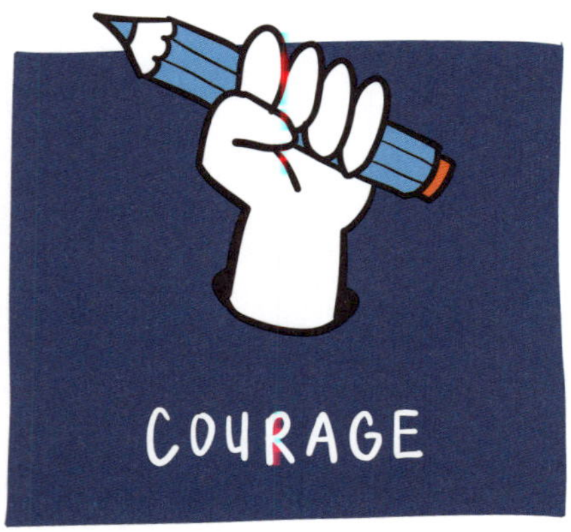

First of all, you must be courageous!
We all know it's difficult to start doing something new and unfamiliar. You might be worried about what others think, worried about your own skills, worried about failing. But to start this journey, you need to open yourself up to change and dare to do something different and new that's outside your comfort zone.
Everyone can start with one courageous step. Actually, you already took that step when opening this book, so you can be proud of yourself!

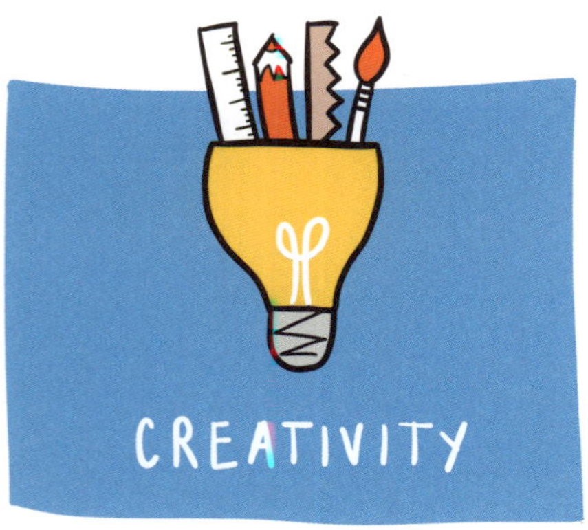

This one you probably expected: creativity. But not necessarily in the way that you'd expect. Creativity is more than making a beautiful painting, piece of music or poem. Creativity also lies in discovering new patterns and connections. Looking at something in a different way.
Being inspired and working from one iteration to the next. In Dutch we say, "Looking beyond your nose", and not just focusing on the obvious. We know for a fact that everyone is creative. It is a skill that anybody can train and develop.

Next to these fundamentals we have created a model that embraces all the possible usages of Visual Thinking. This powerful framework will help you choose which direction you want your visual thinking journey to take. We call it: the Buro BRAND's Five Visual Thinking Types©.

This is a great guide to help you plan your own visual journey. And it is also a useful tool to identify areas of your Visual Thinking you want to develop even further.

We will dive into these types from chapter 6 onwards.

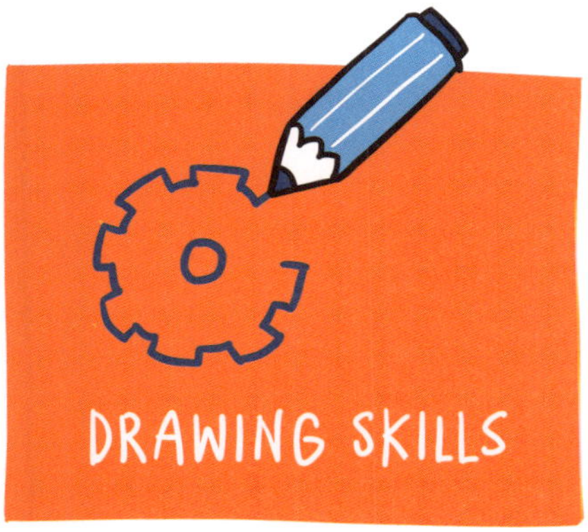

Obviously, being able to draw well is important. When communicating visually, you need some knowledge of basic shapes, icons, figures and interactions. By practicing this often enough, you train your muscle memory and it will become easier and easier.
Visual Thinking can also be applied without drawing, but in this book, we focus on drawing (mostly figuratively). So grab your marker and paper!

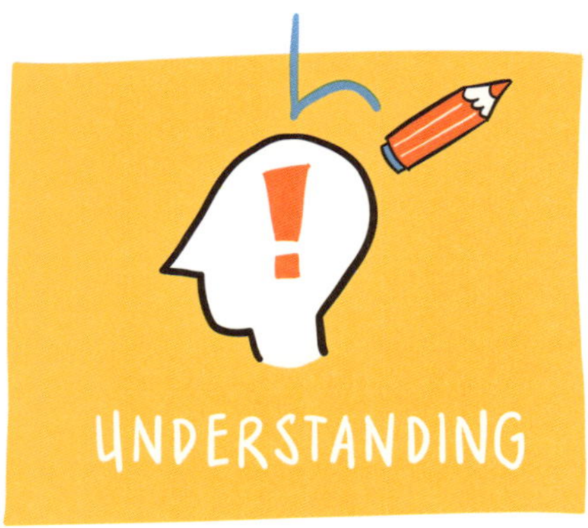

Lastly, you need to develop understanding. Understanding of the power of Visual Thinking. Understanding of the possibilities. And understanding of the moments and settings when it's most effectively applied. When you start to see this, you will start to get more and more ideas on how to apply it in your own situation.
Perhaps you'll even discover ways that we haven't thought of yet!

1.3 HOW TO USE THIS BOOK

This book consists of two parts. In part 1 we give you the confidence to draw. With both theory and a lot of practical assignments you gain the skills needed to express yourself visually.

In part 2 we dive into the Buro BRAND's Five Visual Thinking Types©. We give you examples and inspiration how to implement and use Visual Thinking in business settings as well as more assignments to practice these more specialized skills.

In this second part, the chapters all end with a bigger assignment where we invite you to take your drawings out of this book into the real world.

LEGEND

If you see dotted or squared paper, that's where you can make your own drawings!

Here, written in these colored areas you find assignments that you can do in this (work)book

Sometimes instead of dots and squares, we drew a frame to indicate were you may draw!

TIP Feel free to draw outside-the-box and anywhere you like in this book!

MORE HELP

Combine this book with our e-learnings: 1+1=3

From our experience as trainers in Visual Thinking, we know how powerful it is to see people draw things and to be able to copy their movements when learning to draw.

That's why we created two e-learnings that serve as the perfect companions for this book! In over 50 short videos our Visual Thinking experts explain and show you the ins and outs of Visual Working.

Why you do not want to miss this:

- Step-by-step we show you the ropes with lots of practice, demos, examples and more in-depth explanations.
- The e-learnings follow the same structure as this book, with a video for each paragraph. The part one e-learning matches chapter 2 until 5, and the part two e-learning matches chapter 6 until 12. Together they add up to more than 50 videos!
- Fun is always guaranteed with our Buro BRAND trainers!

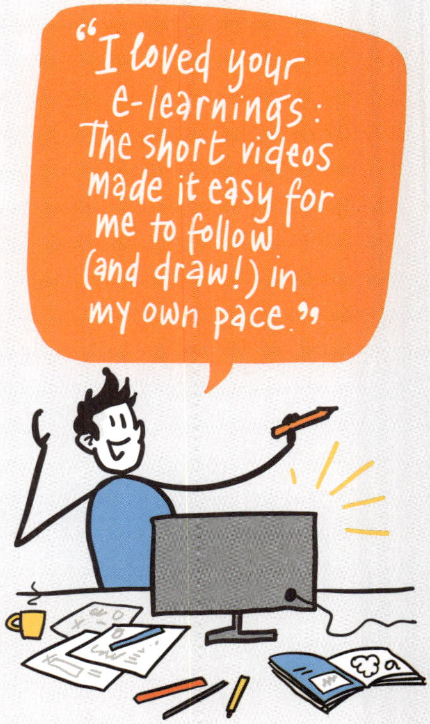

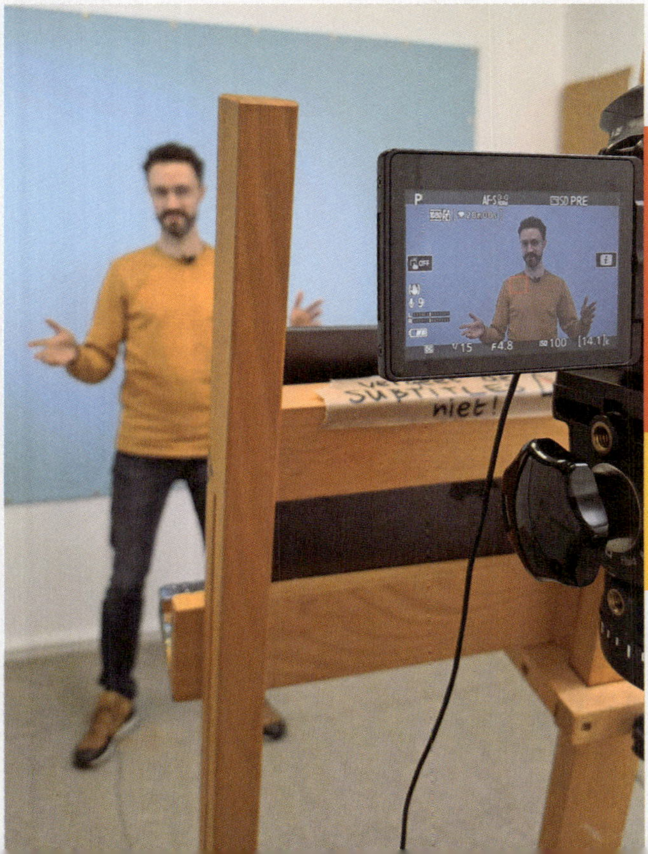

Follow our e-learning to enhance your skills

visualthinkingacademy.burobrand.nl

Use code "visualworking10" for a 10% discount!

PLAY!

BY ~~THE RULES~~

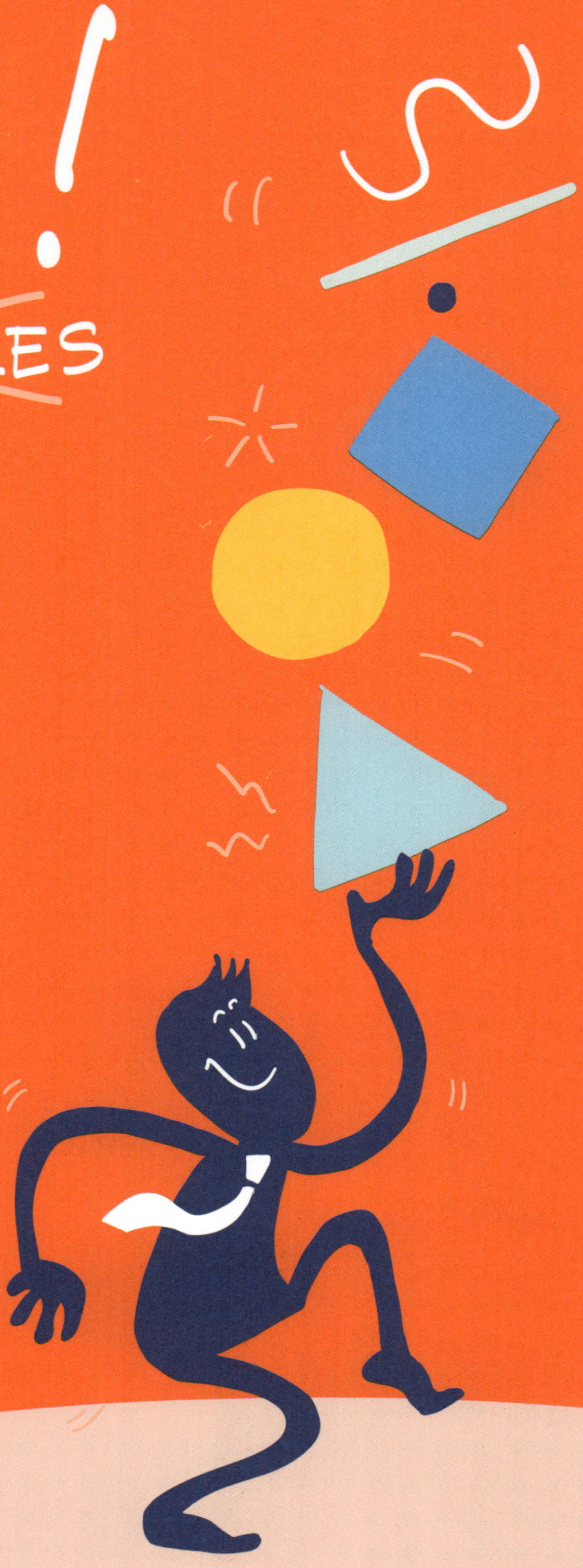

2. BASIC RULES AND SHAPES

Without knowing some of the underlying principles of drawing and visual communication you can only progress so far. We think that what we tell, show and practice in this chapter are the most important rules and principles.

The cornerstone is the notion that we visualize to communicate. There is always another party involved (even if it's just 'future you'). To seduce this other party into looking at what you made, you may want it to look good but, more importantly, you want to be clear in the 'reading' direction of the information. To help them understand and interpret the information, you want to present it as clearly and legibly as possible. To not unnecessarily add to their cognitive load.

In this chapter we will talk about the materials we use, and how visual hierarchy, visual articulation and shadows can help with interpreting a visual. And finally we'll look atbasic shapes and why those are a good foundation for effective communication.

WHAT YOU WILL LEARN

2.1 Materials
2.2 Visual articulation and hierarchy
2.3 Shadows
2.4 Basic shapes
2.5 Effective communication

2.1 MATERIALS

Drawing materials are fun! We usually work with a combination of black and gray markers, and some coloured ones for a bit of extra pop. We will give you a few suggestions that work for us. And don't forget; this book is to work IN. Don't be afraid to fill the blank sections. Just start!

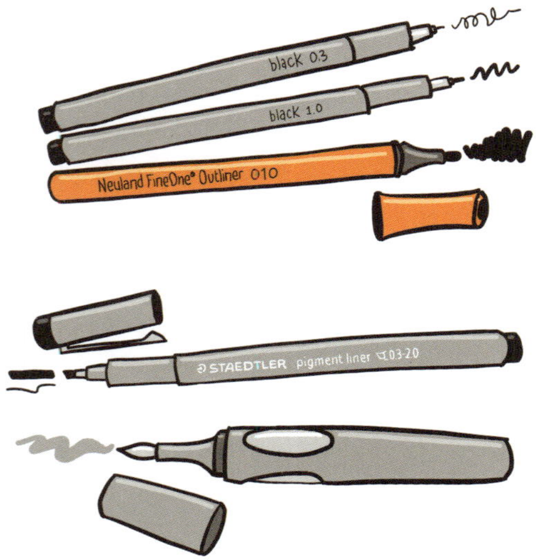

Give them a try

TIP Use a variety of markers. Get familiar with what each one does and figure out what works for you.

BLACK

You need some thin markers for this book. We will start with black ones as they form the base of our drawings. You need them in two or three different thicknesses.

We recommend the following black pens:

- Any fineliner of 0,3 mm
- Any fineliner of 1 mm

We are fans of chisel tip markers like the Steadler 1-3 mm fineliner. Try drawing some lines. One as thick as possible, one as thin as possible. Draw the thickest line by dragging the broader side of the marker across the paper. For the thinnest line, use only the corner of the marker. Et voila; one pen, two lines with two different thicknesses.

Why use so many different black markers? Well... when all lines are one thickness – and one color – the drawing becomes what we call doodle soup! Because everything looks equally important, your brain can't easily distinguish one part from another. That means it takes a bit of mental effort to 'read' the drawing. People don't want to feel like they have to work to understand the message. Some might even give up. That's the opposite of what you want!

Get to know your materials. Grab your markers and some paper. Play around until you find a combination that suits you best! When you copy or redraw on bigger sheets of paper, for example a flipover for a presentation, use bigger pens/markers. That way, even people sitting at the back of the room can see what you're doing.

TIP Switch things up by using a pastel color or even a highlighter instead of a gray marker.

GRAY

You could argue that gray isn't a color. But we love a good gray for sketching, shadowing and for 'less important' elements. This pen has a brush tip. There isn't really a reason why the others are chisel tips and this one is a brush. We just want to show you that there are more options. You can draw different thicknesses with this marker as well.

COLORS

Now you can choose your colors. We usually focus on two colors that complement each other. Which do you prefer? If you need to use more colors, then I'd advise you to pick a range that are in the same color scheme.
So, for example, a range of blues or greens. And perhaps one extra contrasting color. Two colors are plenty. The more color, the more it looks like a child's drawing. The colors will distract from, rather than contribute to, clear communication.

THE WHOLE SET

Just keep in mind that the set that we'll use are black, gray and two colors. You are free to vary with different pens and markers, depending on what's available in your area.

2.2 VISUAL ARTICULATION AND HIERARCHY

ARTICULATION

Visual Articulation is similar to regular articulation. When you talk in public: you want to speak clearly, come across confident and pick the right words so your message really sinks in with the audience. The same applies when we write. We want to write good coherent sentences with proper grammar and understandable language.

The same counts for making understandable drawings.
Let's make sure we also articulate when drawing.

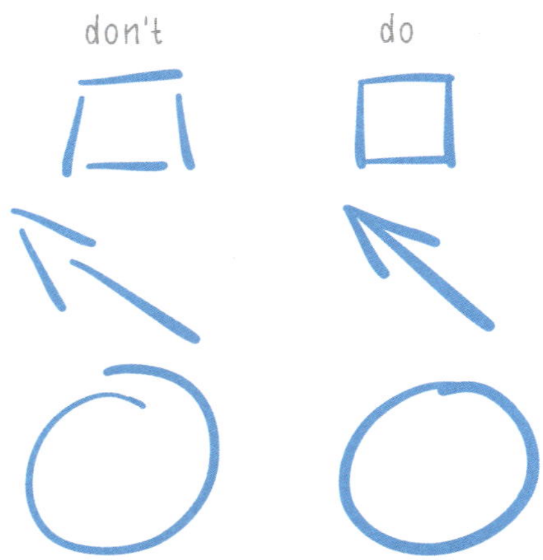

How do you do that? You achieve that by making neat and closed shapes; squares and circles. The quickest way to achieve this, is to always take half a second longer than you would usually do. Even if you're in a hurry or you're live drawing something in front of a group. You always can take that half a second.

Draw a textballoon and arrow for yourself, and take the time to articulate the shapes!

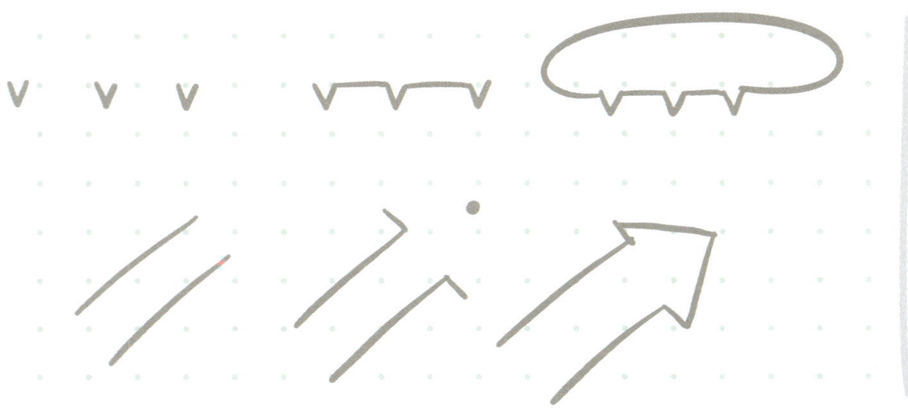

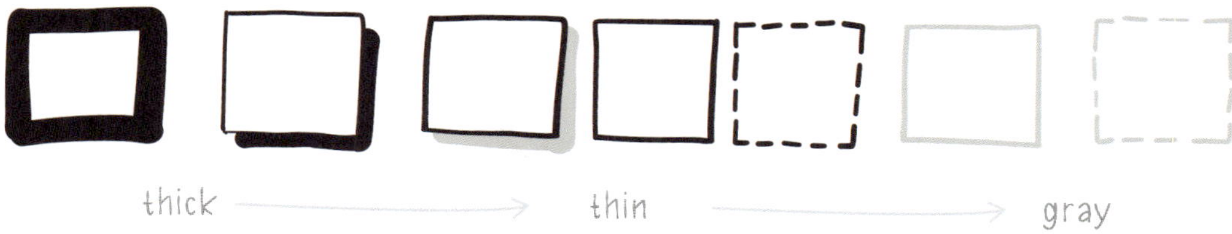

HIERARCHY

To grab and hold your audience's attention you have to create a clearly structured and compelling picture. Balance visual elements and organize them neatly so your audience isn't put off because something 'doesn't feel right' and they don't know where to look. A big help in guiding people through your drawing is the use of visual hierarchy.
Use thick black lines for the main story (the key message) and use thinner lines or even gray (dotted) lines for the secondary layers of information.

Think of how a newspaper is organized. A big, bold headline grabs your attention. Sub-headings break up the main text to quickly draw you into the story. Cursive texts highlight specific quotes and information. Smaller text drills down into the details. This is visual hierarchy.

WEIGHT

Let's consider weight as a tool that can help you create balance. Giving 'weight' to different elements creates an easily readable visual hierarchy. Elements which are smaller, have thin lines or light colors. They feel less heavy and attract less attention.
Big, crowded and dark elements feel heavier and grab your attention immediately.

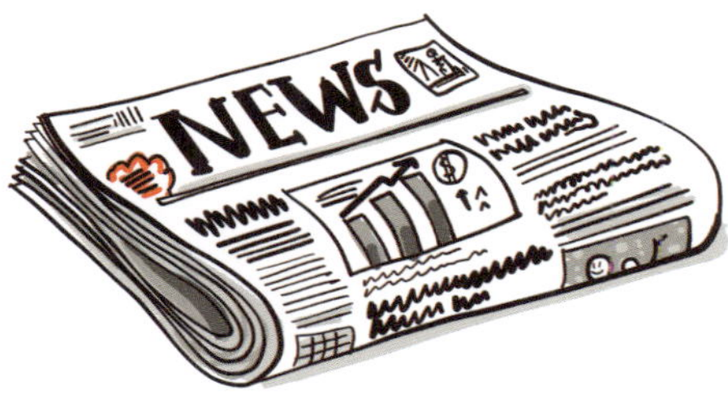

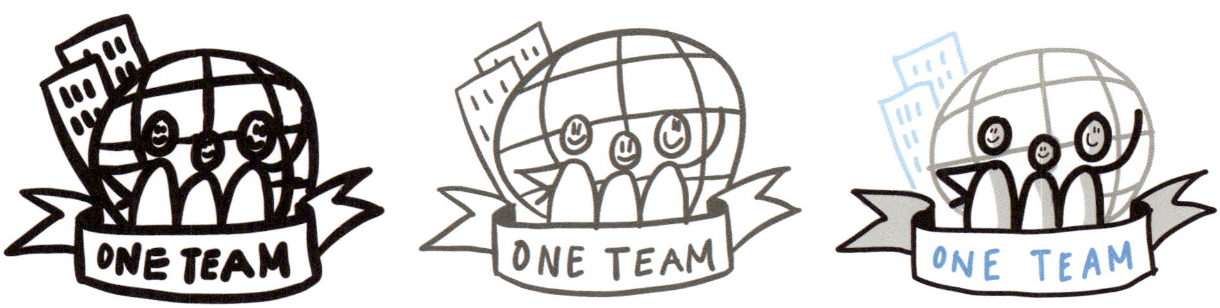

TIP Combine heavy and lighter elements to create a visual hierarchy

HIERARCHY WITHIN YOUR ICON

When making a drawing, there will be some elements that you want to stand out, and others that are supporting details. Here you see the effect of using only thick black, or only thin gray. You want to make it clear to your audience what the most important part of your visual is, and what the details are. Or at least you want to create contrast between the elements. So use thicker, darker colors for important elements, with gray and light colors for less important parts.

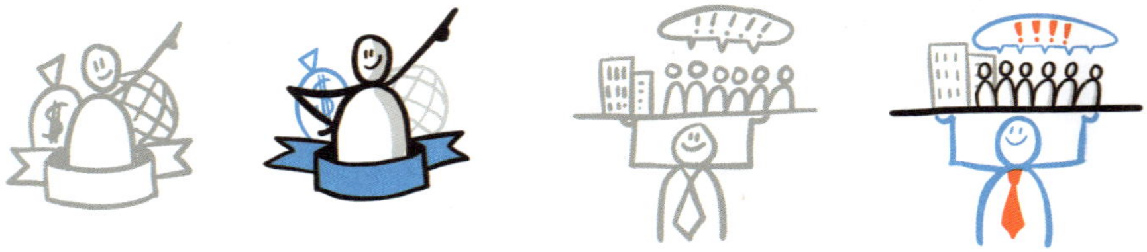

Use a black, gray and colored marker to manipulate the drawings below and create a visual hierarchy within your icon. (Some lines are allowed to stay gray!) You will see how you instantly create a more dynamic, clear and engaging drawing.

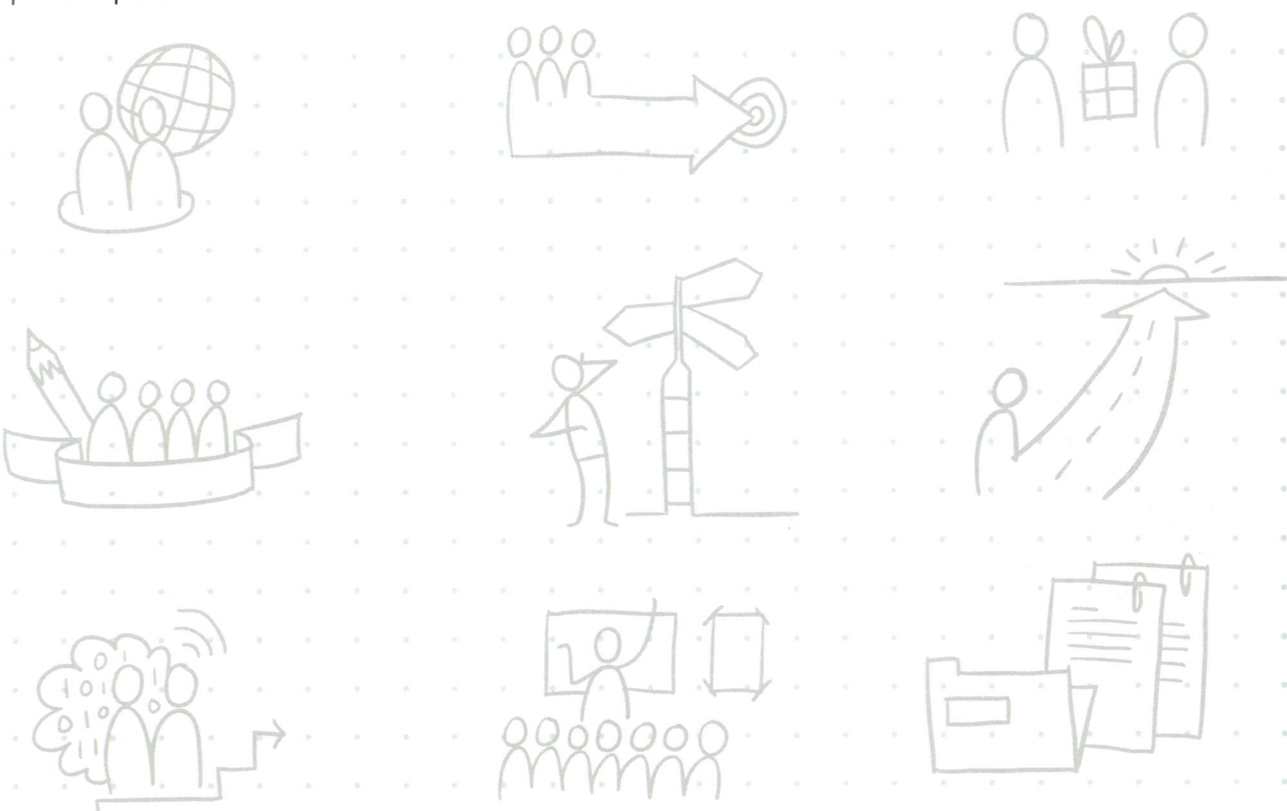

Combine the following icons with the gray icons below to tell and enrich a story yourself! There are multiple combinations possible, depending on what you want to show. Add them to the gray icons and create a clear hierarchy!

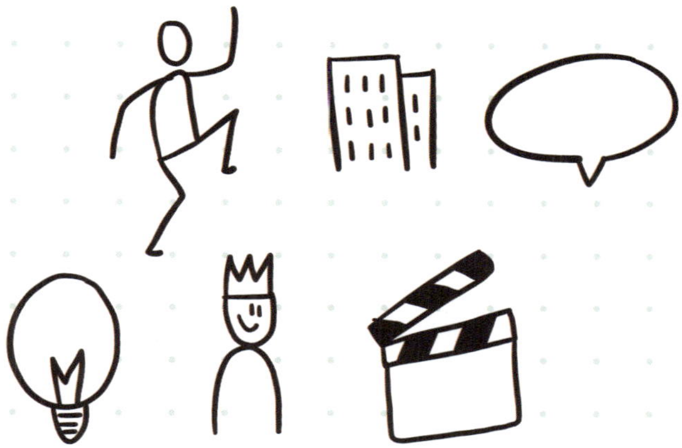

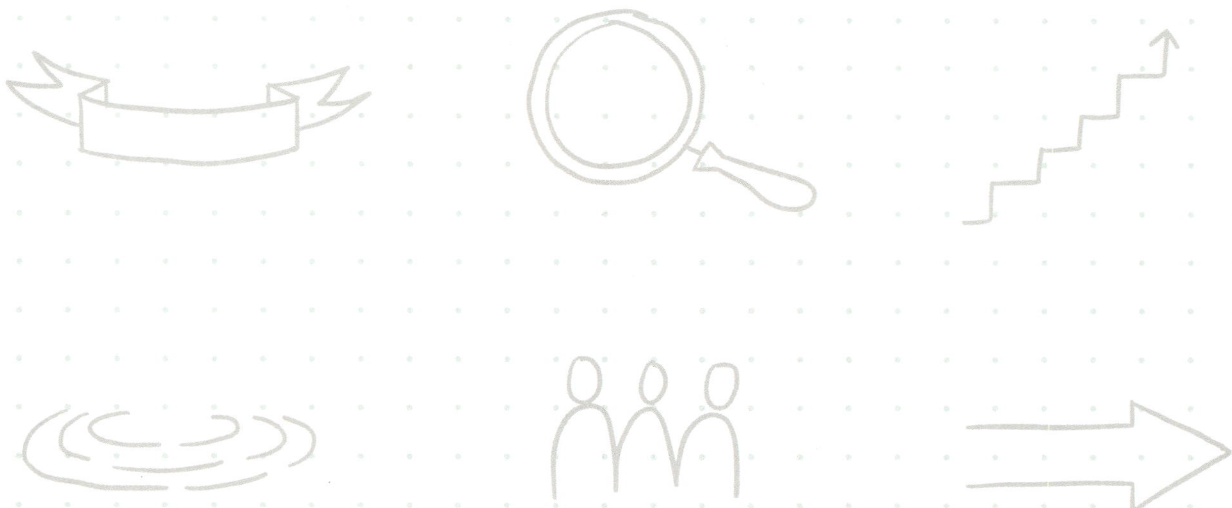

thick over thin lines | black over gray | color

TIP Variation! Both in thickness and in color, helps people distinguish between the different parts within a drawing and therefore, "read" it with less effort.

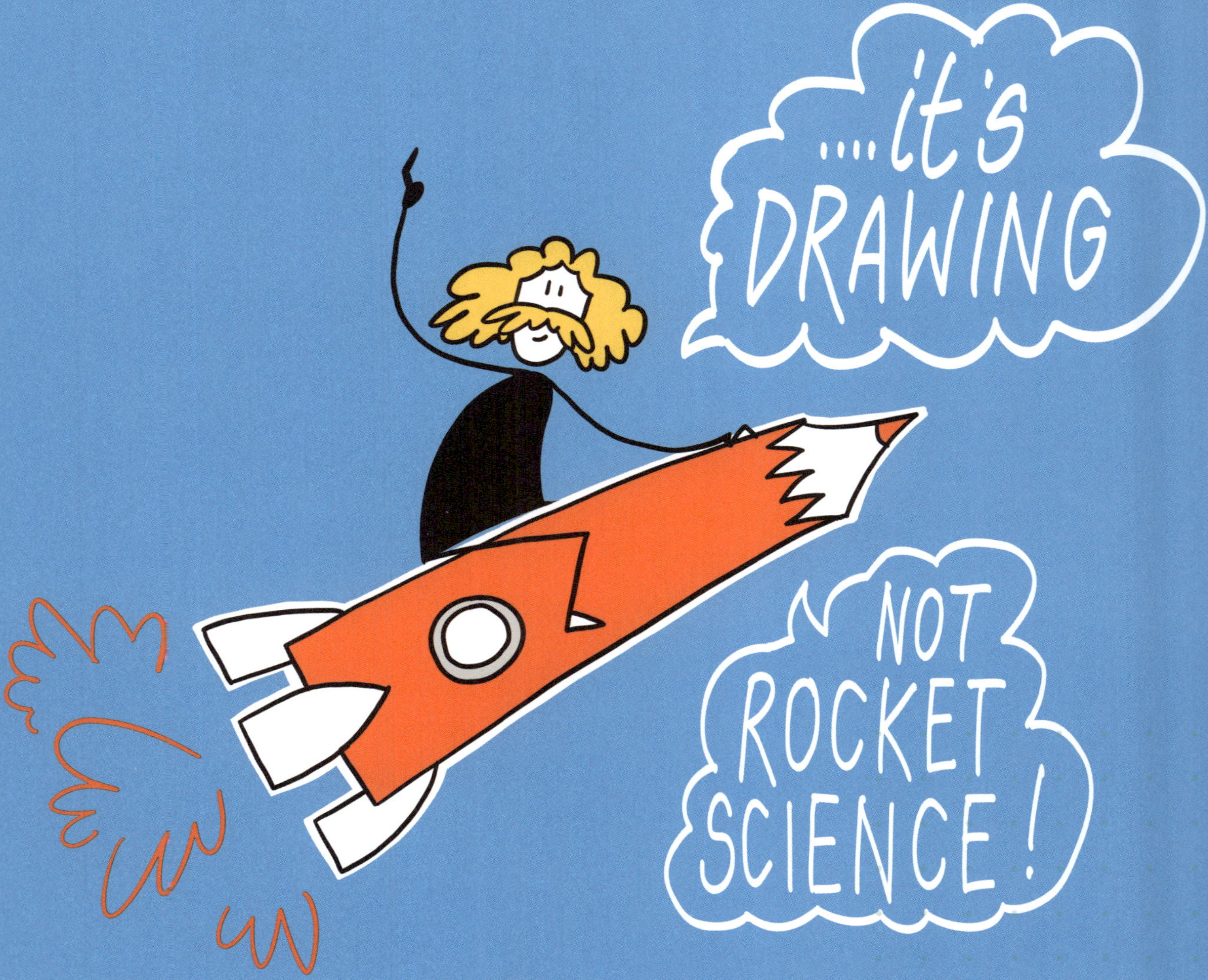
....it's DRAWING
NOT ROCKET SCIENCE!

2.3 SHADOWS

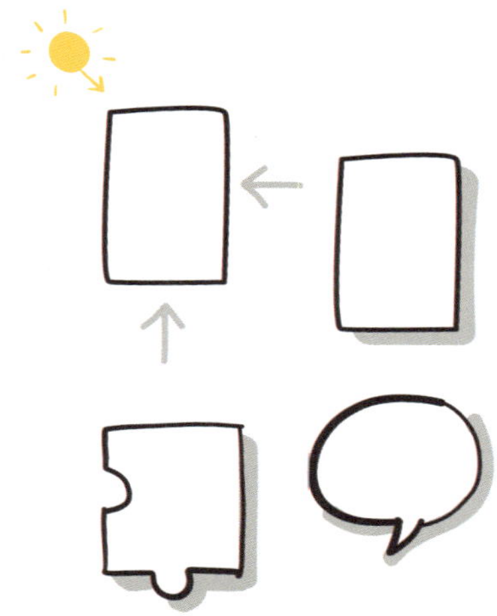

Shadow makes your drawing richer, clearer and more dynamic. Having trouble figuring out which side your shadow should go? Our rule of thumb is to consistently draw the shadow on one side – we use the right side but it could also be left – of the object and possibly also underneath. There needs to be a compelling reason to break this rule, such as a drawing with a whole bunch of lightbulbs!

We're not too worried about how exactly the light falls on an object. We're not trying to emulate Rembrandt! We're drawing to communicate and elaborate, so the shadow doesn't have to be completely correct.

TIP You can use gray or a nice pastel color for your shadow. A light highlight marker also works well!

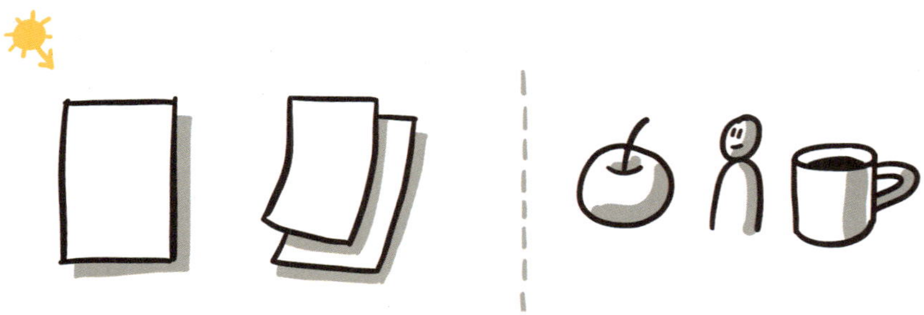

With static objects that have 'flatter' surfaces, such as paper, boxes and rectangular shapes, we usually draw the shadow behind it. With people, apples and other 3D and rounded shapes we always draw shadow on the 'inside' to emphasize the roundness.

Add shadows to the icons you see here. Be aware, they are not all as straightforward as they might seem.

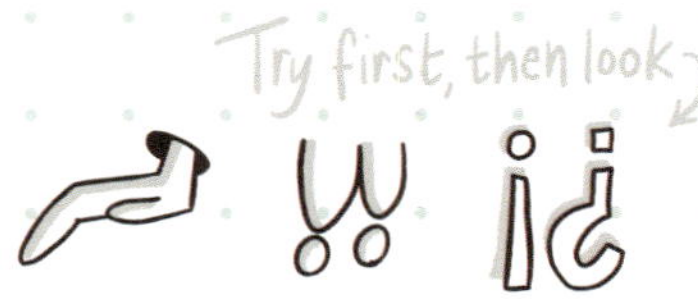

2.4 BASIC SHAPES

We all learned the alphabet and how to write as children. Now you can use those same basic skills as building blocks for drawing! This idea comes from the author Martin Haussmann. For example, if you take the letters U, Z, M, O, you can already draw a basic icon, the lightbulb! By resizing, rotating and combining them, we can create a recognizable object. If you ever have to convince somebody they can draw too, just let them write UZMO!

How easy it would be, if you could just learn a simple visual alphabet, so you could draw anything you wanted? Well you can! There are actually multiple visual alphabets around the world. The one we use is our six-piece Basic Shape Alphabet.

Repeat drawing each shape to get the hang of your newly found alphabet. You can also stretch the shapes, or cut them in half.

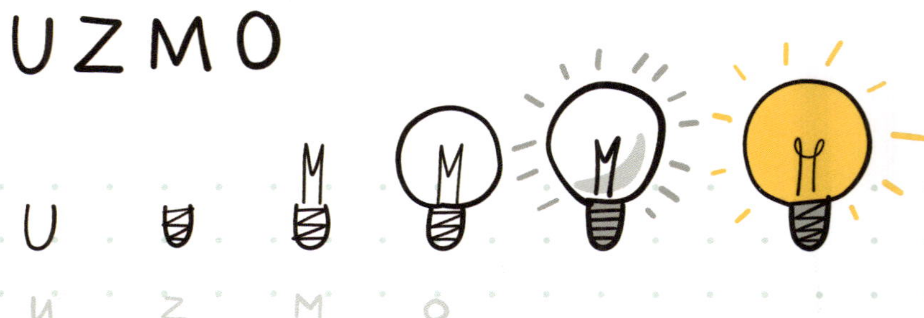

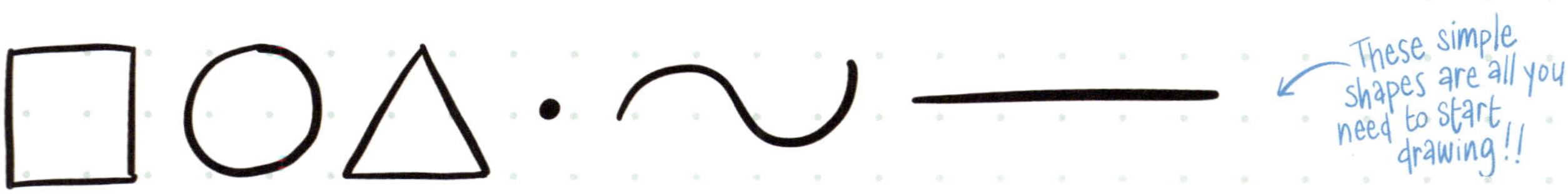

Let's do the visual math. As soon as you start seeing objects as combinations of basic shapes – or letters – drawing becomes a whole lot easier. If you can break down objects and images into basic shapes, you can draw almost anything.

We're starting with the basic shapes here and show you what you can make with only a few shapes. It's not rocket science, it's just: visual mathematics.

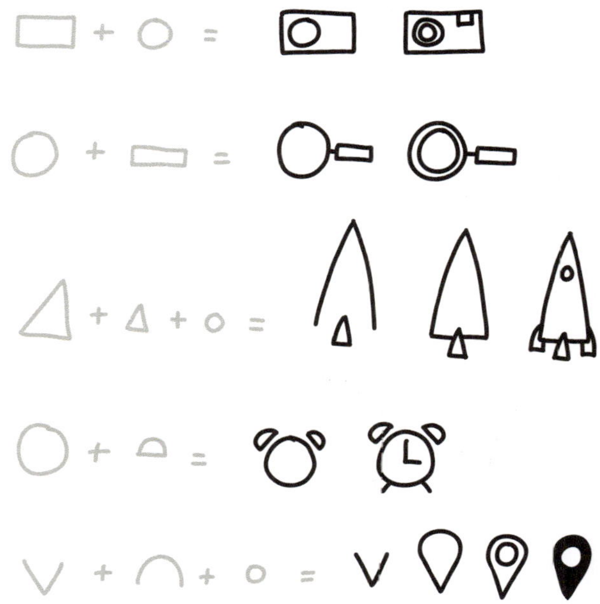

Now you do the visual math! What do you get when you combine a triangle with a circle? Draw your combination here!

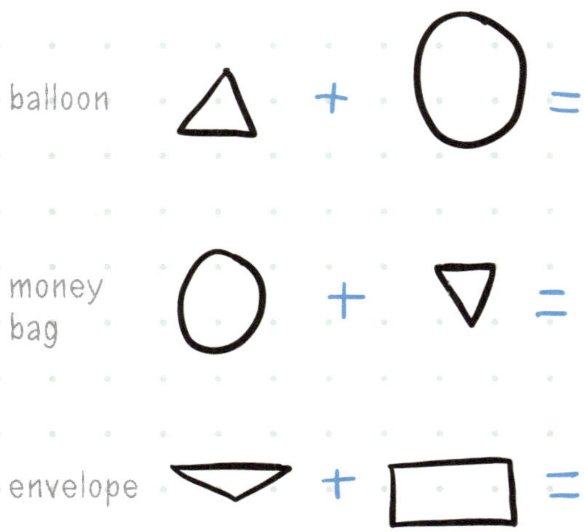

TIP Feel free to use color!

2.5 EFFECTIVE COMMUNICATION

Usually, when you want to draw something for the first time, you look it up and copy what you see, whether it's an actual object, a picture or something in your imagination. So let's try that!

Ignore everything we just told you about basic shapes and try to copy this fish as beautifully and realistically as possible! Take 2 minutes max.

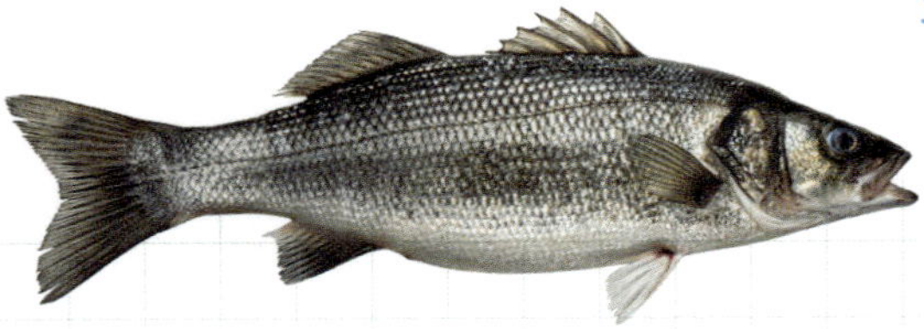

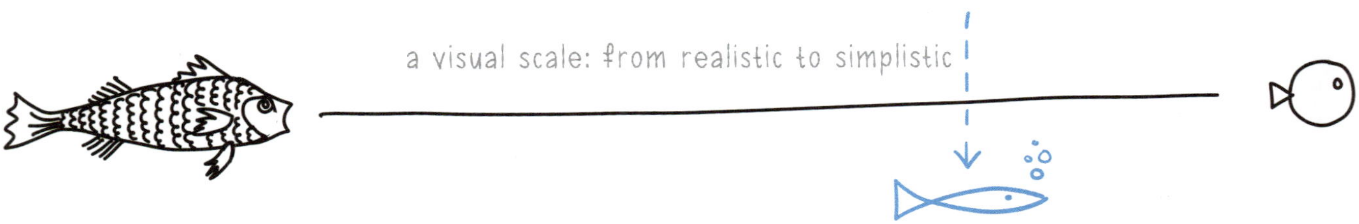

Whenever I have to draw something realistically it generally takes far more time than I want and I obsess over every tiny detail. I end up believing I can't really draw. Sound familiar?

If you want to communicate that you're talking about a fish, you can draw a fish with all its life-like fishy features. But why make it hard when you could simply draw it as a circle, triangle and a dot for the eye?

Now if we were to ask random people in the street what this super simple drawing represents, I think most would guess it's a fish. A more realistic depiction will be instantly recognizable, but it takes a lot more time to draw.

Since the goal is to communicate 'a fish', we want to draw exactly enough for people to immediately understand it's a fish. So, we

Let's simplify the pictures on the right. Make it as simple as possible, but ensure it is definitely recognizable. Use the basic shapes we learned in the previous chapter!

TIP Look up icons in our My Icon Library book.

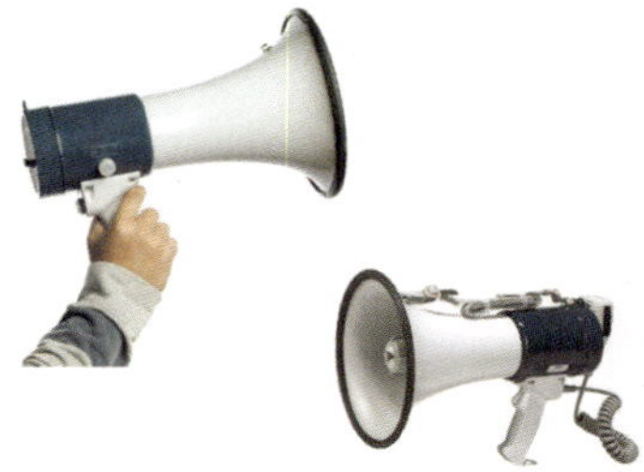

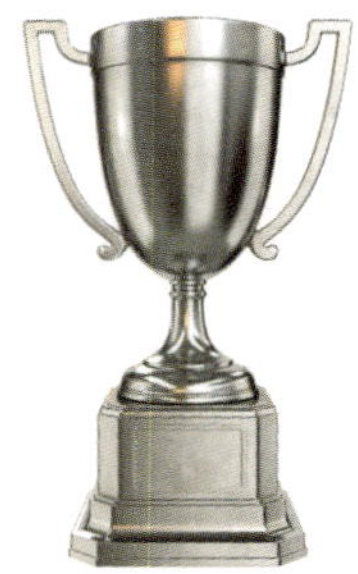

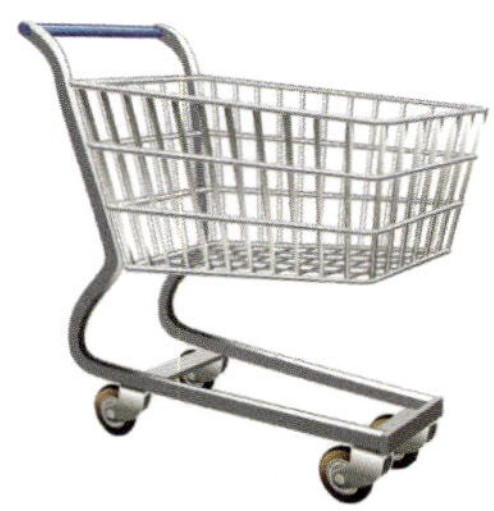

want to add a bit more detail to this fish, but still keep it simple and quick to draw.

The shape of a fish is something we all have etched into our memory. Now you've seen how easy drawing can be, don't ever say you can't draw! You can absolutely draw for communication purposes, using simple and clean drawings based on basic shapes.

TIP Check out our e-learning to see what we focus on when drawing these visuals.

EMBRACE YOUR OWN STYLE

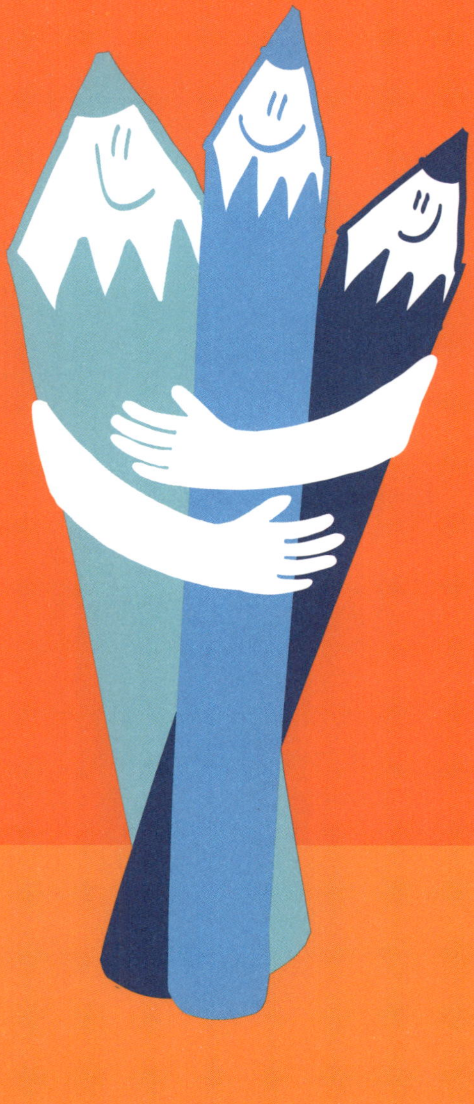

3. DRAWING PEOPLE

A lot of people never got past the stick figure way of drawing people. Some are convinced that they can't draw something more human-like, and the fear of not being able to draw often comes from drawing people.

With only a small adjustment to the stick figure, you can actually draw quite decent people to help you tell your story. We think it is very important to practice drawing people. For one, because it really helps with people's confidence about their drawing skills. Secondly, drawing people is a great tool to make things personal and to show not only facts and information, but also behavior and emotion.

In this chapter we will focus on the face first and practice emotion and interaction. We look at comic books and how they use speech bubbles to let people say or think something. Now you can draw entire scenes of people doing something. Finally we practice drawing the entire body, in different poses. And how you can quickly draw multiple people.

Get familiar with drawing people in all sorts of (business) settings. Make this style your own, or develop your own personal style.

WHAT YOU WILL LEARN

3.1 Emotion
3.2 Interaction
3.3 Speech bubbles
3.4 Drawing a scene
3.5 The entire body
3.6 Poses
3.7 Multiple people

3.1 EMOTION

When you are drawing people, you want to be able to express how they feel. You only need a few lines to tell a story!

Look at the angry and mean/evil faces below. A tiny change – flipping the mouth – can have a huge impact!

Mix and match the eyebrows and mouths to create different facial expressions below. When you've created a new facial expression, don't forget to name it!

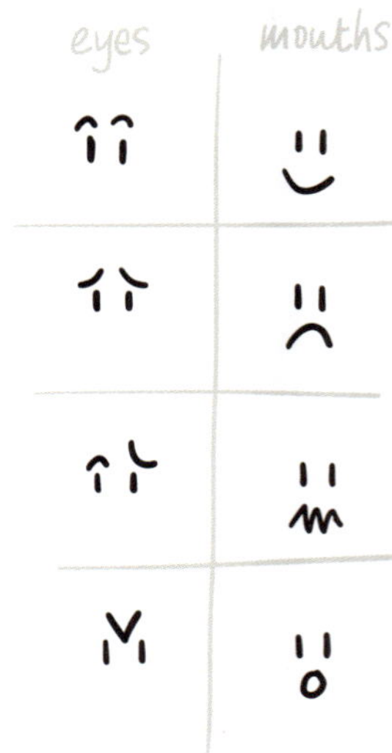

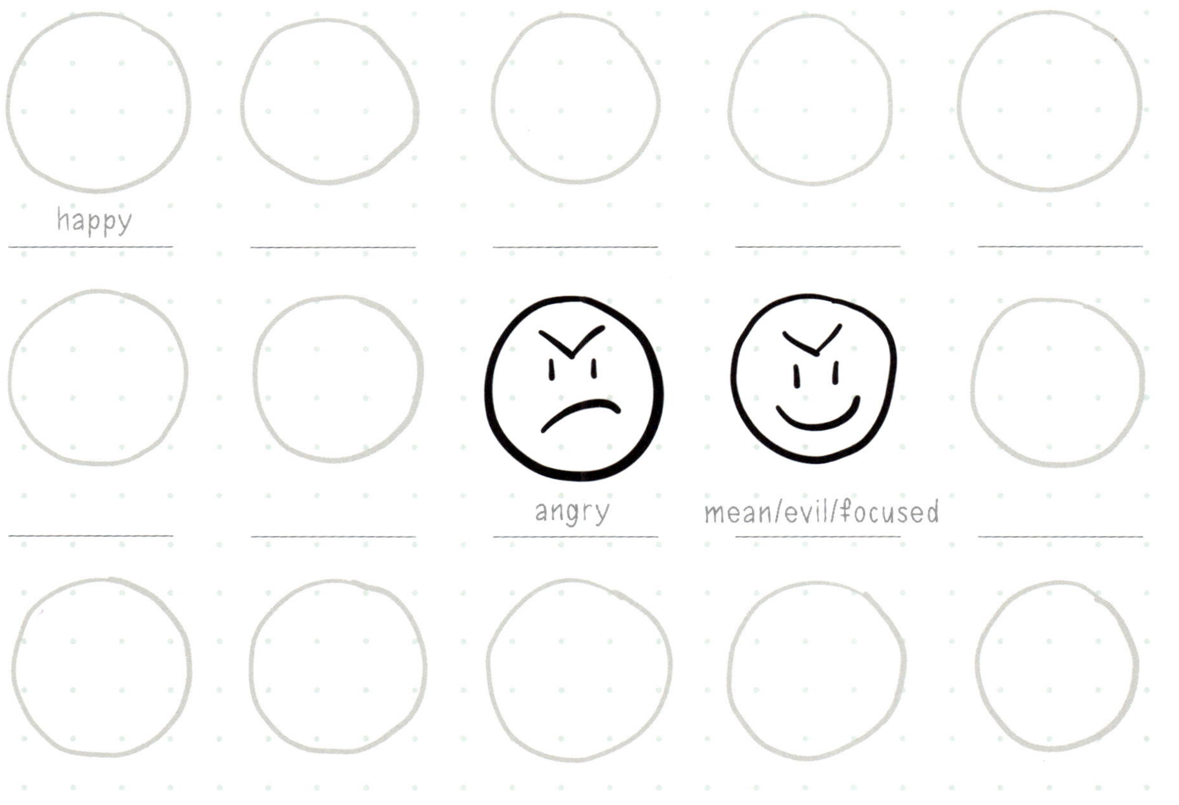

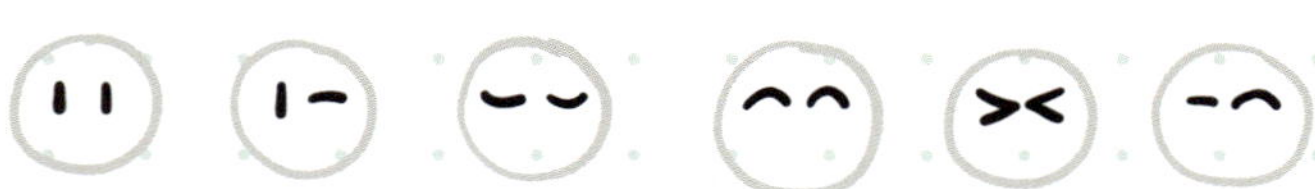

TIP Yes, you can sometimes use other shapes for eyes. Just look at the emojis on your phone for inspiration!

3.2 INTERACTION

Now we know how to draw emotion, it's also useful to know how to direct it. So let's create new interactions by positioning the eyes in different ways.

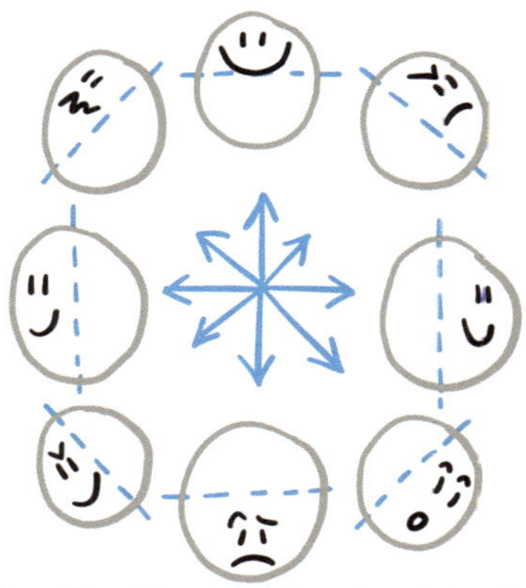

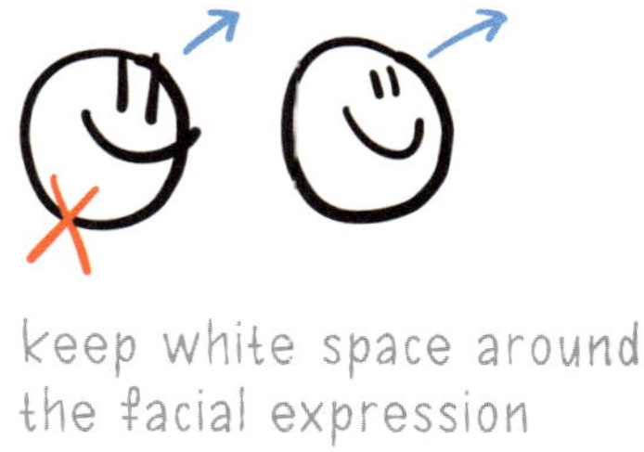

All the faces are looking at the lightbulb. Fill in the faces (eyes and mouth) looking in the right direction.

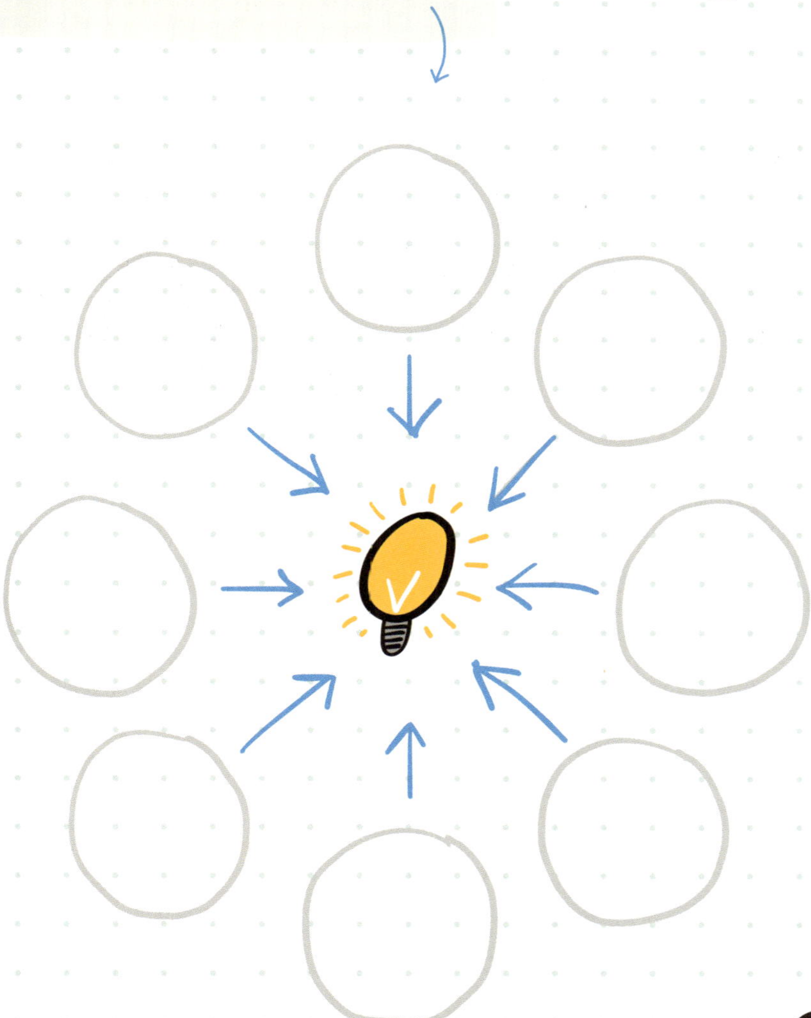

How are you feeling? Let's try drawing the following emotions in the empty outlines. Add whatever you need, but make sure the faces look in the right direction to interact and express the emotion. If you're not happy, just try again! You could also add icons, speech balloons or expression lines to amplify feelings (or come back later to add these once you've practiced them on the following pages).

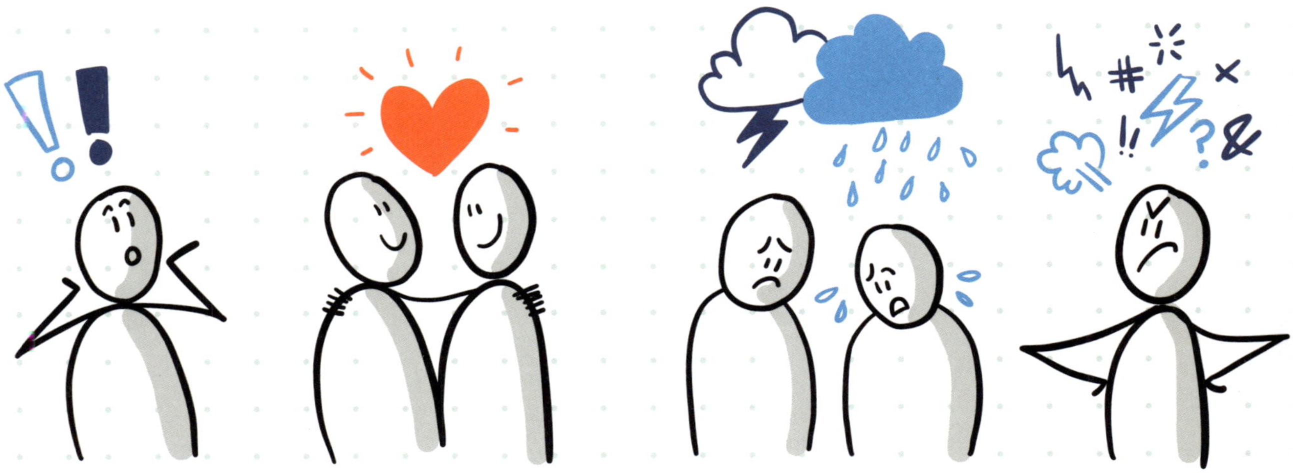

surprised   so in love   sad and crying   very angry

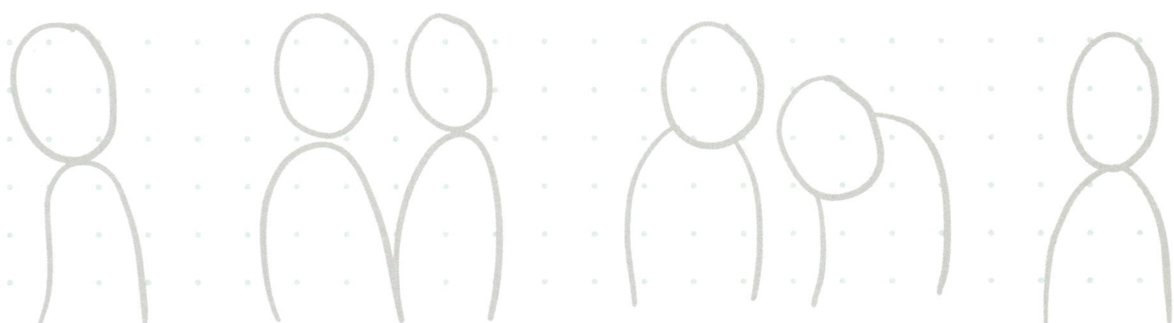

surprised   so in love   sad and crying   very angry

Complete the drawing so it matches with the prompt underneath.

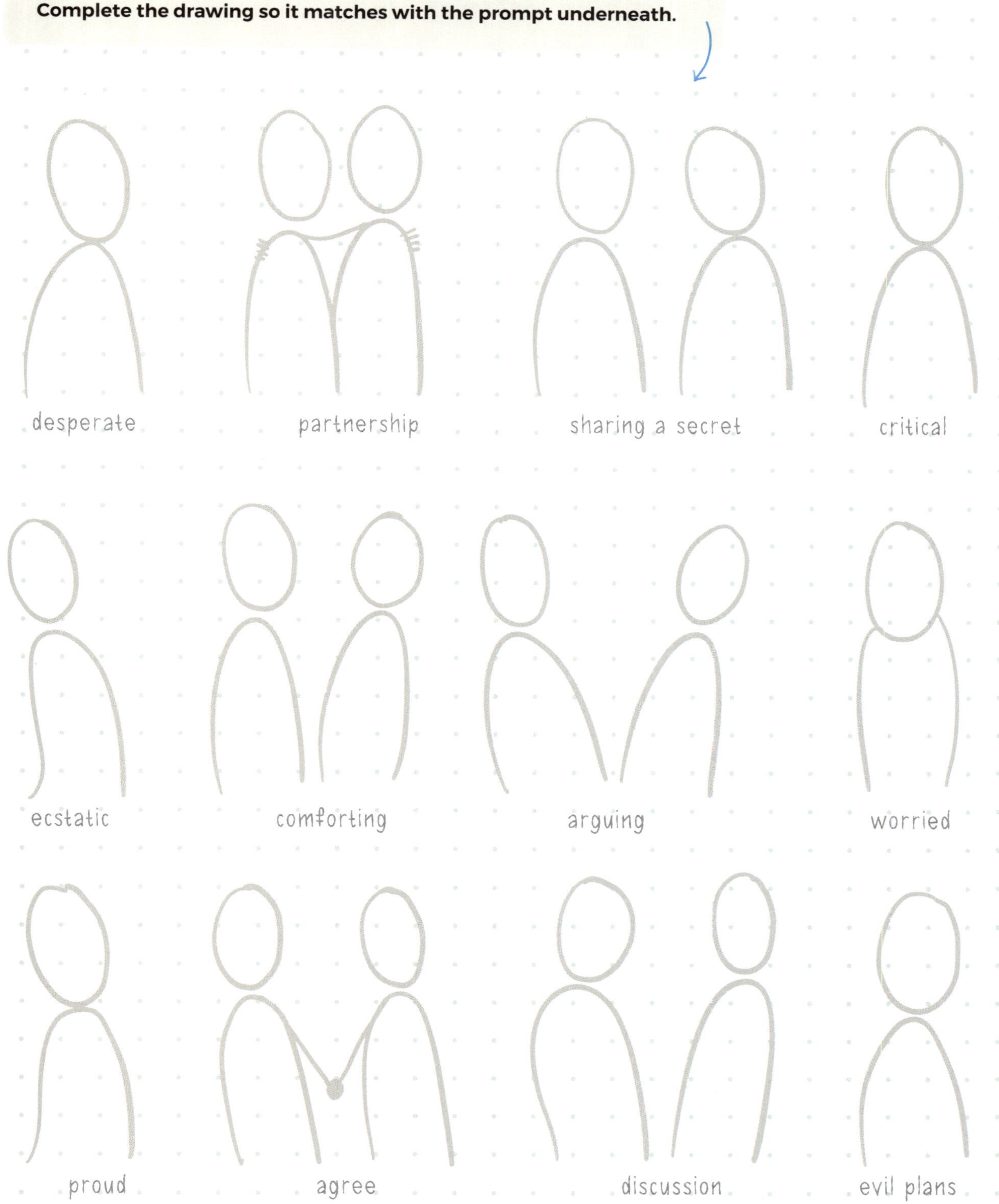

3.3 SPEECH BUBBLES

When drawing people and interaction, speech bubbles or balloons are essential! Even on their own, the balloons can express a feeling or story. When combined with people and/or text they are even more powerful.

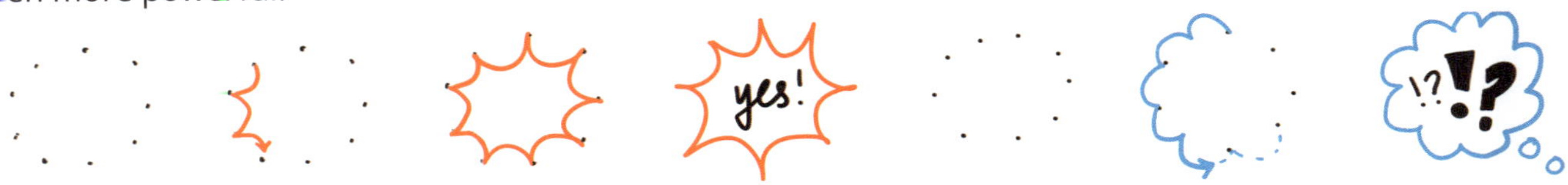

Copy the balloons below to practice!

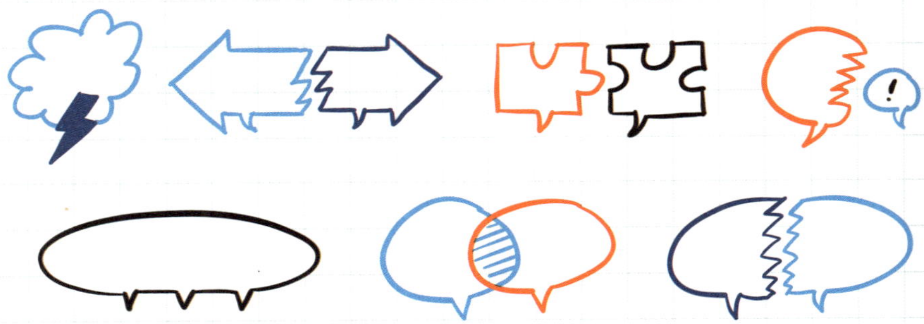

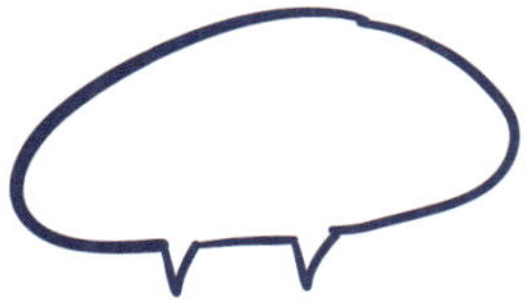

empty

with icon

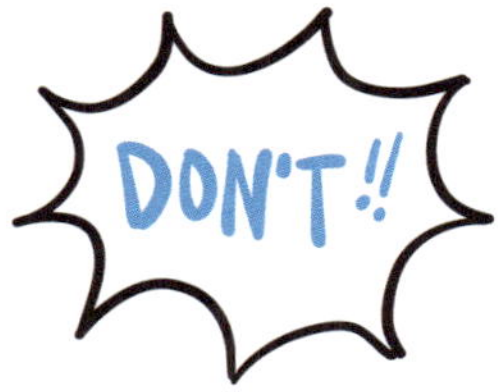

with text

TIP Either leave the balloons empty, make a drawing inside, or write something in there! Write big enough so people can actually read it.

TIP Think of comic books!

Invent your own unique balloons. Try variations in size, shape and structure and see if you can combine them with icons. Also try drawing people with your balloons.

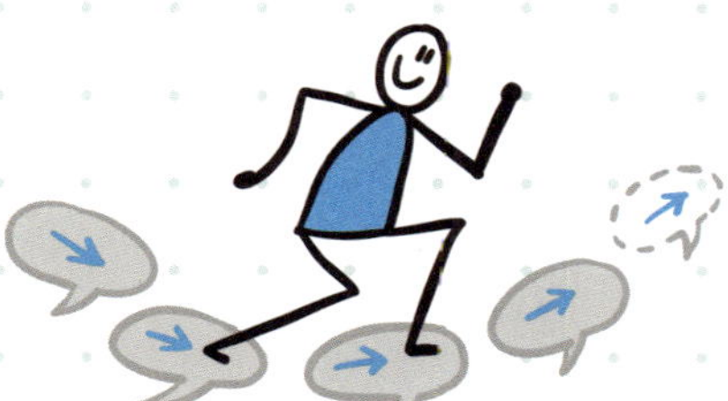

walk the talk

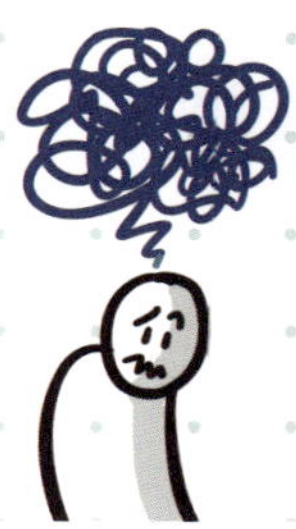

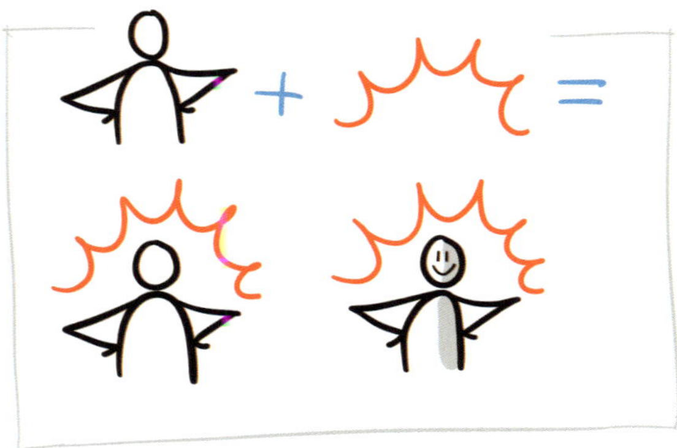

Speech bubbles aren't the only way of enriching visuals! How about adding expression lines? Look at the drawings and describe below what type of situation you could use them for. Practice more poses underneath! Don't forget your visual hierarchy. Try to use a different color (or gray) for the expression lines. You can also use much thinner black lines.

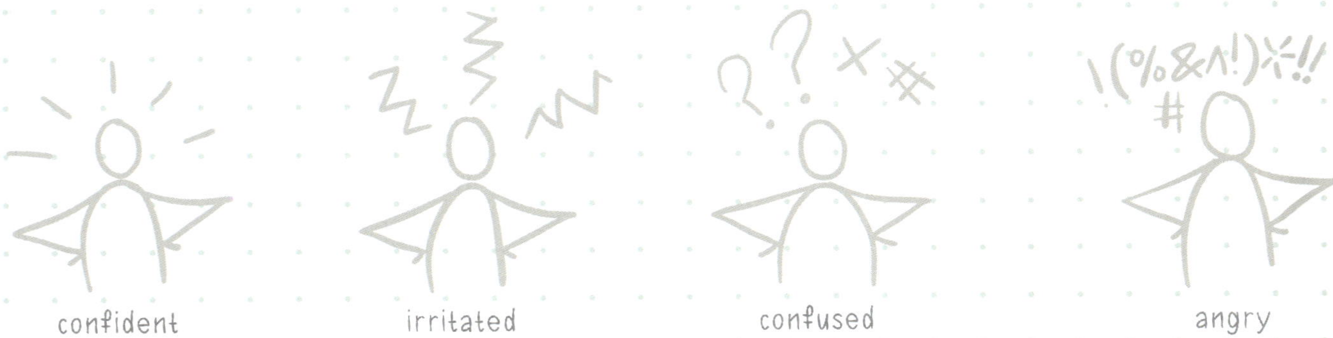

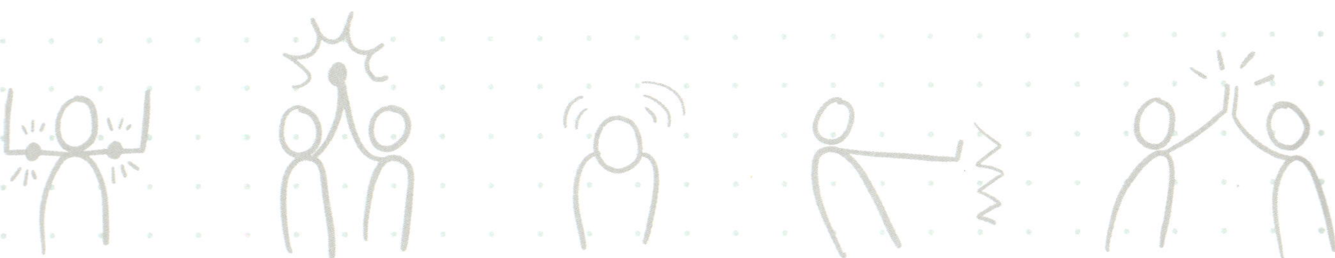

Look at the people below. Try to amplify their emotions by adding expression lines. Use gray and/or a bright color.

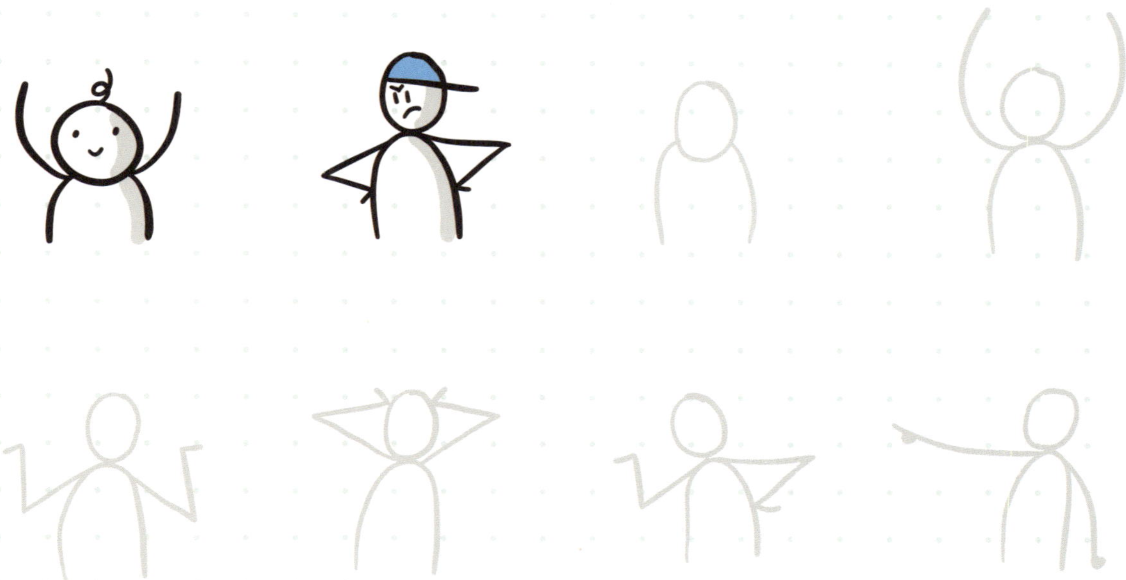

TIP To keep it simple and clear, try to draw things like ancient Egyptian symbols/hieroglyphs: with a flatter or 2D feel. Keep the arms away from the body as much as possible and draw people next to each other instead of behind each other.

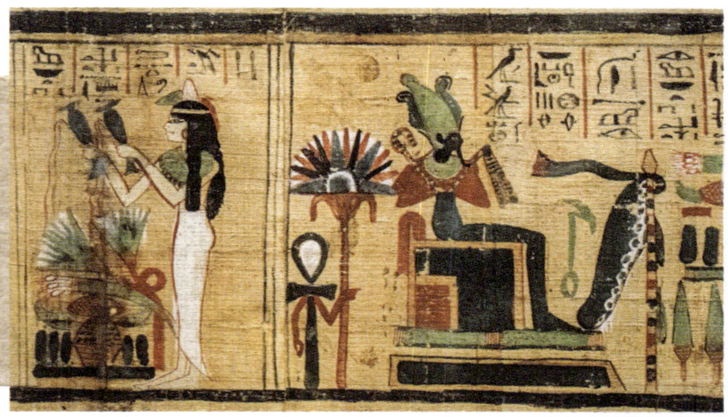

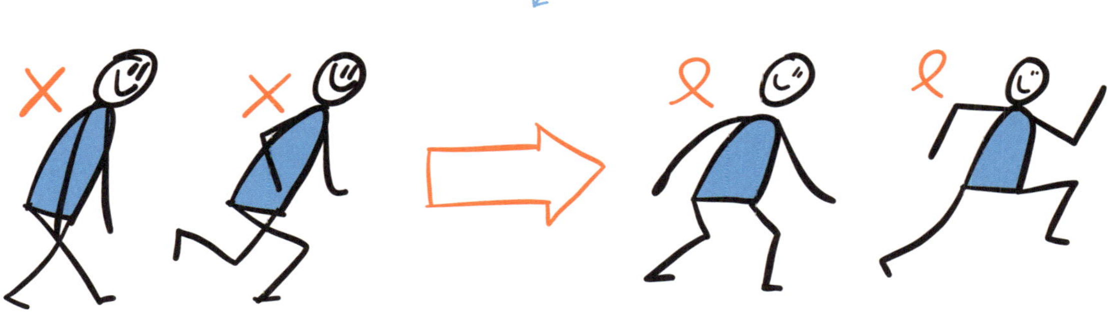

3.4 DRAWING A SCENE

Can you draw the following situations? Try to use facial expressions, additional expression lines or speech bubbles and maybe other icons if needed. Consider whether or not to draw legs: nine times out of ten you don't really need them!

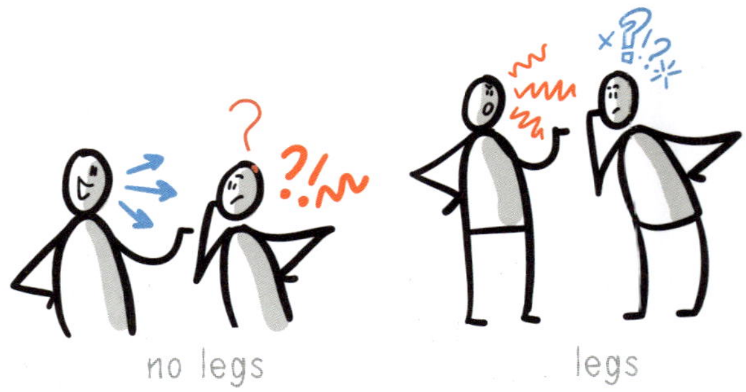

decision making

miscommunication

brainstorming

celebrating success

arguing

Have confidence in your skills

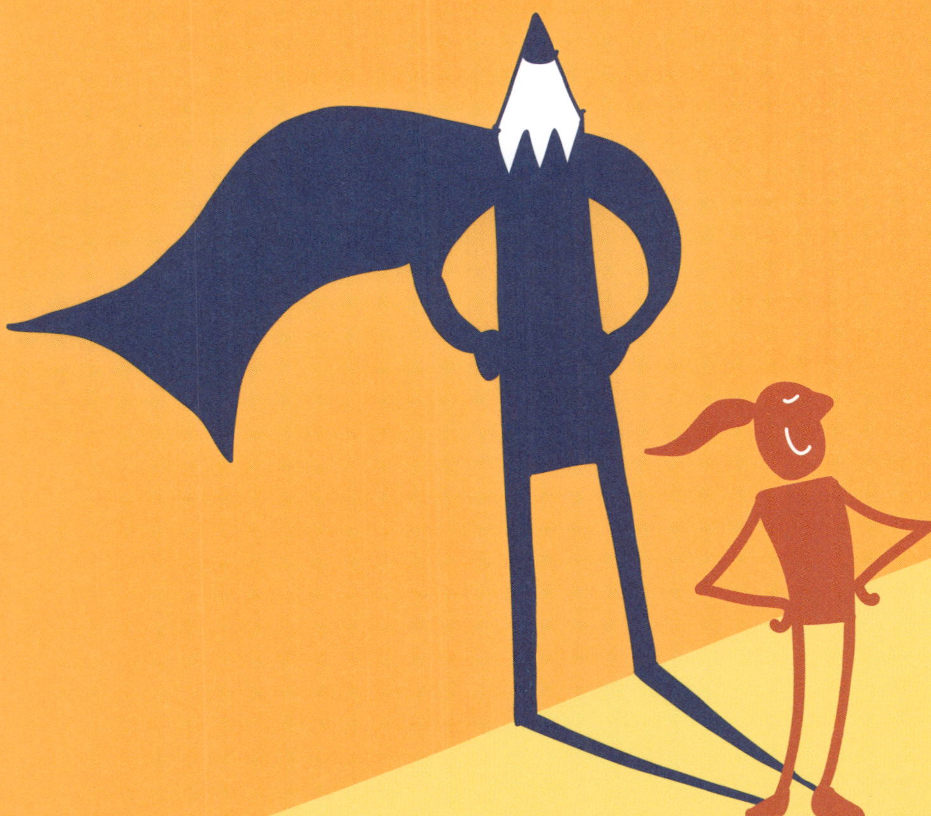

3.5 THE ENTIRE BODY

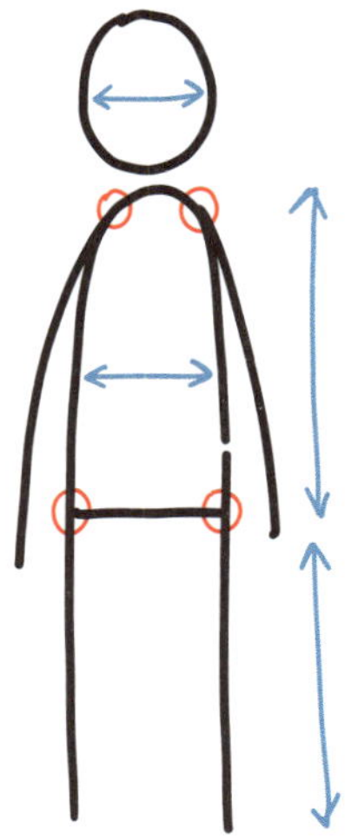

When drawing an entire person, make sure the body is closed. The arms come from the shoulder joints, the legs come from the hips. We try not to draw hands, but when we do, we keep it simple! Lines, a zigzag or mittens are all you need.

Look at how we draw hands in these situations. Just draw the hand as a basic shape; a circle for a fist, or a short line for an openhand.

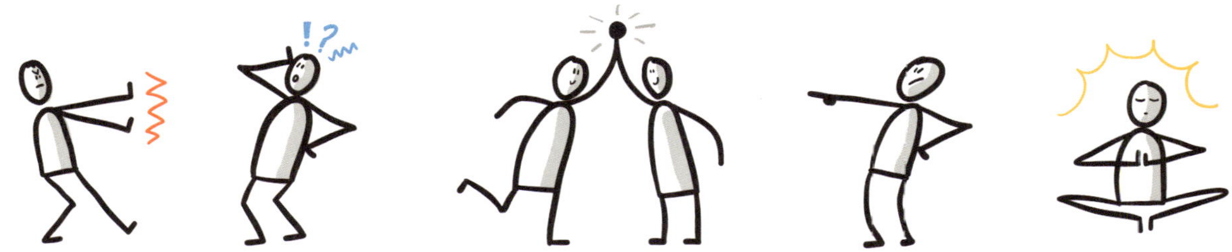

Copy to practice!

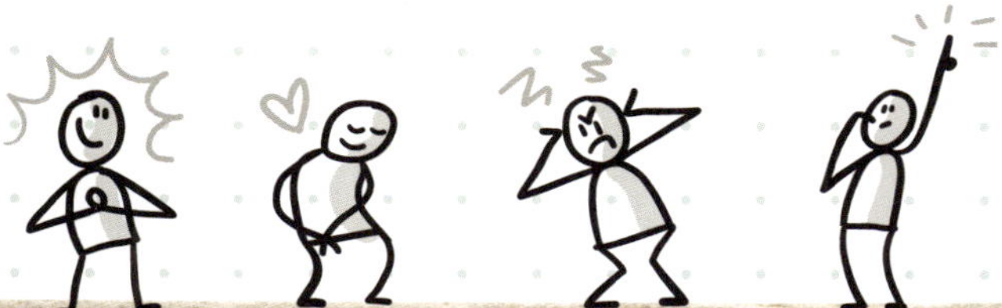

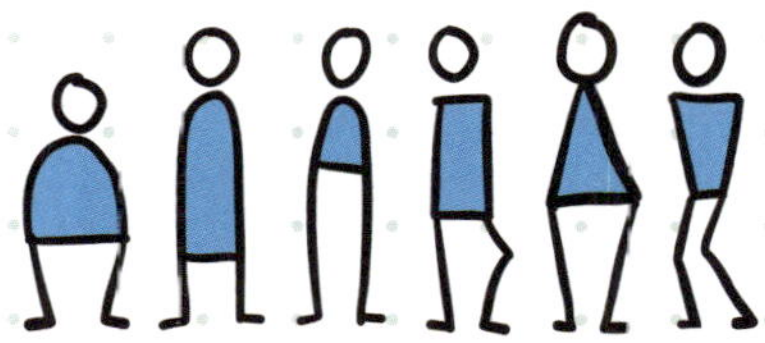

TIP Look in the mirror while posing as the person you want to draw and really study your reflection.

TIP You can also use a different shape for the body, or experiment with different proportions

3.6 POSES

If you want to draw a person on the move, start with the torso at the correct angle. Next add the head and finish with arms and legs. You can include extra details such as facial expressions and movement/expression lines later.

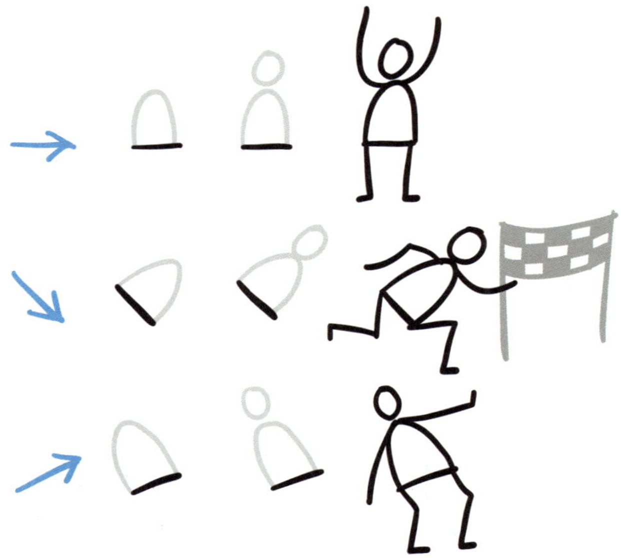

We've drawn the bottom lines of the torso for you. Can you finish the people yourself, including arms and legs? Play around!

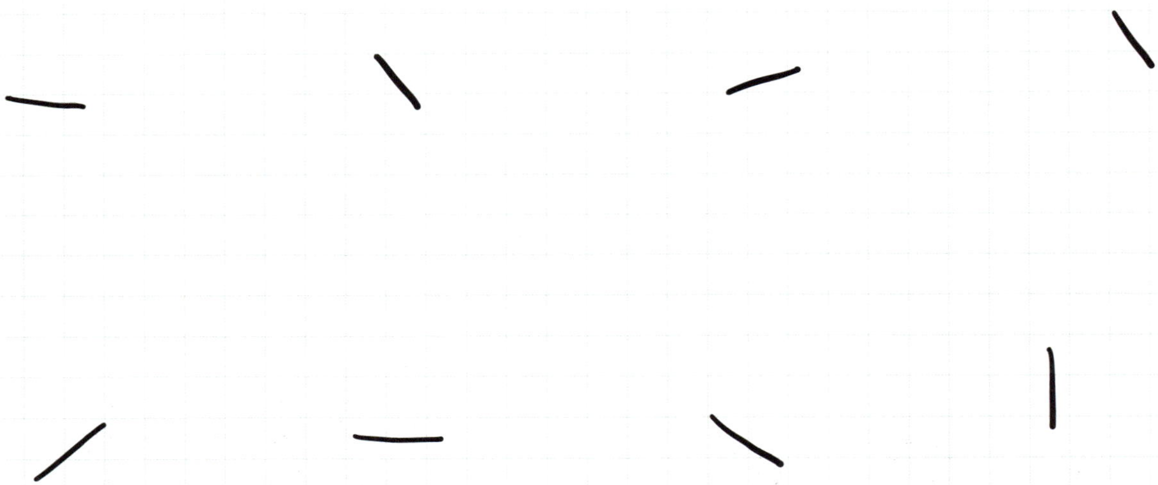

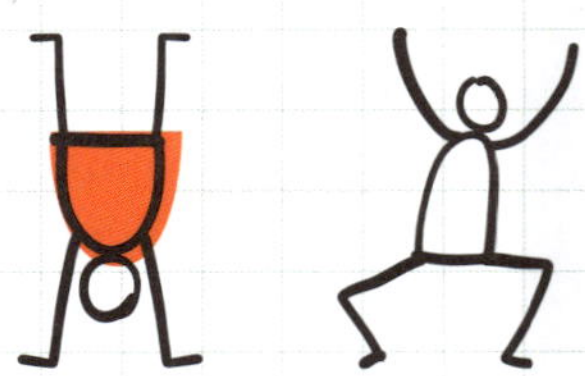

People on the move and in action seem hard to draw, yet practice makes perfect! Trace the drawings to get a feeling for the line directions and shapes.

sitting

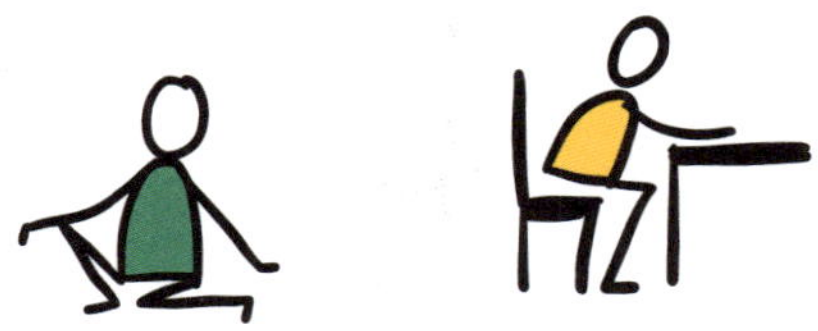

walking

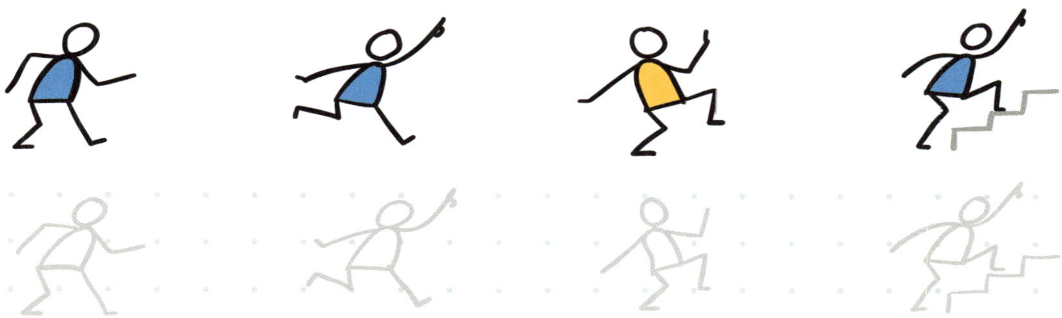

running

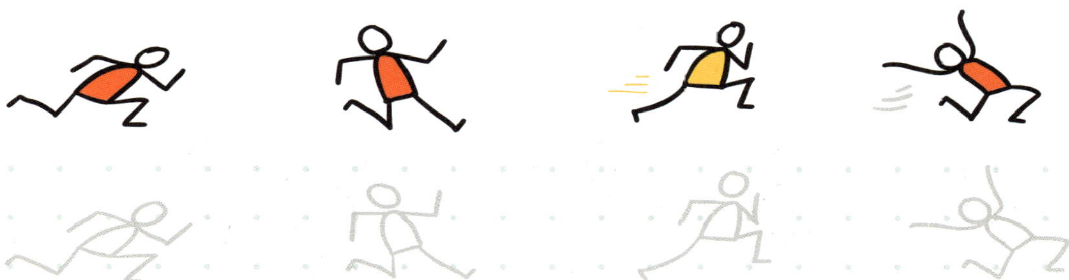

jumping

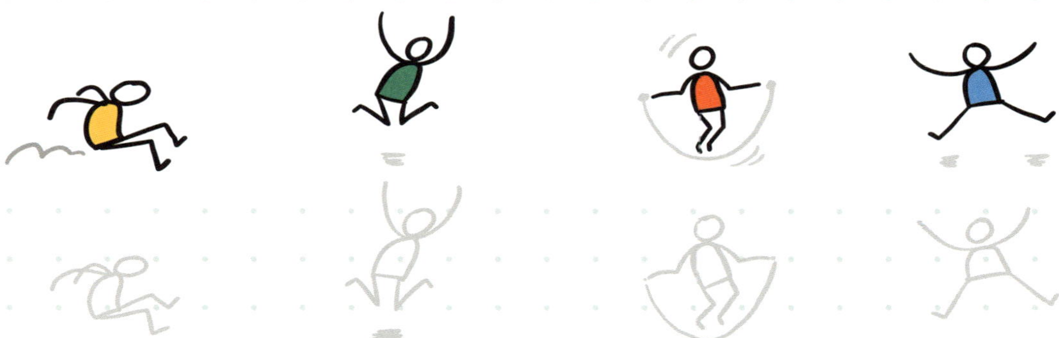

Trace the gray line to get a feeling for the pose.

sports

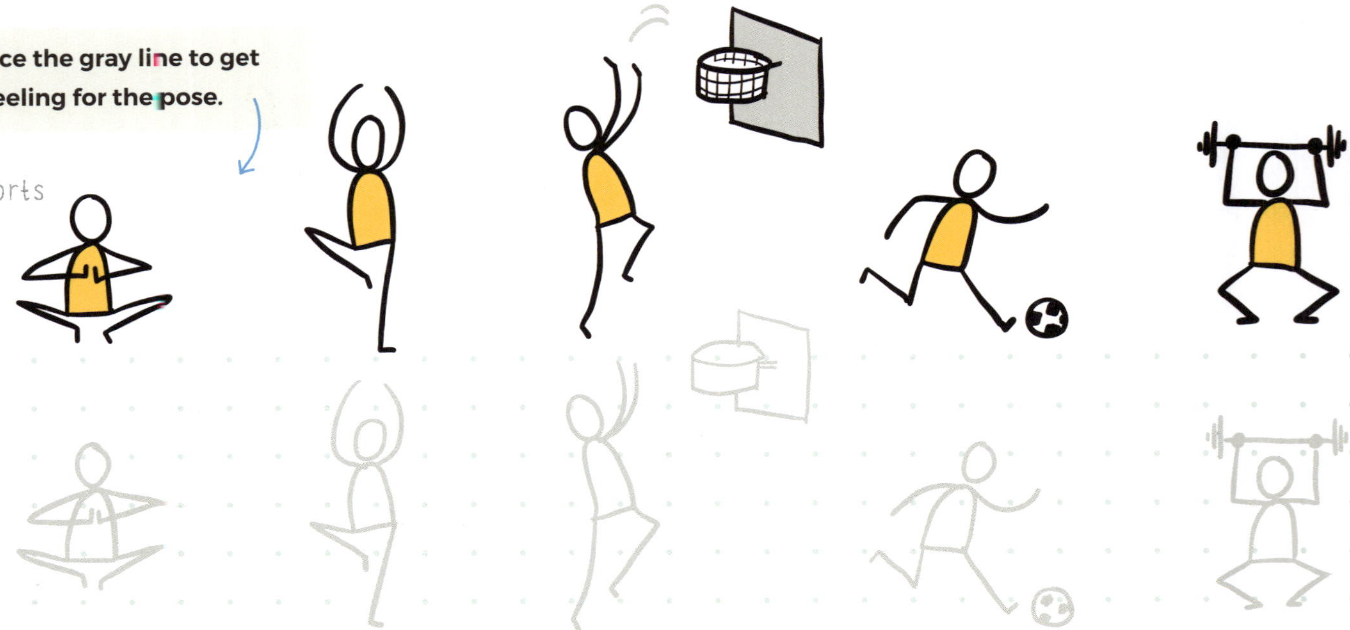

Now do it yourself!

fighting

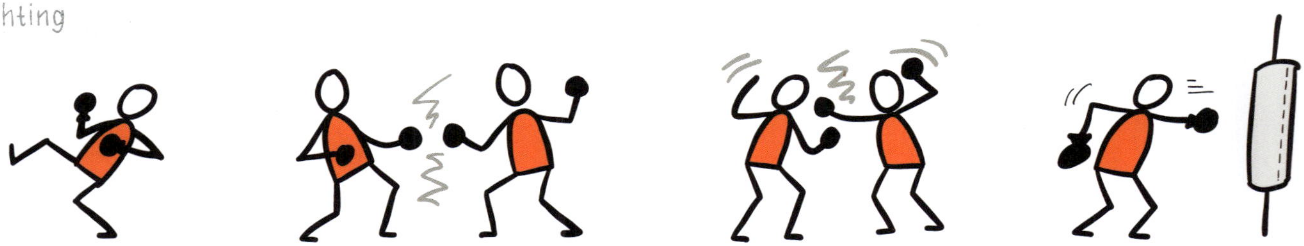

dancing

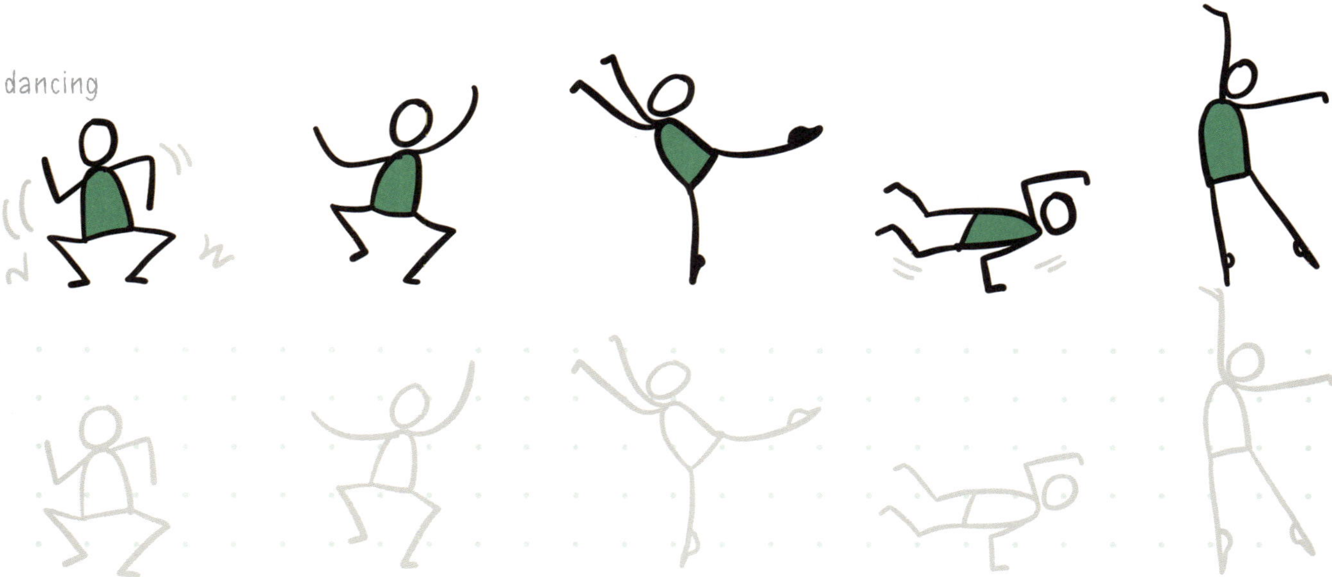

striking a pose

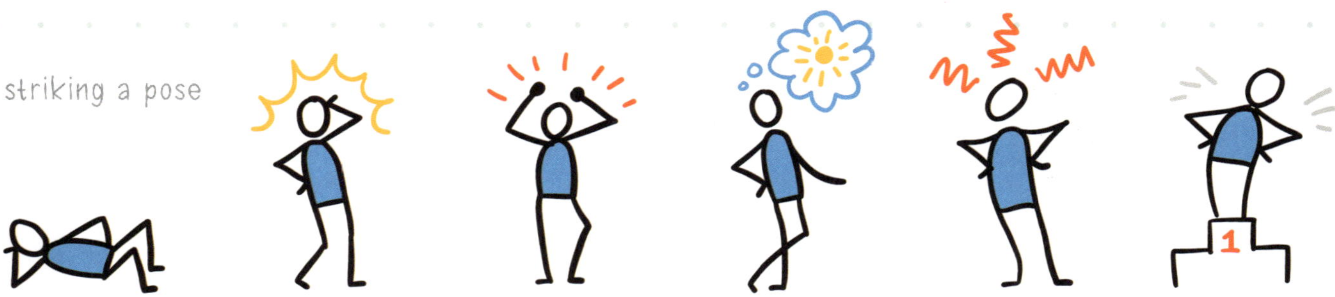

The pitfall. Let's practice some postures combined with your ability to think visually! The superhero stands at the end of the pitfall… what happens in between?

Draw at least five other people in different positions.

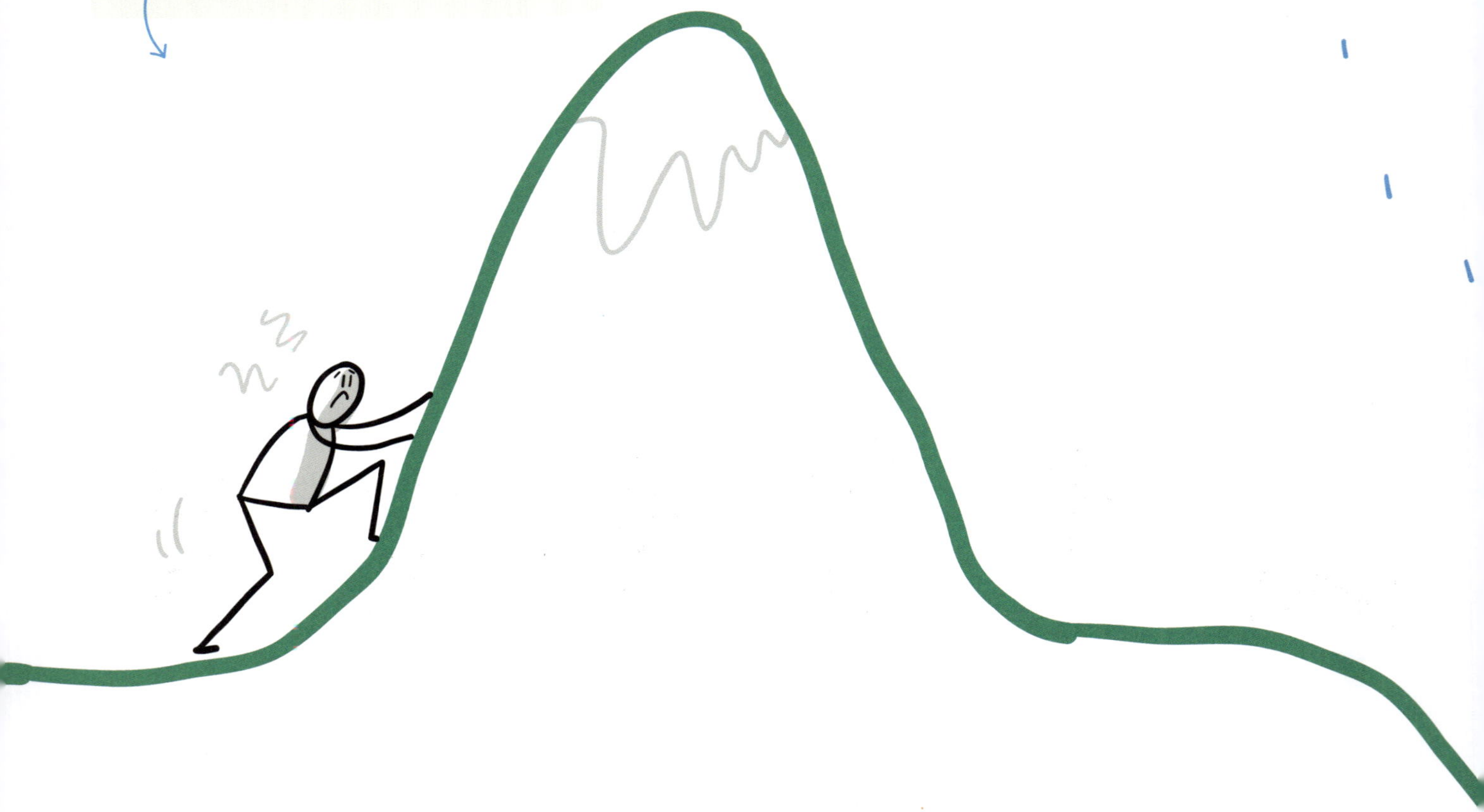

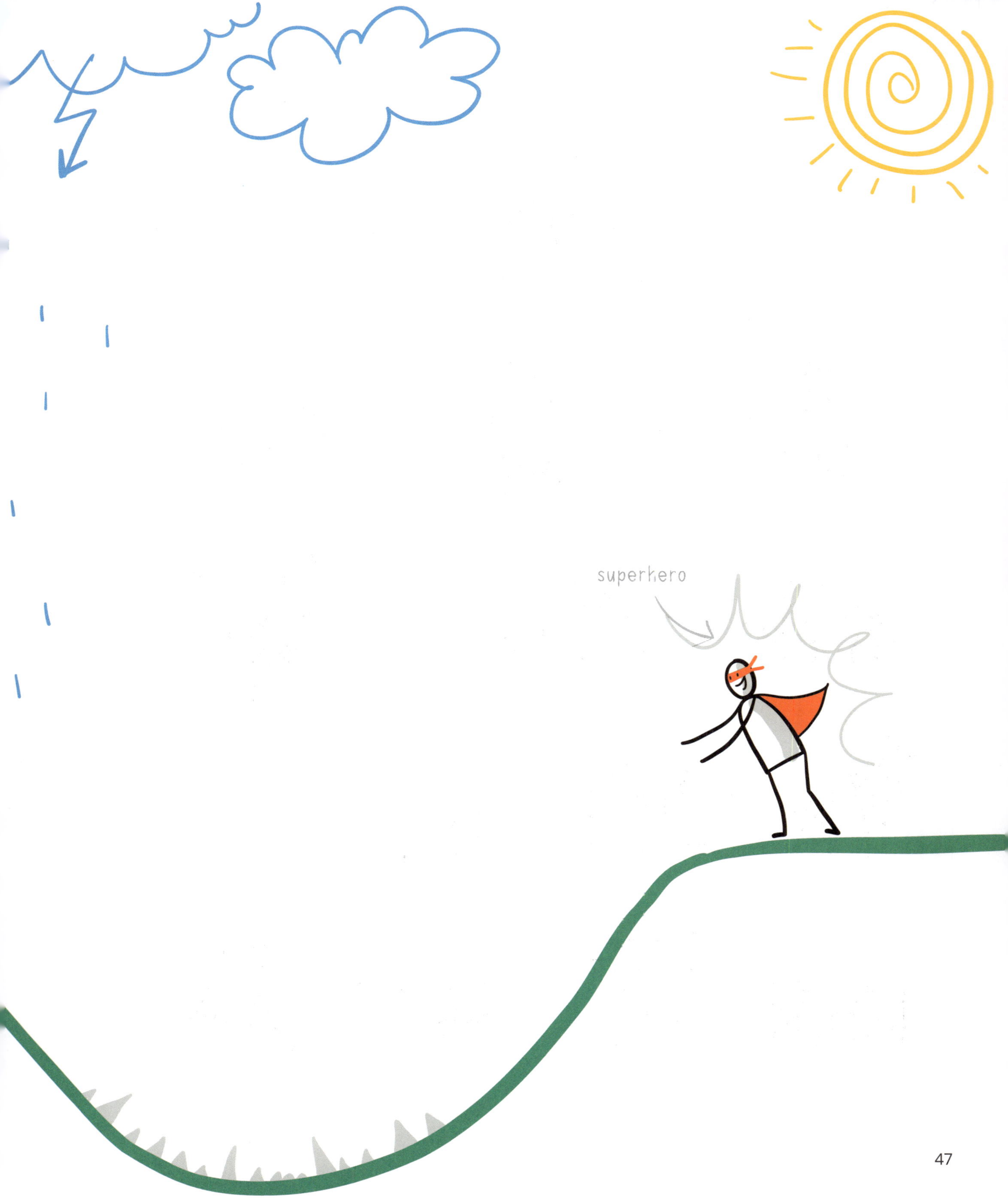
superhero

3.7 MULTIPLE PEOPLE

To quickly draw multiple people, just repeat the arc of the body for each person and add the heads afterwards.

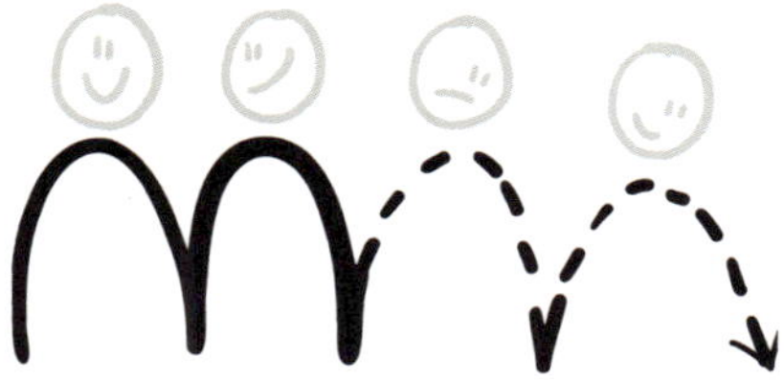

teams / multiple people

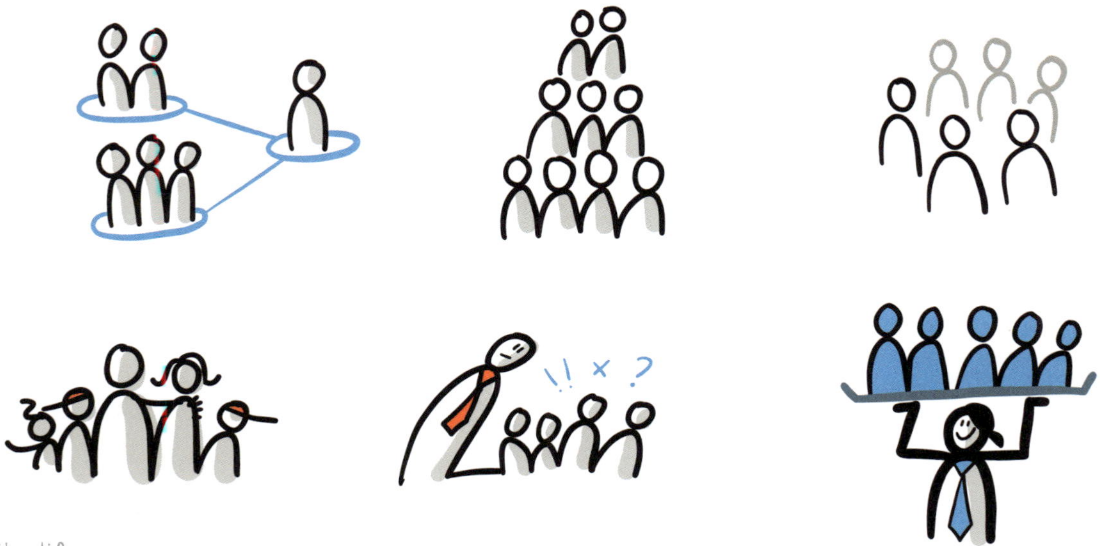

family life

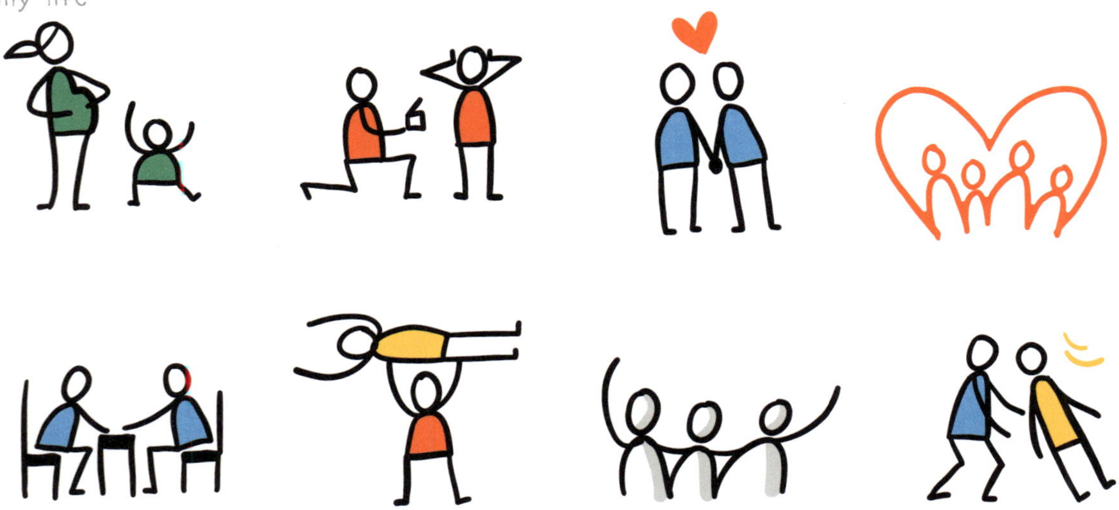

Copy your favorites from the left page or make up your own!

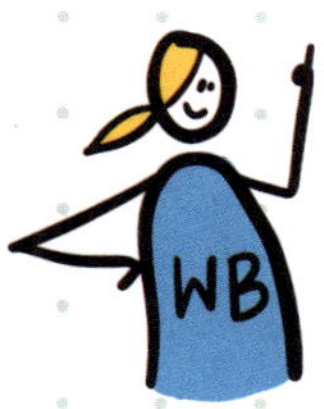

TIP If you want to personalize a figure you could write their initials in the body. You could also characterize them, check chapter 8.2 for more inspiration!

work life

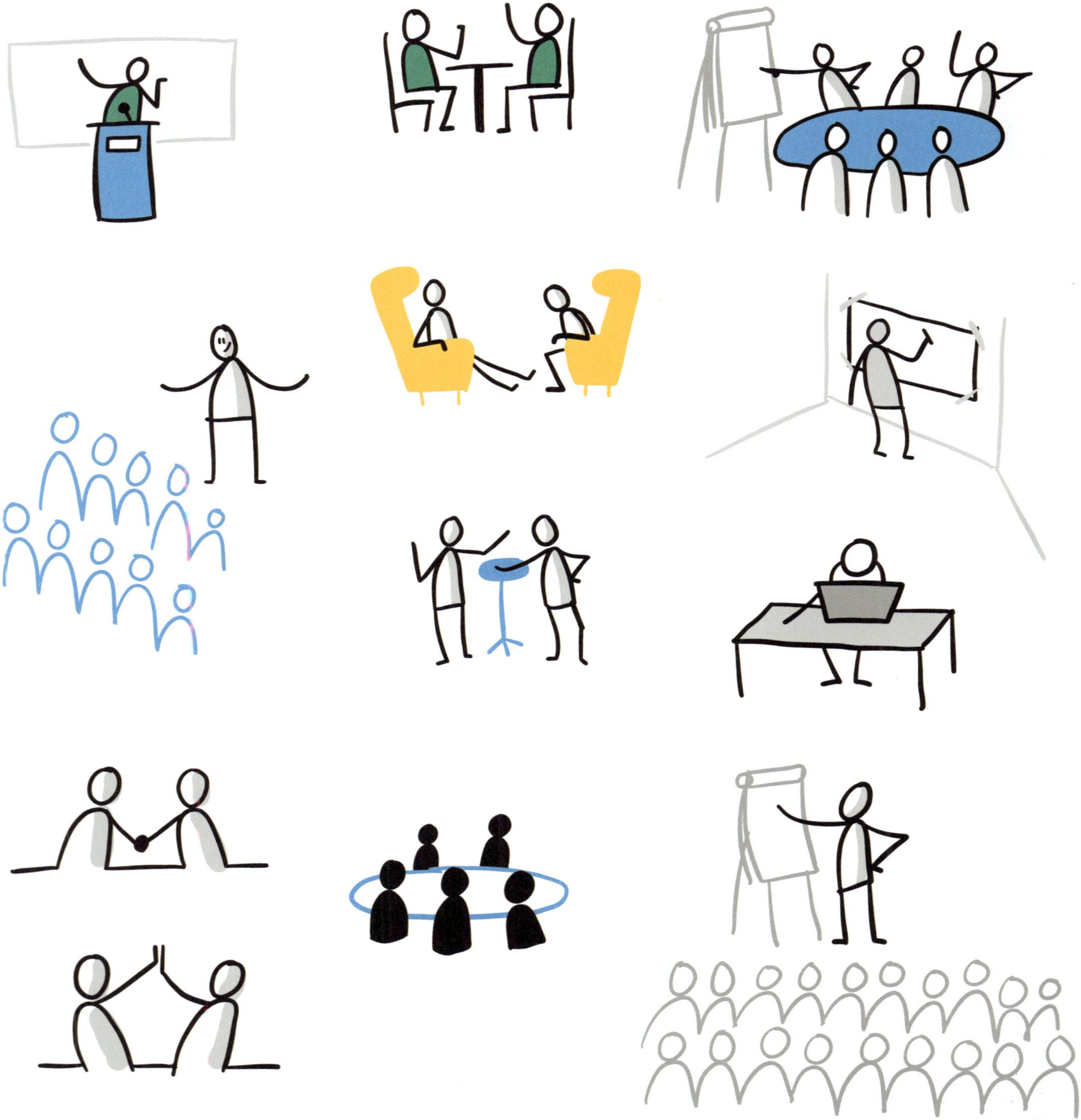

What does your workplace look like? How do you interact with your colleagues and where do you draw?

Draw your favorite settings from the left page below and think of some interactions yourself.

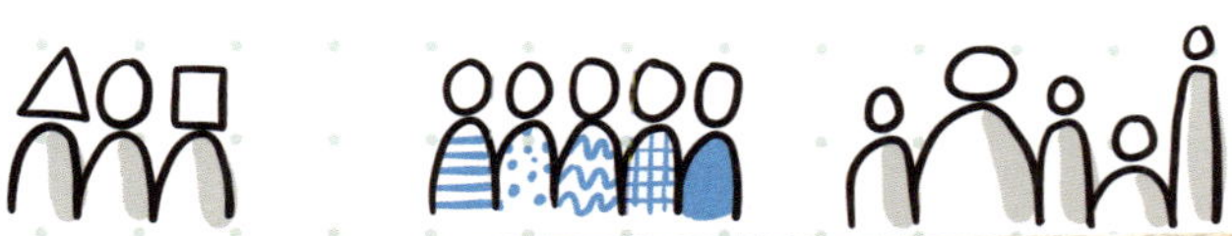

TIP Want to show diversity in a group? Different skills, backgrounds or cultures? Try these!

You can draw a team striving to move forward or a team that's holding back by drawing the bodies at an angle.

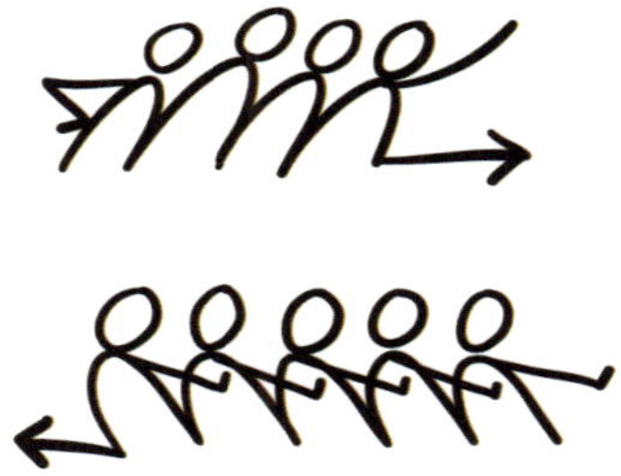

Make drawings based on these prompts. Don't forget you can use speech bubbles, facial expressions and even icons or other drawings as well!

sharing the same vision

collaborating

aiming for a shared goal

team resistance

Draw the one you support or hold close to your heart on top of the bar.

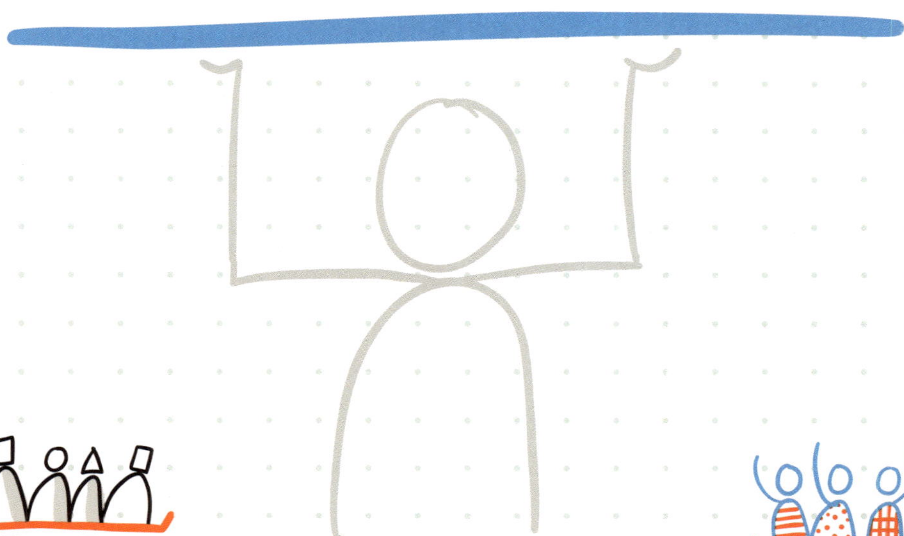

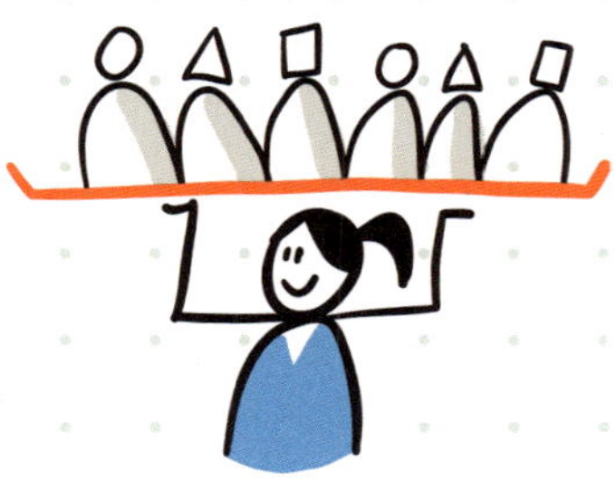

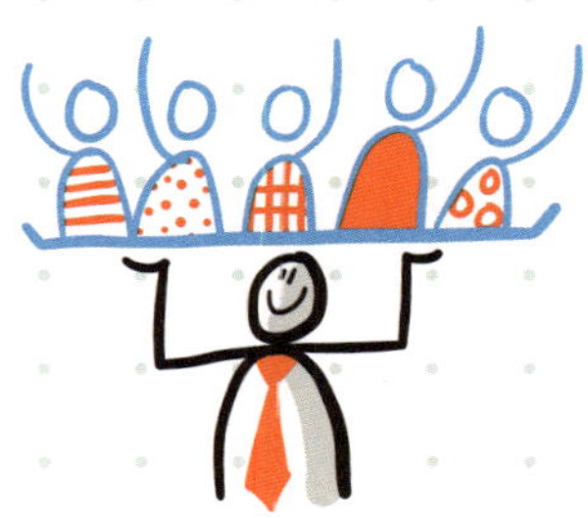

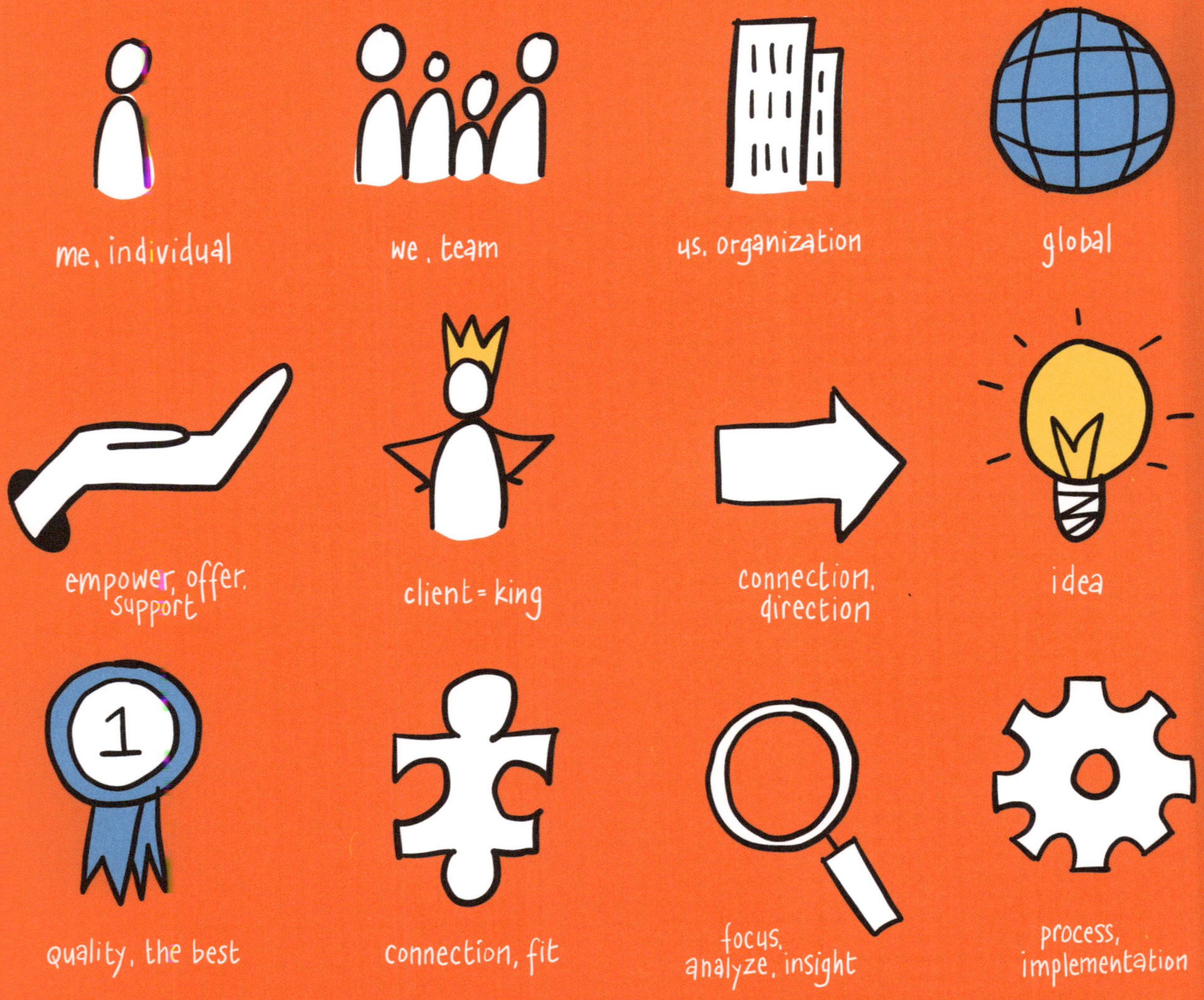

Basic icons from our book 'My Icon Library'.

4. BASIC ICONS

We have noticed that when you challenge people to draw a word or concept they can often express themselves visually, even if they only know some basic icons. That's why we believe it is very useful to master some essential icons that fit almost every environment.

You can transform a drawing of something as basic as a stack of paper into a strategic plan, a to-do list or a document with important data.

They are effective on their own, but you will also see them popping up in a lot of combined icons, which we will talk about in chapter 5. With these icons in your visual library, you will be able to make endless iterations and combinations!

In this chapter we will practice a range of basic icons that we've come across often, when drawing in a business context. We've clustered them into three groups, circle-based icons, rectangular icons, and arrow-based icons.

Basic icons are a foundation for your creativity. Build on them!

WHAT YOU WILL LEARN

4.1 Circles
4.2 Rectangles
4.3 Arrows

4.1 CIRCLES

The starting point for these basic icons is a circle. Start with the circle and add to it, step-by-step. When you've mastered drawing the basic icon, try adding more elements.

Copy the icon here

magnifying glass: research, analysis, focus

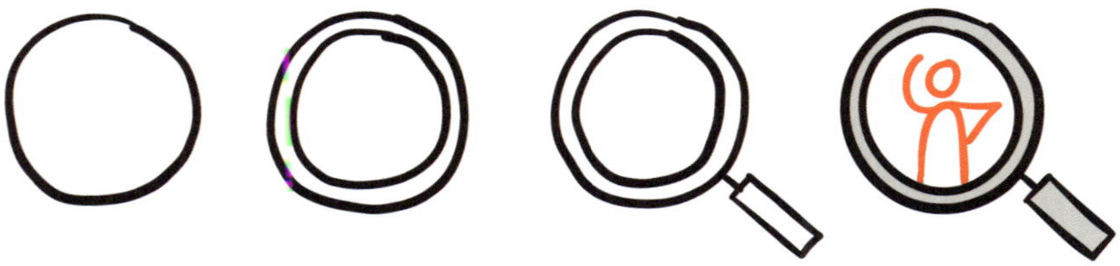

gear: how things work, processes, working like an oiled machine

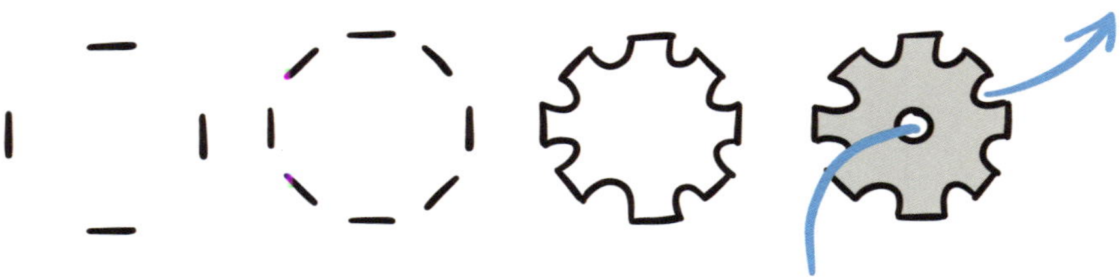

globe: earth, globalization, virtual

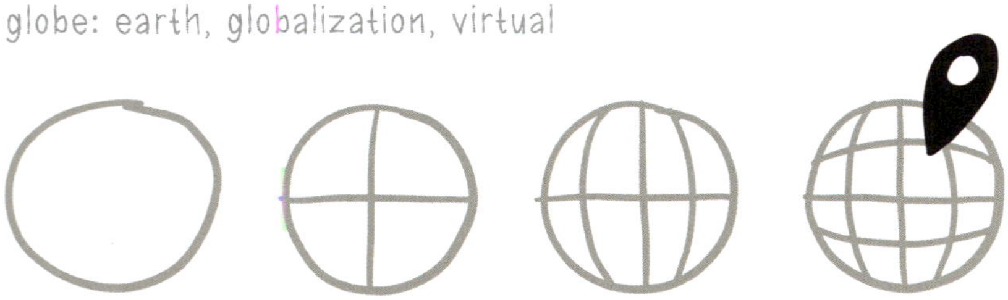

target: goals, targets, the 'why'

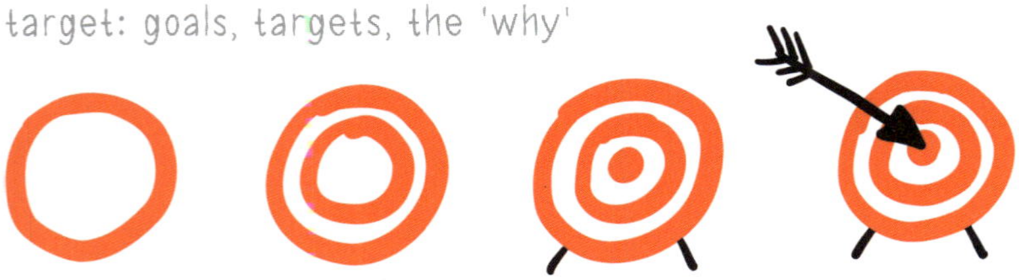

Experiment with other circle-based drawings, by transforming all of these circles into something recognizable. You can also combine circles. Be creative! To push yourself, set a timer for two minutes and see how far you get.

TIP Let yourself be inspired by your previous ideas!

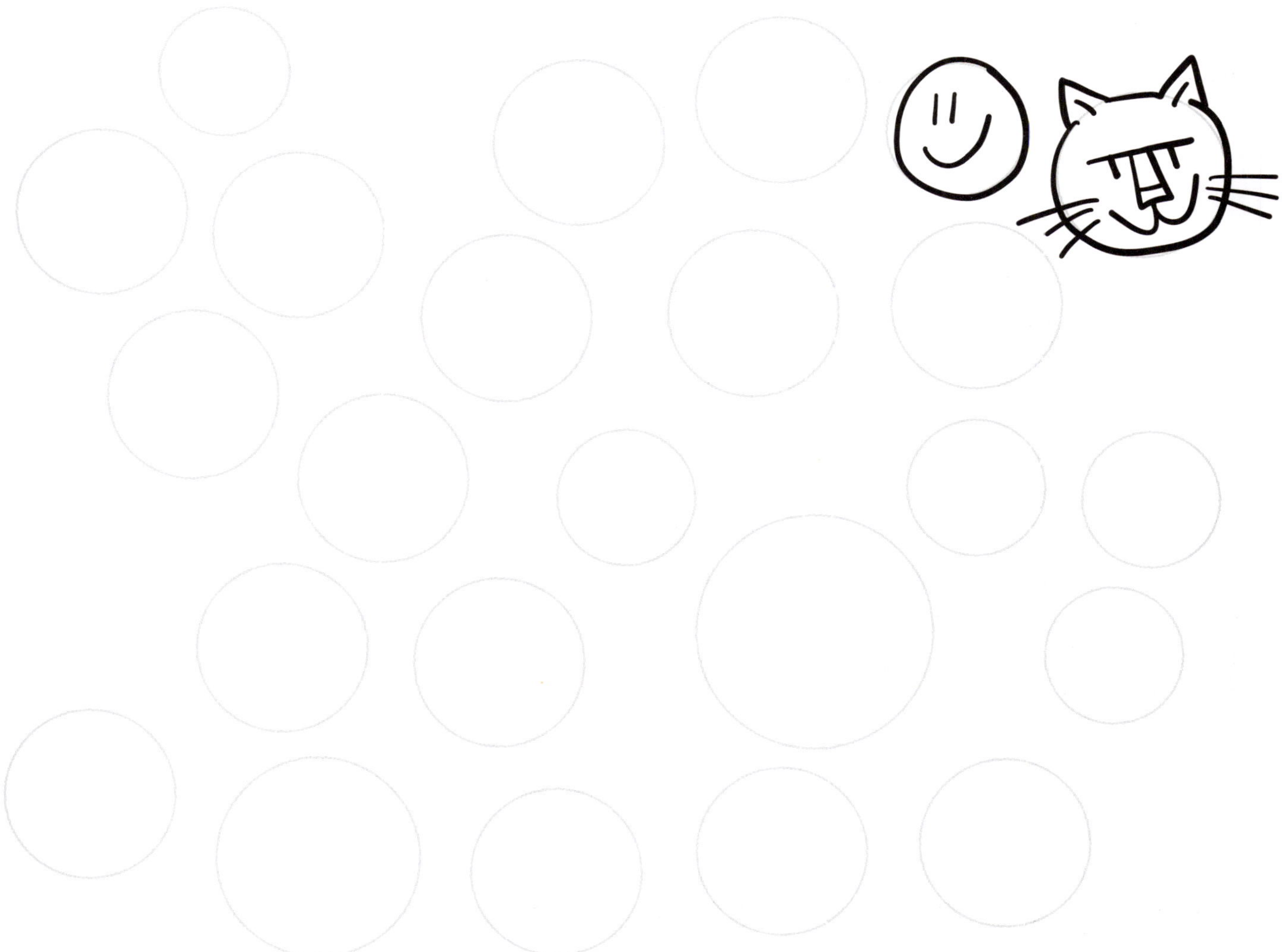

4.2 RECTANGLES

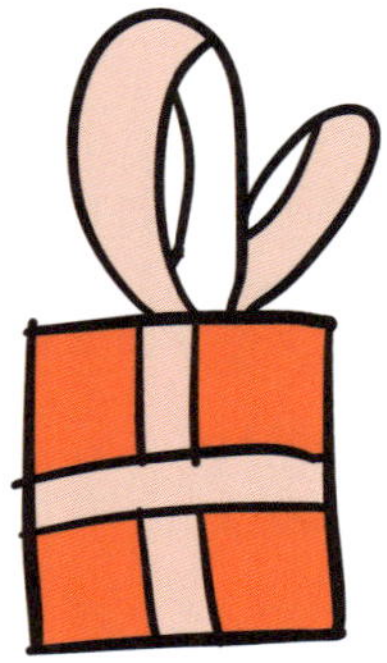

A few of the most simple icons are based on a rectangle.

Copy the icon here

a stack of paper: documents, information, a plan, a report

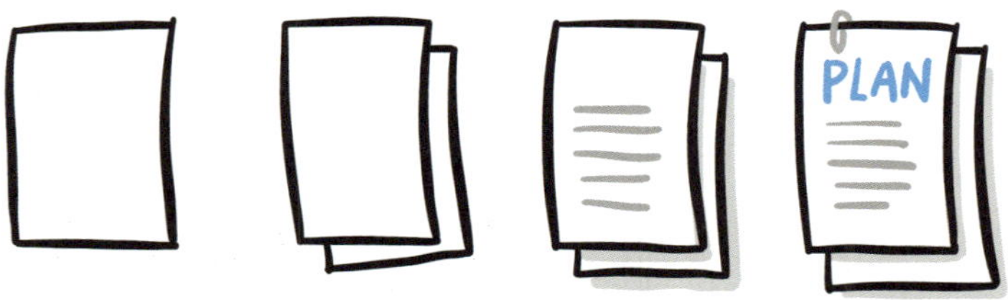

a puzzle piece: part of a process, co-creation, solution, finding the missing puzzle piece

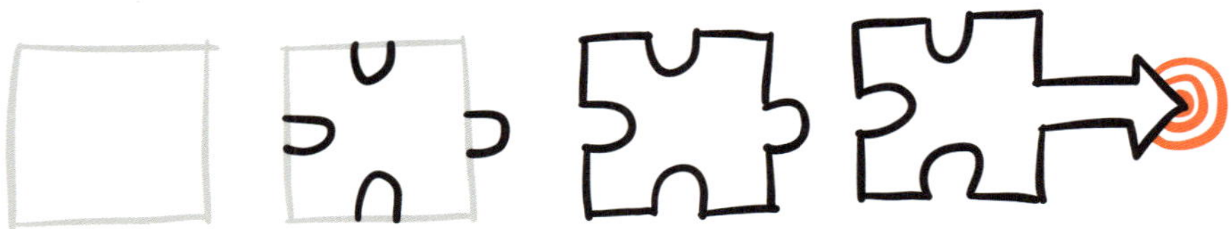

a building: organization, location, company

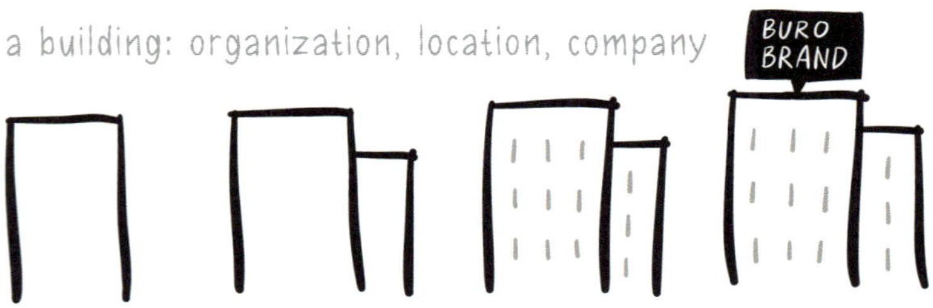

Make it a building you visit regularly

a rectangle: computer monitor, quarterly report

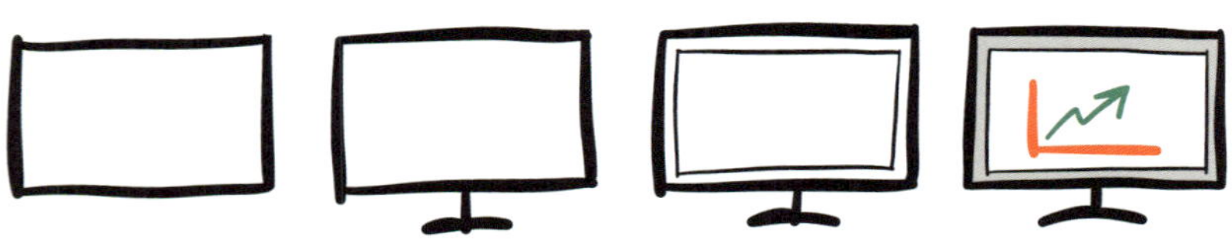

Personalize and specify the basic rectangular icons that you already know. That way you learn to use the basic icons for different purposes. Or come up with some totally new icons!

TIP See episode 'rectangles' in our e-learning for more inspiration and basic icons.

TIP Look around you, do you see anything lying around that resembles a rectangle? For example, a camera, or a present?

4.3 ARROWS

TIP Don't forget visual articulation! Draw a neat arrowhead.

Even the simplest arrow can point you from A to B. But arrows can represent so much more and help you tell so many visual stories. Try out different shapes, lines and colors, and see how an arrow can give your visuals a sense of direction.

Copy the arrows from the right

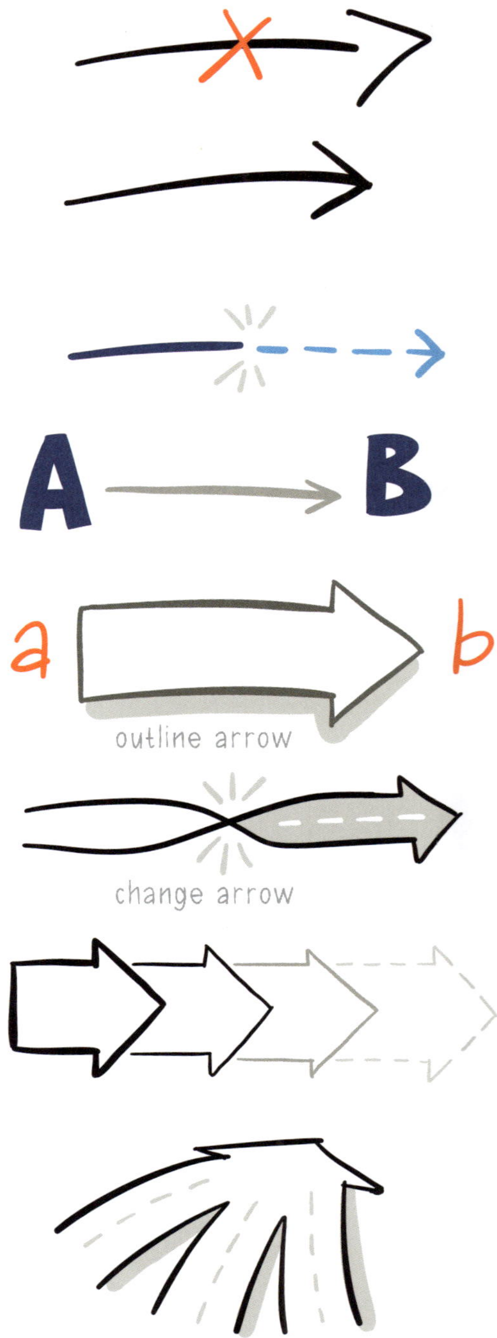

Different arrows, different meanings. A light or dotted line makes something 'unsure' or 'not yet existing', while the outline arrow is almost an icon in itself and focusses attention.

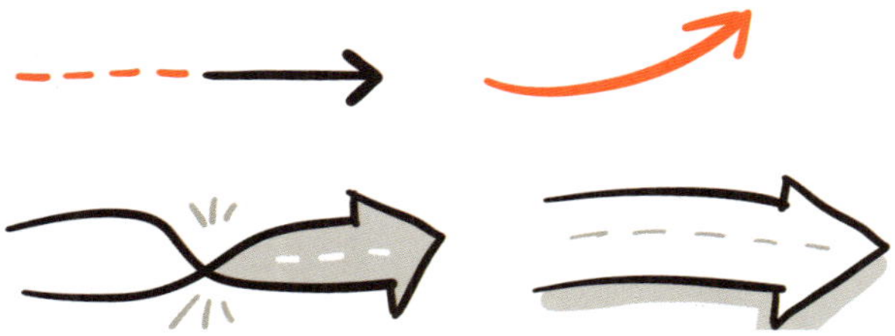

These four scenes are missing an arrow. What arrow best connects each pair? Keep in mind visual hierarchy. Choose from the four arrows on the left.

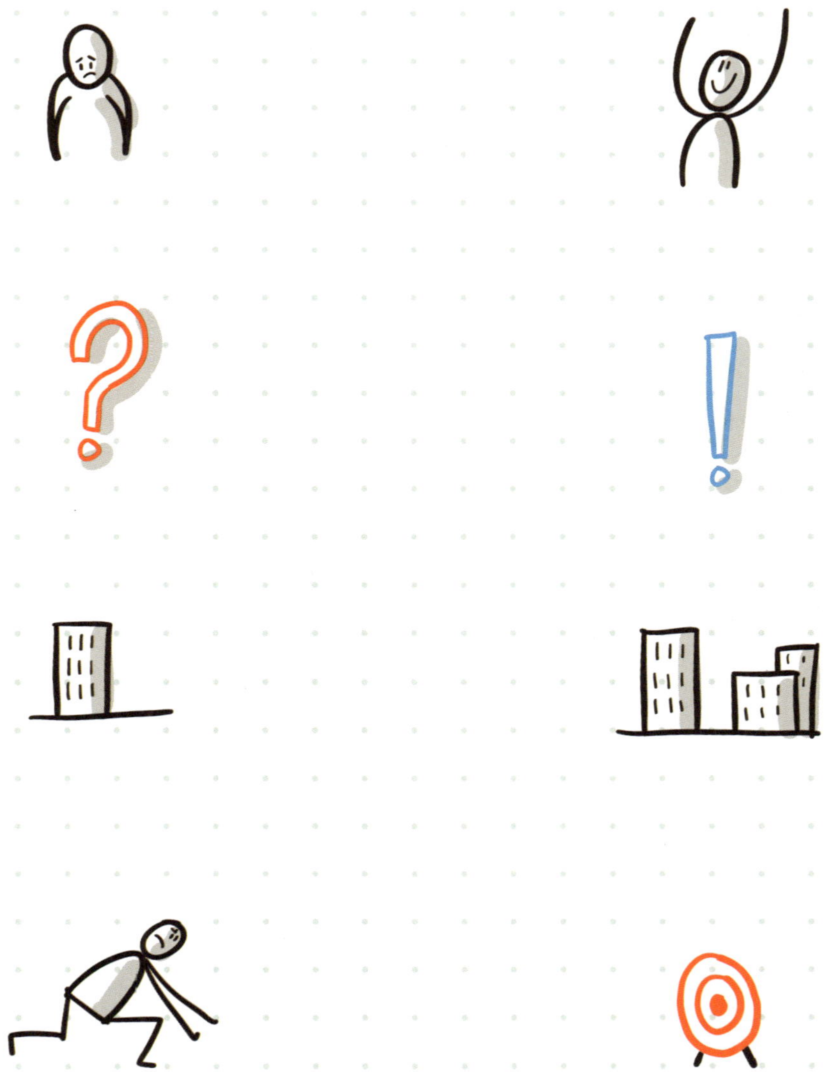

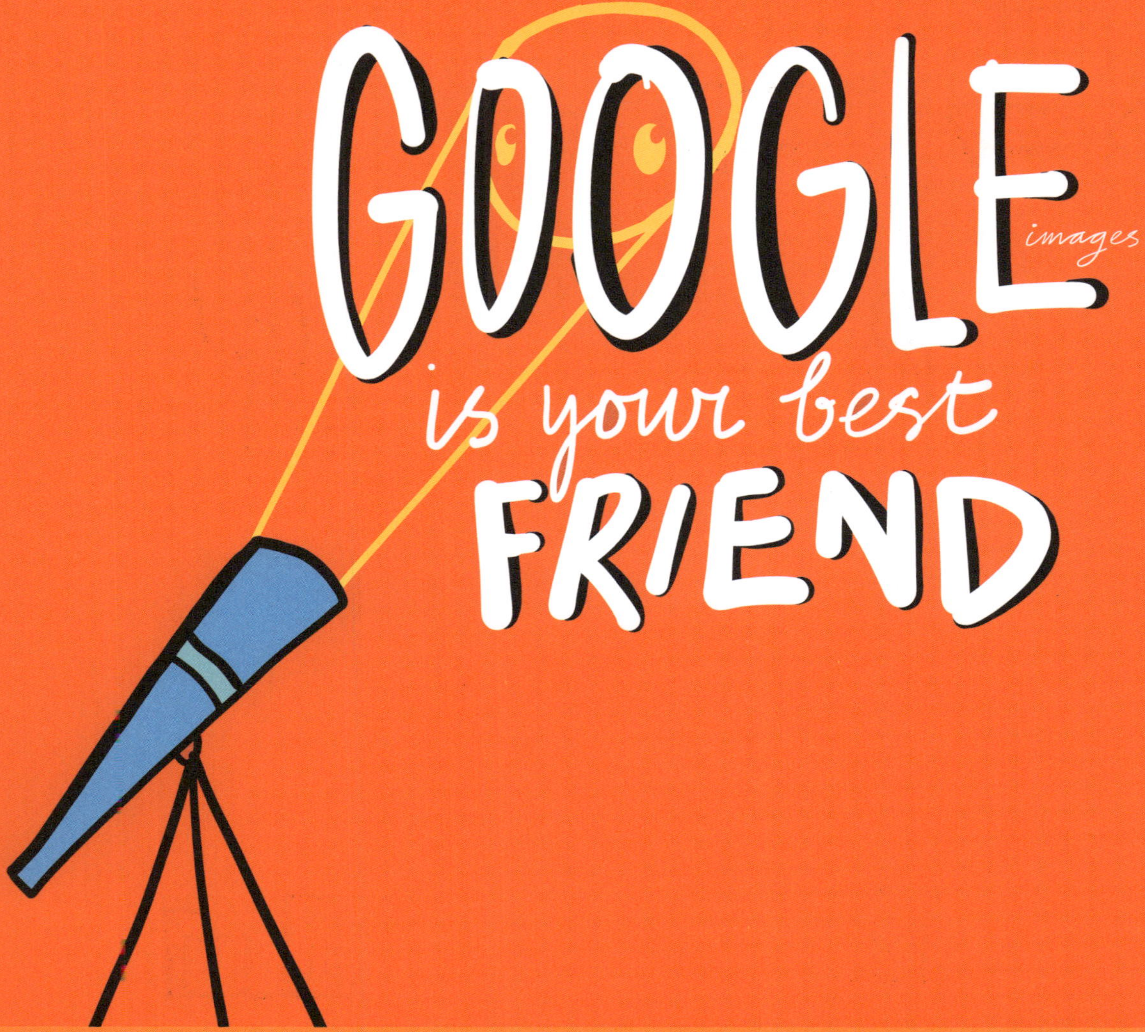
GOOGLE
images
is your best
FRIEND

5. COMBINED ICONS

You can find all sorts of basic icons online. So you might wonder: 'Why bother drawing?' Well, you might not be able to find exactly the icon you need to help explain your concept or story. This is where things gets interesting!

Just as you combine shapes to create an icon, you can also combine icons to create a more complex drawing. When you combine icons, a more layered story unfolds. It becomes a visual. These types of visuals cannot be found on the internet. They help you tell your own unique story. People recognize what you say, understand and remember it better and are able to share your story with others.

In this chapter we let you play around with combined icons, both dissecting and combining them. Finally, you'll be challenged to create your own (combined) icon library that can become a personal resource for your story telling.

WHAT YOU WILL LEARN

5.1 How to combine
5.2 Creative exercises
5.3 Assignment: Create your icon library

Imagine someone tells you a story about 'insights' and they show you this icon to illustrate the point they want to make.

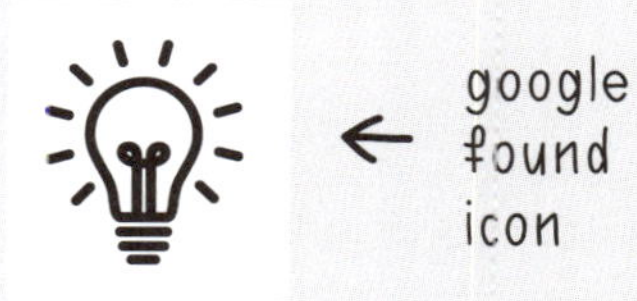

If you look at this again a few days later, chances are you won't be able to clearly recall the insight. However, if you use a more tailored (and combined) visual that fits your story – you'll still need some text and explanation to fully understand the visual – it will be far easier to remember the message.

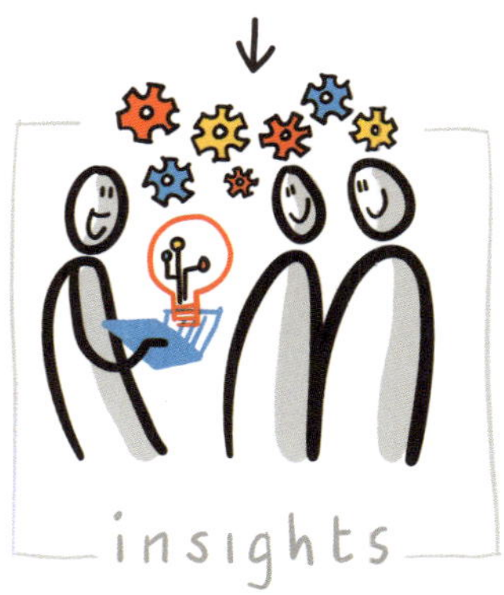

5.1 HOW TO COMBINE

When you start combining icons, you can of course use basic icons that you already know, or new ones that might pop into your head. But, since this is a new language for you and your visual vocabulary isn't that big, chances are you will have to look for inspiration elsewhere.

Google is a great place to start... Just make sure you search for images and type 'icon' behind your search word. You'll get all kinds of small visuals that represent your search word.

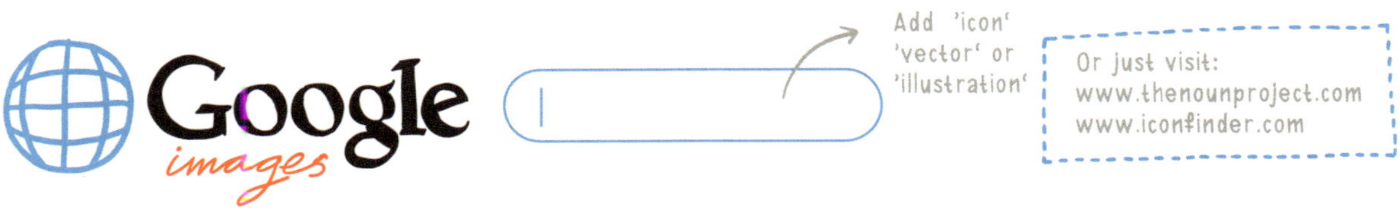

STEP 1

Write down key words linked to the story you want to tell. If you have only one word, try to visualize using synonyms, opposites, associated words, etc.

STEP 2

Look for icons generated by your key words that best fit your story and copy them into your notebook.

STEP 3

Sketch, experiment and make your own combined icon.

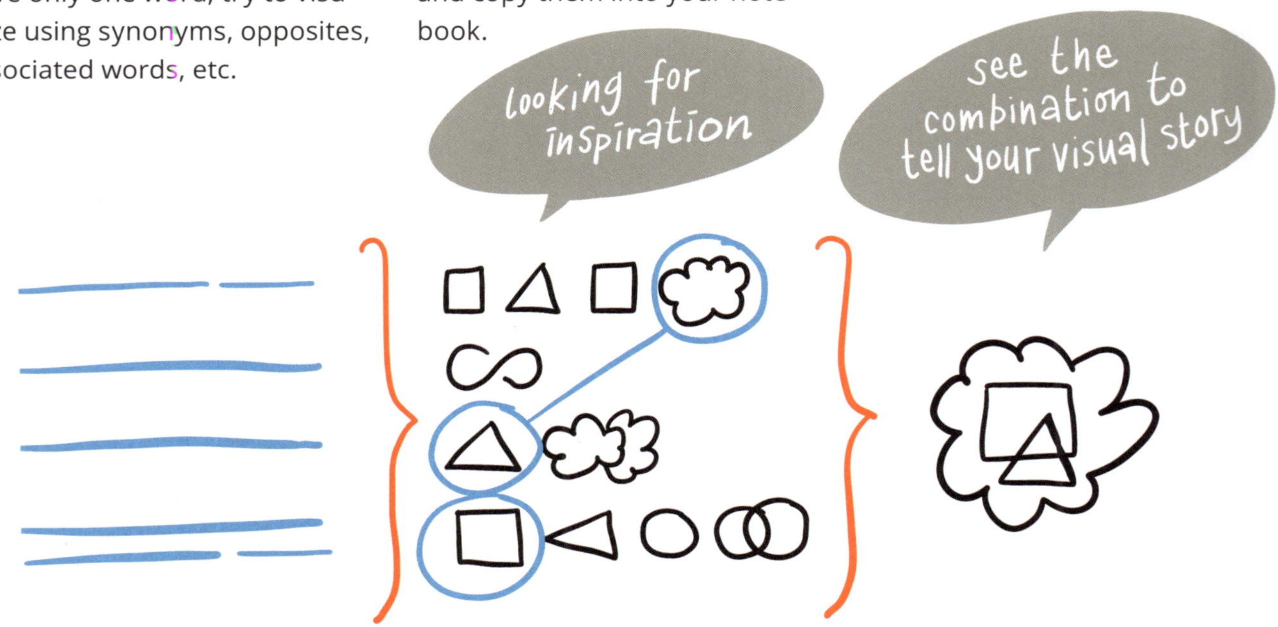

TIP Make your icons overlap and think of what should be in the foreground and what in the background (visual hierarchy!).

Let's look at two examples. They start with key words that lead us to a variety of different icons. These are merged in preliminary sketches that are distilled into a final combined icon.

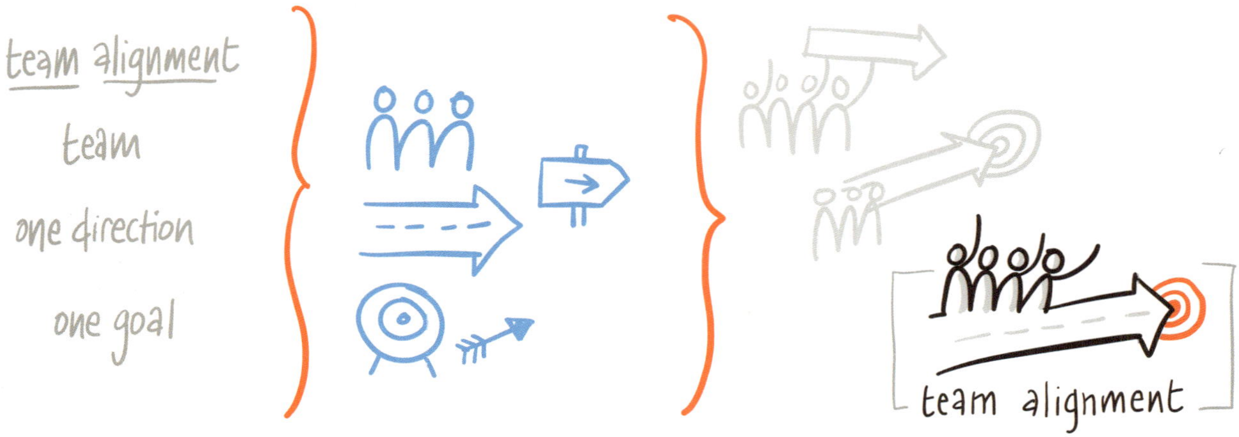

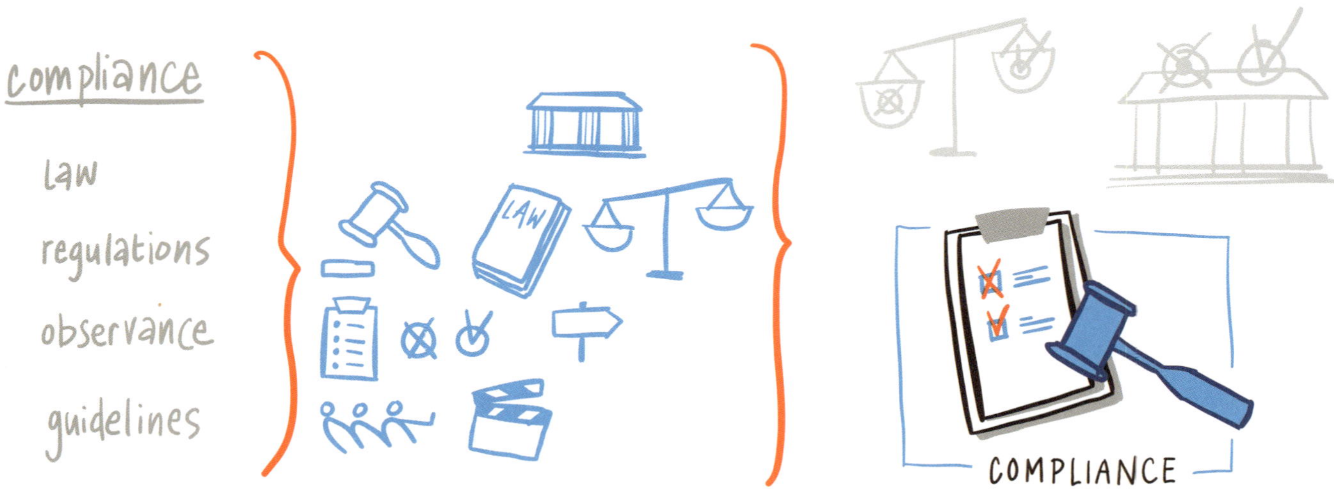

TIP As you can see, sketching and experimenting is a big part of learning how to communicate with (the right) drawings.

In our book "My Icon Library," we show you, step by step, how we went from a single word to several combined icons, and also how you can draw some of them yourself.

For example, for the word ACTION. At the top of the page, you see some icons found on the internet for the keyword 'action.' In the middle, there are four different sets of 'combined icons.'

As you can see, there is no single solution (there are many more than shown here!). Depending on the context, a certain drawing might or might not fit your story.

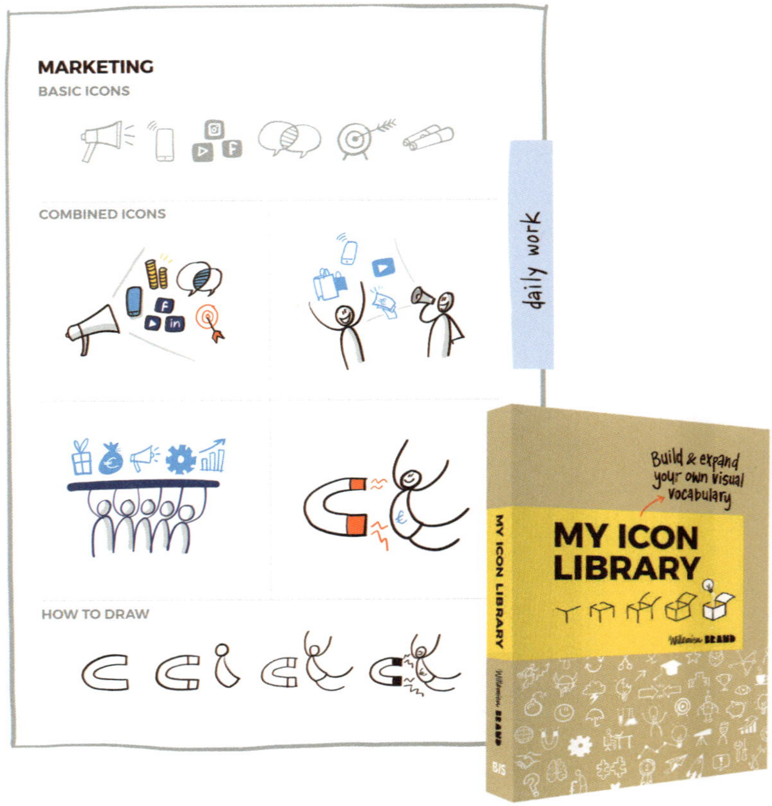

ACHIEVEMENT

BASIC ICONS

Draw a couple of different icons you see when you look up 'achievement' on the internet.

On the right, draw four ideas for a combined icon that could fit the concept 'achievement'.

COMBINED ICONS

Copy these combined icons with a gear as a basic icon.

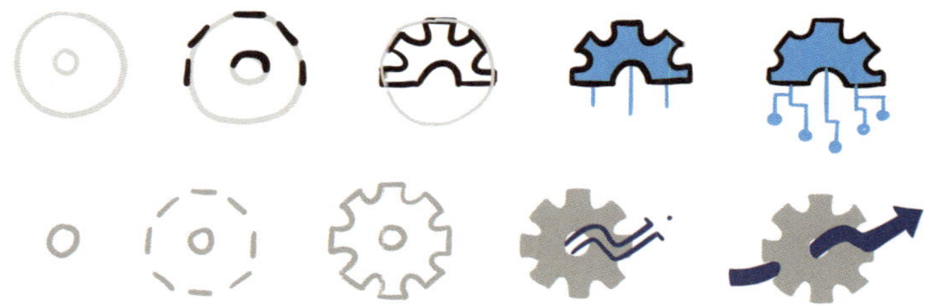

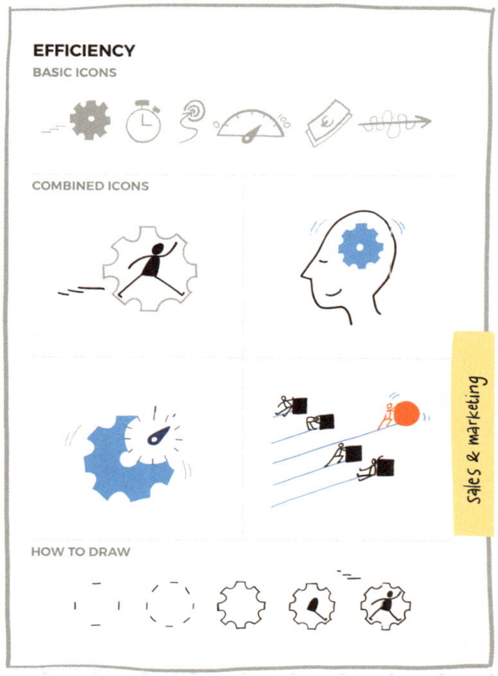

Sometimes it's even more impactful to draw the opposite of something you are describing. Or you can draw both to emphasize the difference. Try to draw both!

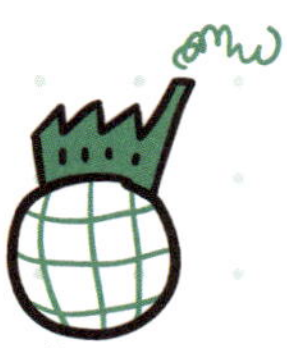

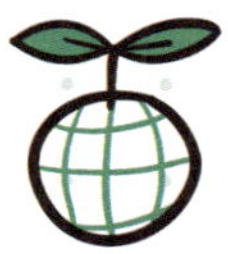

pollution → sustainable

miscommunication → understanding

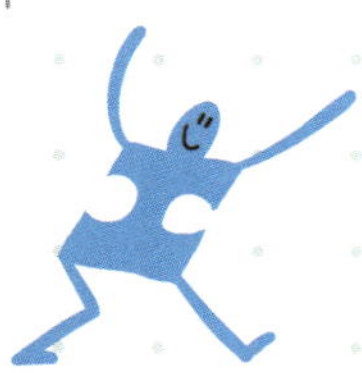

missing piece → complete puzzle

concept → final product

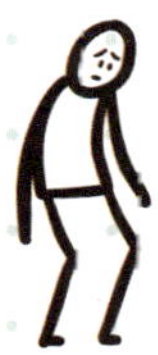

disagree → agree

alone → together

5.2 CREATIVE EXERCISES

Let's get your creative juices flowing! When you are combining icons, you sometimes have to think out-of-the-box, both conceptually as well as visually. Conceptually you can, for example, think of metaphors and other ways to tell your story.

Visually, you can think of creative ways to combine different drawings. On this page, everything is possible. Try not to overthink things. Just do it. Surprising things might happen!

Let's break down the drawings on the left into their two, three or even four elements.

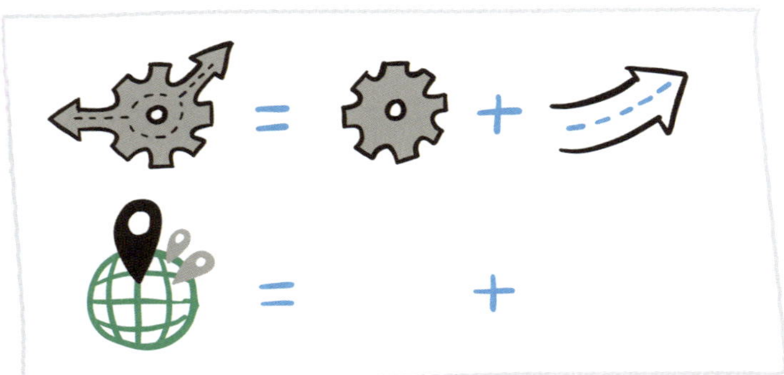

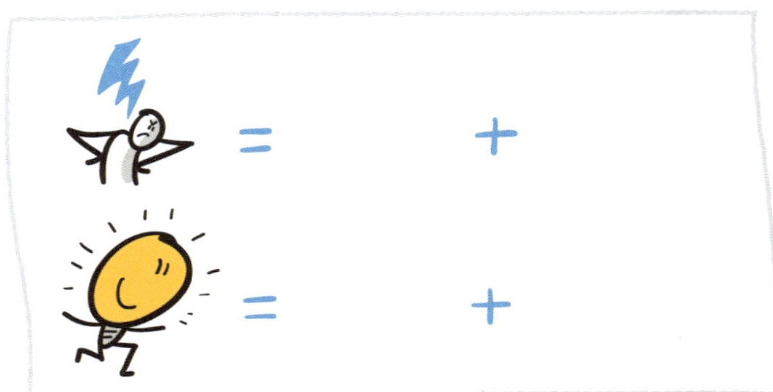

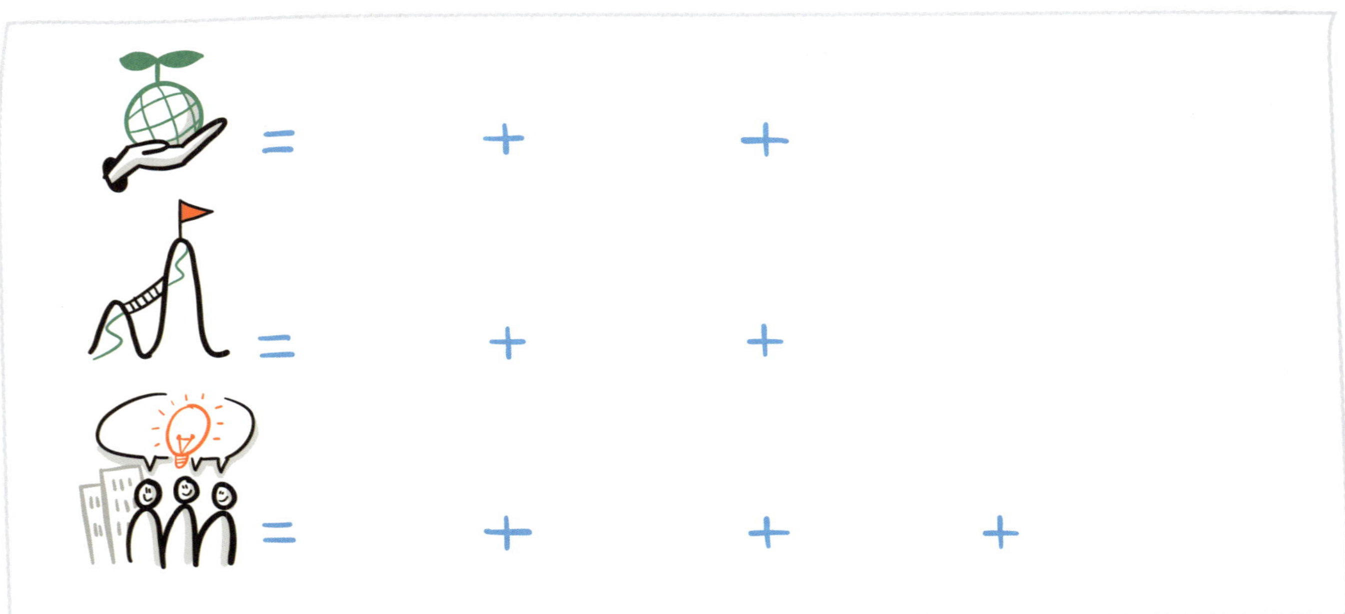

Fill in the empty boxes and combine the visuals to create something new!

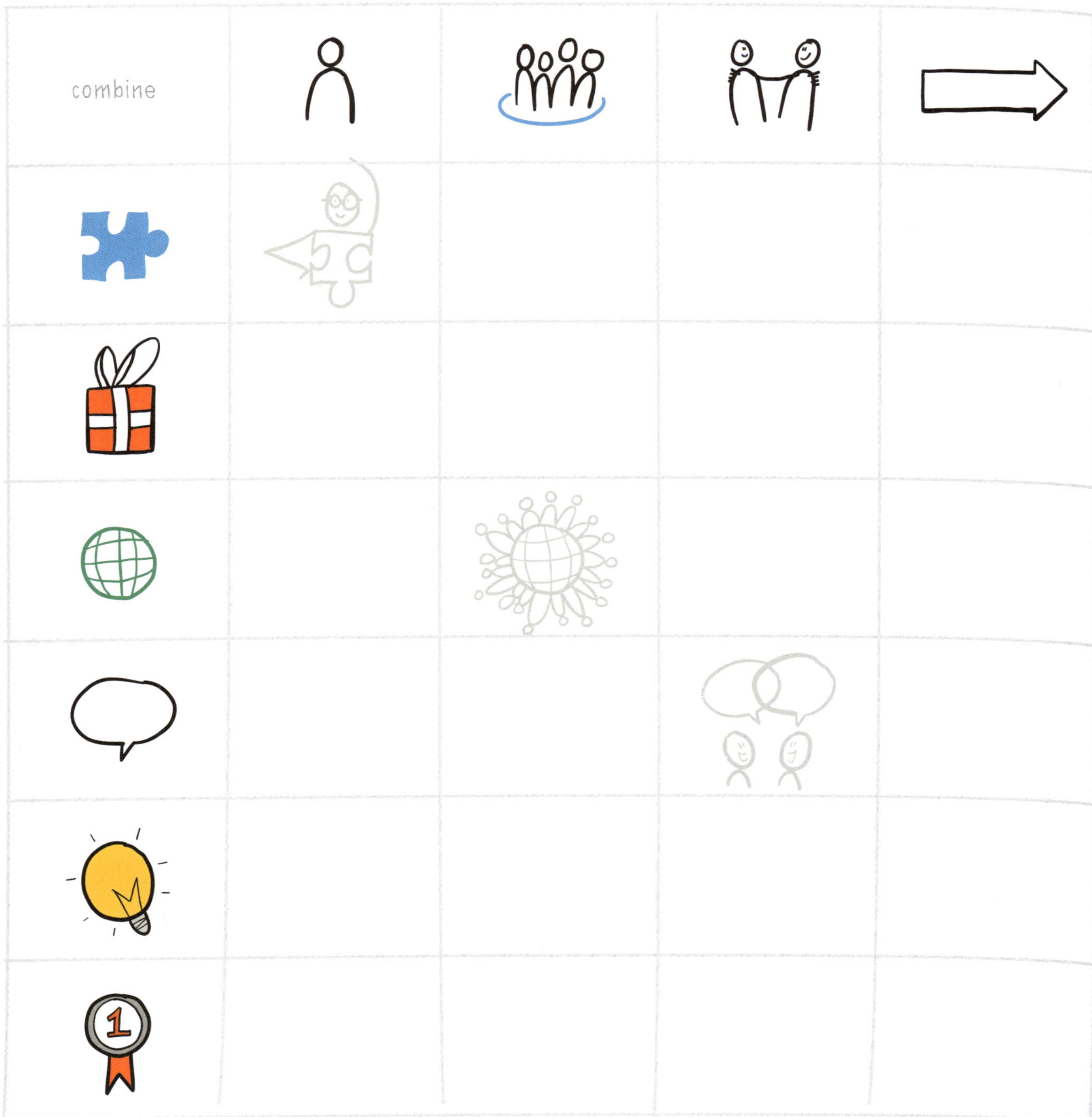

5.3 ASSIGNMENT: CREATE YOUR ICON LIBRARY

Let's start building your own visual library. We all have words that we often see or hear in your line of work. Words or concepts you often have to explain to people or jargon whose meaning isn't necessarily clear to everyone. Let's visualize them!

Make a couple of sketches/iterations of a combined icon that helps to clarify one of these words. Always keep the goal and target group in mind (Why do you want to communicate this?).

Write down some words for which you would like to have a visual.

When you have decided which sketch you like best, draw it again on the right page. Give it a title and draw a frame around it.

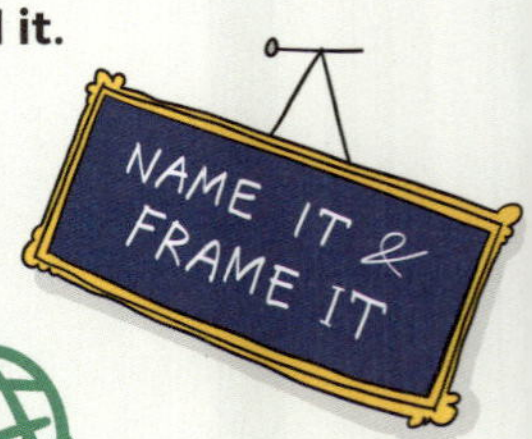

your illustration

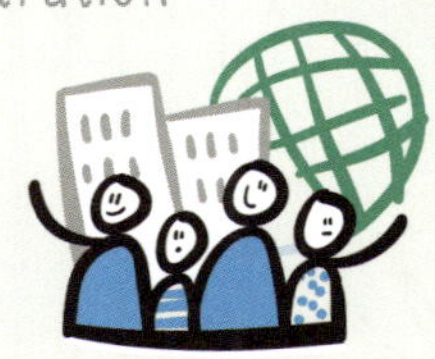

tiltle

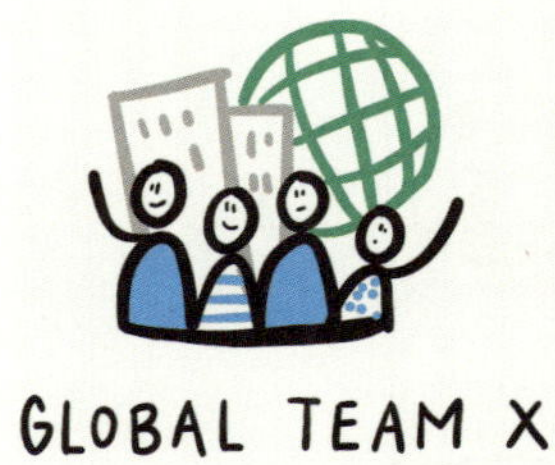

frame

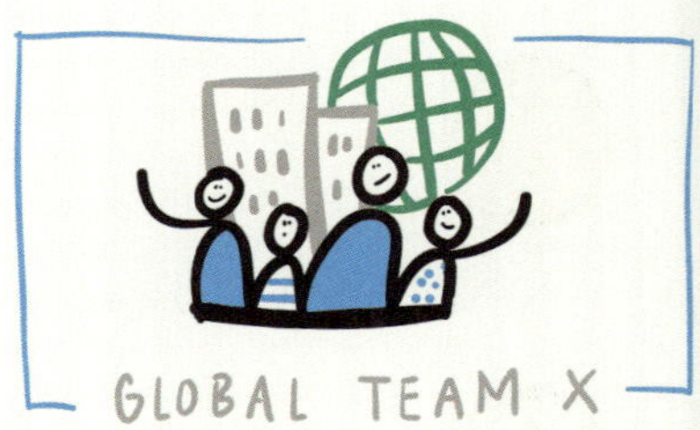

TIP Take a picture of your drawing and save it in a designated folder on your phone. That way, you always have your visual library at hand!

Draw your combined icon here

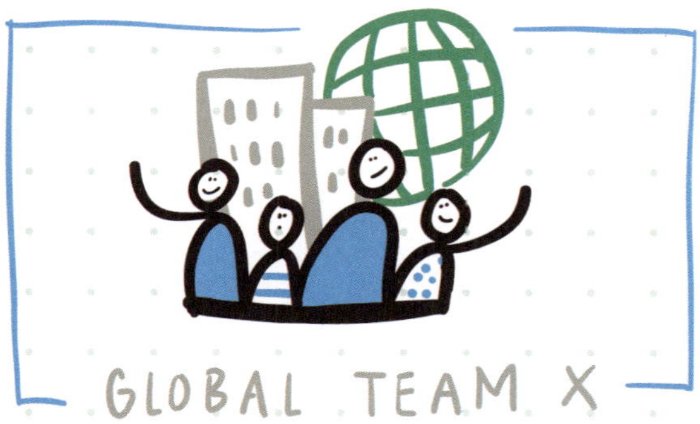

Write your topic here

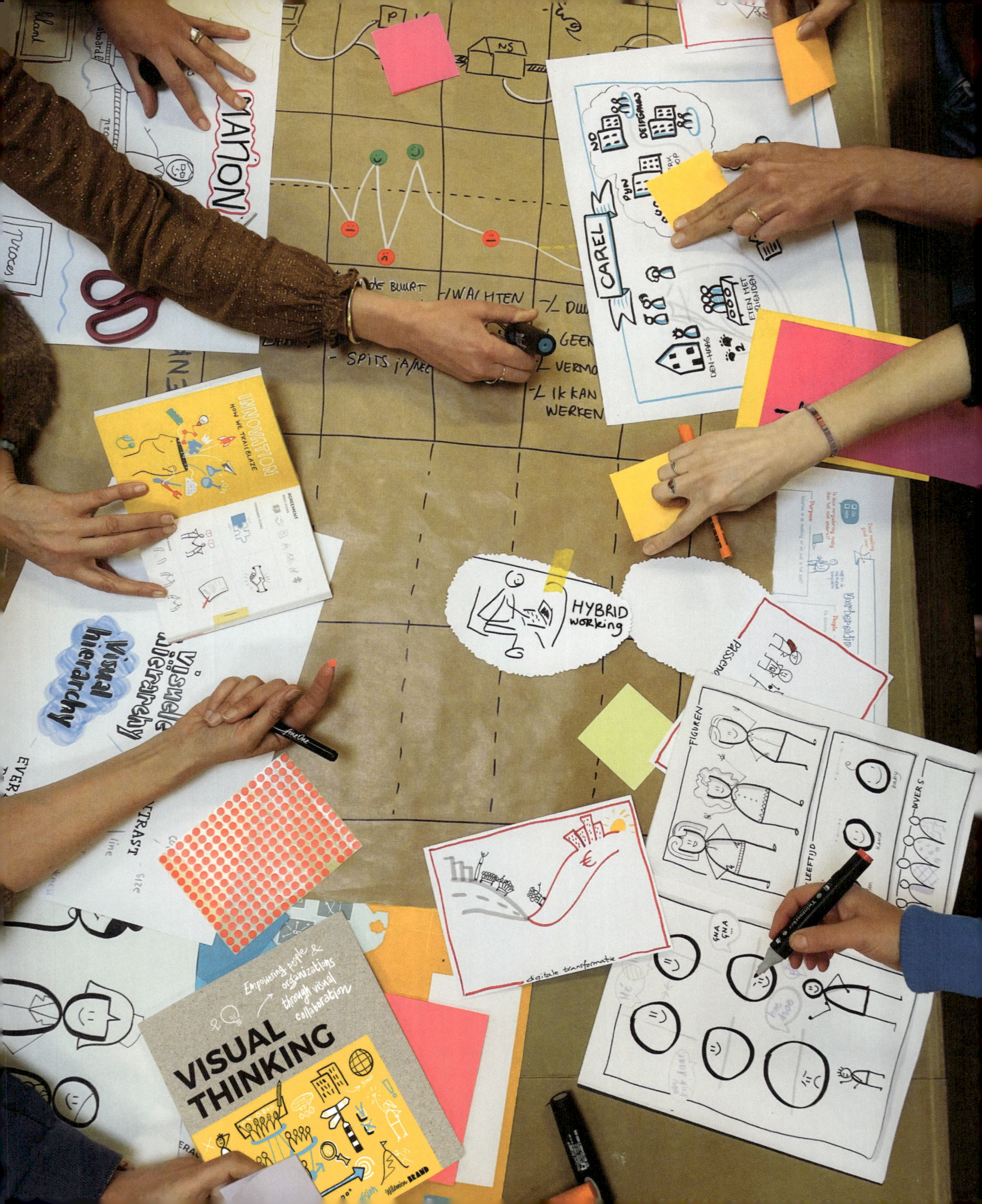
VISUAL THINKING
Empowering people & organizations through visual collaboration
HYBRID working
CAREL
Visual hierarchy
FIGUREN
LEEFTIJD
digitale transformatie

6. BURO BRAND'S FIVE VISUAL THINKING TYPES©

There is no longer any debate about the value of Visual Thinking in corporate settings. Big Tech and large corporations have embraced the power of working visually, and countless books have been written about how to use drawing, doodling and visualization in the workspace.

These days, nobody will laugh at you if you suggest drawing your team's problems. Visual Facilitators are common at brainstorming sessions. But even though we have seen thousands of people become inspired by the power and possibilities of Visual Thinking in the past 15 years, we've also seen a disconcerting trend. While people are excited about the opportunities Visual Thinking creates, only a few know how to tap its full potential in a practical sense.

In our trainings we are often asked these questions:

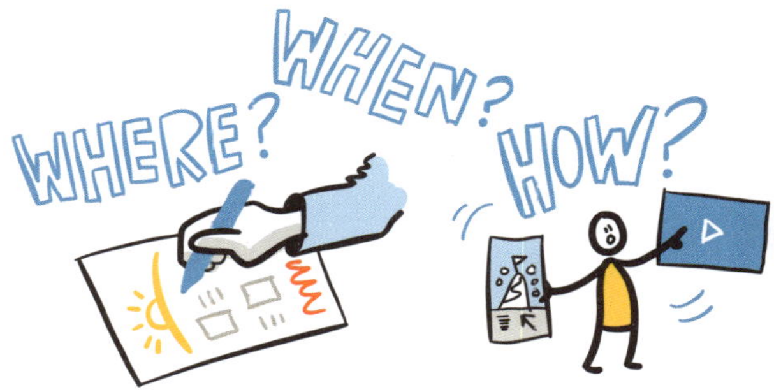

As you can see, there are a LOT of different questions about Visual Thinking because there are a LOT of different ways to implement Visual Thinking. To help you, we have developed Buro BRAND's Five Visual Thinking Types©!

In earlier chapters, we learned the basics and fundamentals of Visual Thinking. Starting with this chapter, we will take you through the five different directions of Visual Thinking and the ways you can use them. It's time to discover what kind of visual thinker you are!

How do I apply these techniques when I'm giving a short presentation?

I don't really care about all this fancy drawing, I just want to know how I can use it to work together with my team.

Where do I start when I want to make visual notes from my meetings?

How does this stuff help me present complex data in a clear and easy way?

6.1 LET'S MEET OUR FAVORITE FIVE

When looking at how you can apply Visual Thinking, we see five main types of application or, to put it another way, five goals that you might have with Visual Thinking. To make it easier to understand, we've formulated this into 'Buro BRAND's Five Visual Thinking Types©'. As soon as you understand what you want to 'get out of' Visual Thinking, you can start developing and practicing the necessary skills.

Whether it's generating a deeper layer of input from your co-creators, organizing thoughts and information, or inspiring people, there's a Visual Thinking Type for everyone. And if you can't choose, don't worry; you don't have to! See these types as temporary visual 'hats' you put on. You won't always want to use Visual Thinking the same way. Now let's introduce you to the five types!

VISUAL STORYTELLER

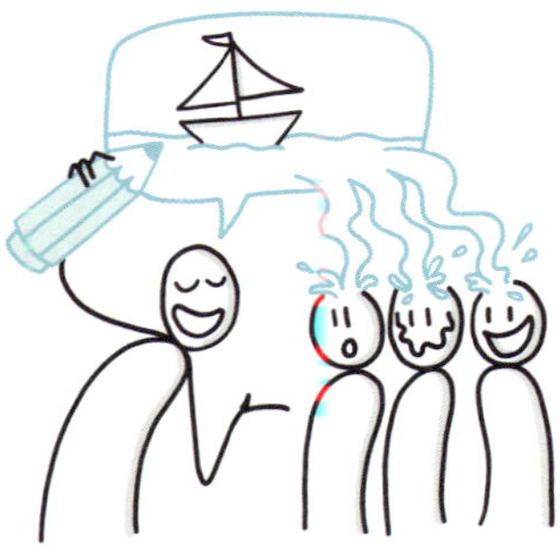

This type wants to use Visual Thinking to quickly convey ideas, inspire people and communicate visually. You want to use metaphors to draw people into a story and, most of all, make ideas and information stick!

TIP Look for analogies in your daily work: take any objective/hurdle/process and try to find a symbol, image or allegory that (roughly) corresponds to it. Read more about the Visual Storyteller in Chapter 7!

TIP Complete Part 2 of our e-learning to learn all about the different Visual Thinking Types, and about other courses that can help you develop your drawing skills.

VISUAL DESIGNER

A Visual Designer wants to use Visual Thinking to develop concepts into cool, sleek publications. Do you love design and focusing on details? Perhaps this is your type.

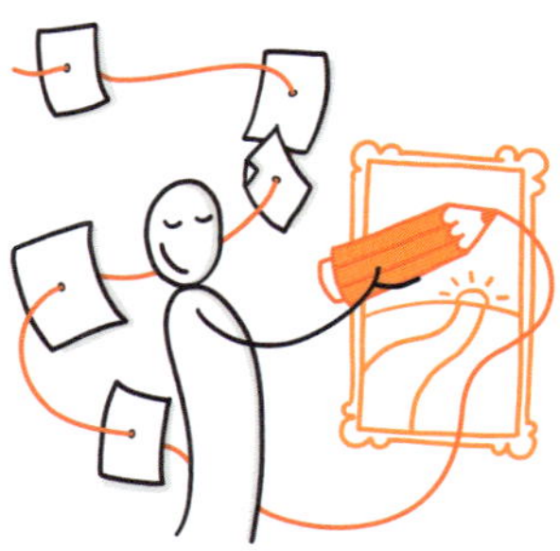

TIP Drawing every day, but also drawing the same thing over and over (and over) again is a great way to start. Read more about the Visual Designer in Chapter 8!

VISUAL REPORTER

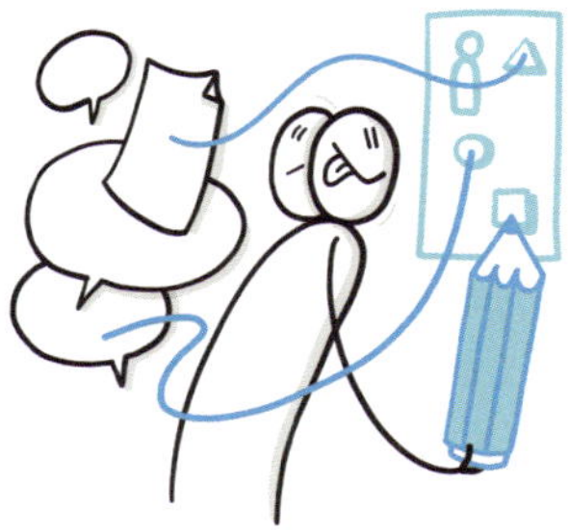

The Visual Reporter wants more than anything to get to the core of a story. To summarize it and make the information manageable. To better understand it.

TIP Practice writing by hand, and make your own Visual Minutes of news items or an inspiring TED talk. Read all about it and the Visual Reporter in Chapter 9!

VISUAL CO-CREATOR

Are you interested in developing your internal Visual Co-Creator? If you want to use Visual Thinking to make progress together with others and want to give everyone a (visual) voice, start by delving into the world of the Visual Co-Creator.

TIP Start out by learning how to make your own visual templates. Maybe plan a creative session, and use a self-made format to gather input or feedback. Read more about the Visual Co-creator in Chapter 10!

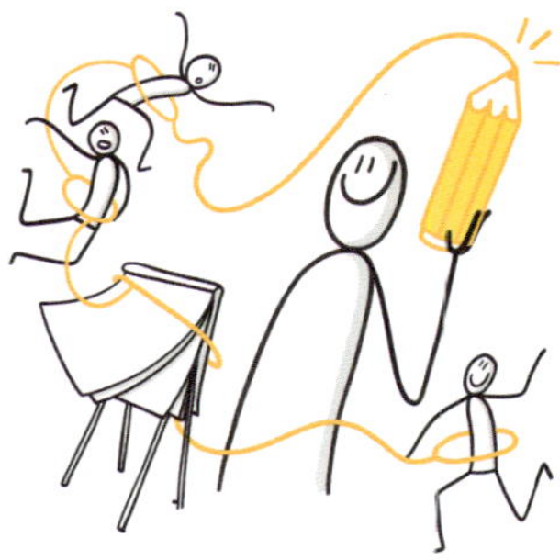

VISUAL ANALYST

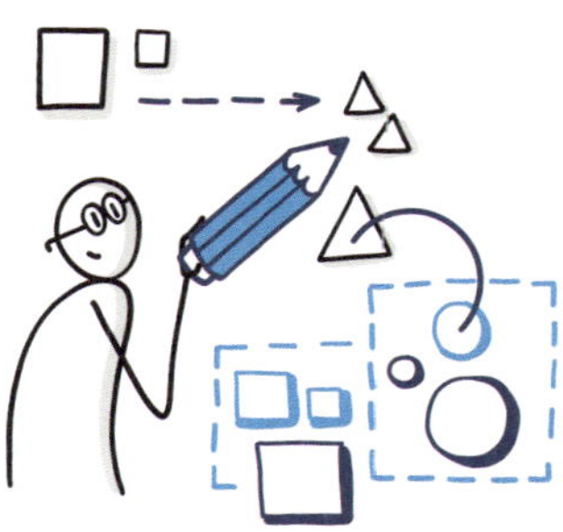

Do you want to get a clear overview of complex processes? This type focuses on the analytical side of Visual Thinking, and the use of visual structures to organize text or information.

TIP Start to drill down into this type by using colors, symbols and size to structure information. It can be as complex as your team's weekly workload or as simple as your daily morning routine. Read how to do this in the Visual Analyst in Chapter 11!

Buro BRAND's Five Visual Thinking Types© cover the entire spectrum of Visual Thinking and all its possible directions. It's not a linear path: you can develop your Visual Thinking skills in any (or all) of the five directions. As you gain more experience, knowledge and skills your Visual Thinking profile will become richer, and you will turn into a more all-round Visual Thinker. Check out a few examples below.

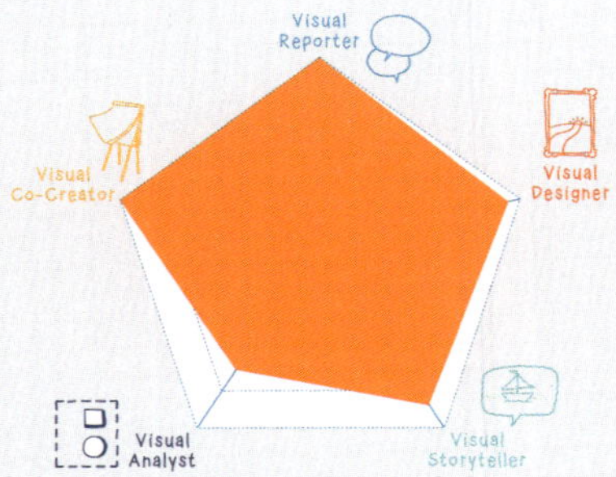

Willemien Brand, a Visual Thinker pur sang

Fluent in a lot of the directions, but has a sharper focus on visual recording, visual workshops and creating beautiful visualizations.

A facilitator of creative workshops

Has the tools to create sparkling workshops and templates, and uses their visual analyst skills to cluster and categorize input, to gain insights. Is also able to use a visual to summarize a workshop and share this with the participants.

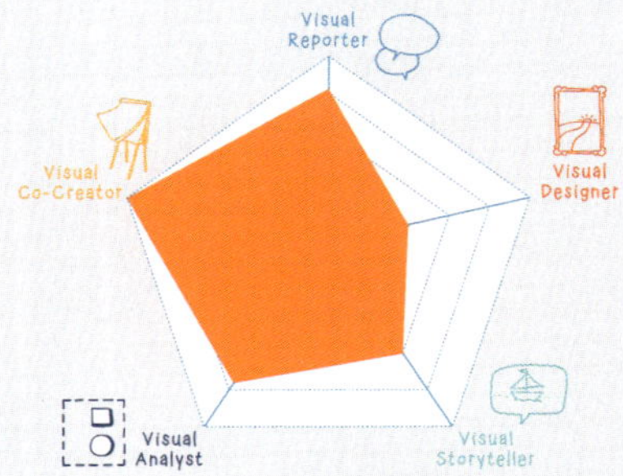

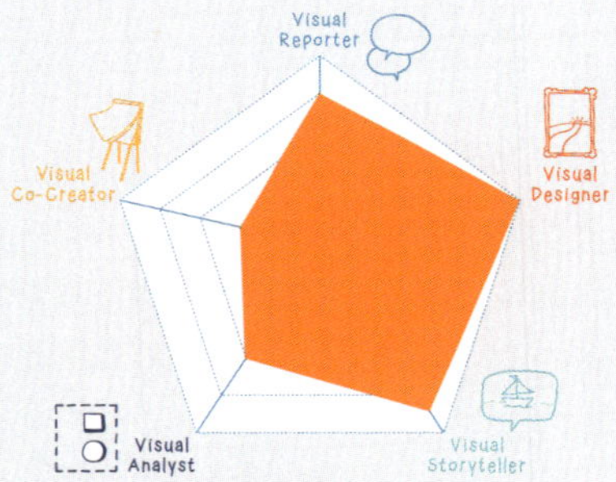

A marketing or communication strategist

Is focused on expressing a distinct message and setting up clear, cohesive marketing campaigns. Uses their visual design skills to create appealing visualizations and knows how to apply interesting metaphors to focus an audience's attention on the essence.

TIP As you can see, you will likely need more than one way of using Visual Thinking to achieve your goals. It is completely fine, and actually valuable, to focus on one or more specific Types that interest you.

WHICH TYPE ARE YOU?

Now that you've got to know the five types, reflect on your work and what you want to achieve with Visual Thinking.

Do you want to inspire people during your presentations? Translate dull text into gripping visuals? You might even see a bit of yourself in every type.

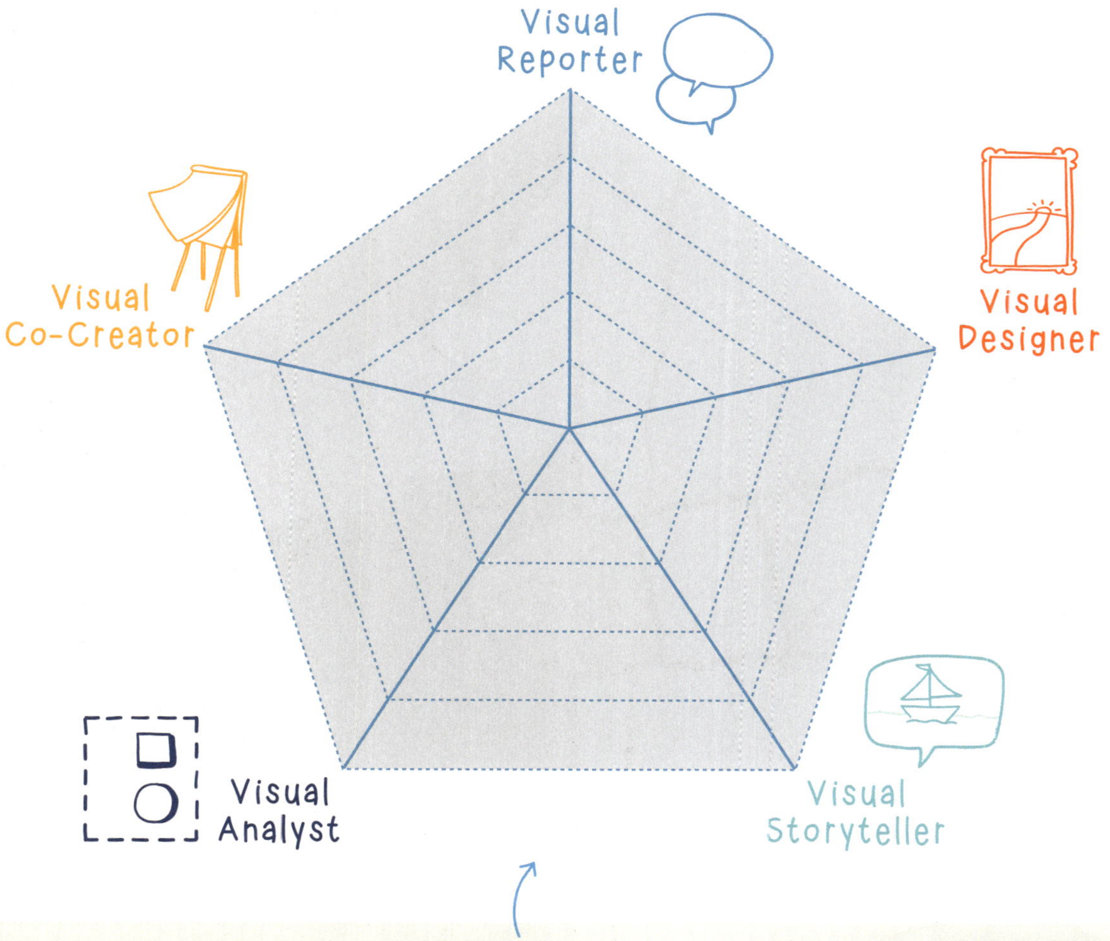

1. Take a pencil or marker and draw a line to indicate where you feel your skills are now.

2. With a different color, indicate how much you want to delve deeper into the different types. Be strict and don't say you want to be an expert in every type ;)

3. When you've finished this book, come back to this page, and see how much progress you've made, and where you still have room to grow.

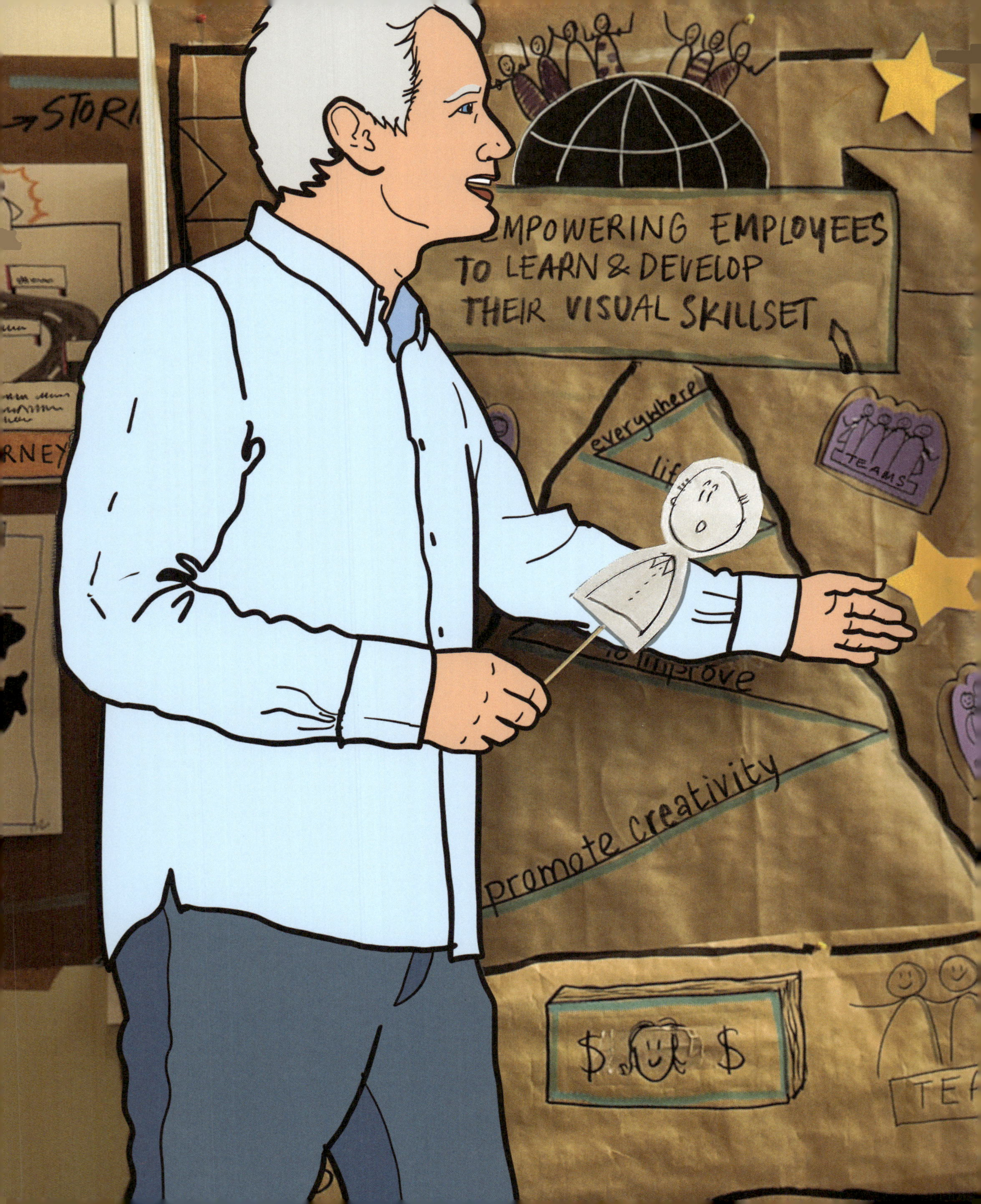

EMPOWERING EMPLOYEES
TO LEARN & DEVELOP
THEIR VISUAL SKILLSET
everywhere
promote creativity
TEAMS

7. VISUAL STORYTELLER

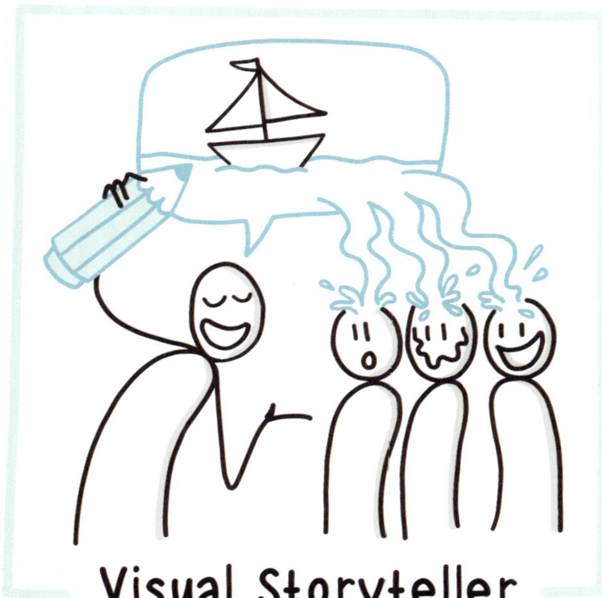

A Visual Storyteller uses Visual Thinking to quickly convey ideas, inspire people and 'talk' visually. They focus on using metaphors and visualizations to engage people in a story and to make ideas memorable.

They often show leadership through their inspirational stories. They can communicate strategy or change by visualizing the desired future, impact or outcome. Thinking in pictures and being able to use them to explain things or stimulate the imagination of others is also a great coaching tool.

It's important to be able to grab your audience's attention with a recognizable and relatable storyline. That way, they will remember your story much better and understand the interplay of different elements. To help you tell this sort of visual story, we are going to show you how to find and use metaphors!

In this chapter we will give you inspiration for metaphors, set you some creative exercises and do an assignment to find and visualize your own metaphors in a presentation about yourself.

WHAT YOU WILL LEARN

7.1 Creative examples
7.2 Metaphor hunting
7.3 Assignment: Introduce yourself

TIP Make a prototype to test your story! This is how you can check whether it resonates with your audience.

7.1 CREATIVE EXAMPLES

You may not realize it, but we already use metaphors a lot in business language.

"This process is like a 'journey' towards our final goal; we will encounter uncharted paths, and we have to watch out for 'hurdles' along the road." Or: "We want to work together like 'a well-oiled machine'".

A common metaphor is 'the tree'. People say: "We want to grow as a team or organization. To do that, we need resources!"

We can break down each element of the tree metaphor and how it applies to daily work.

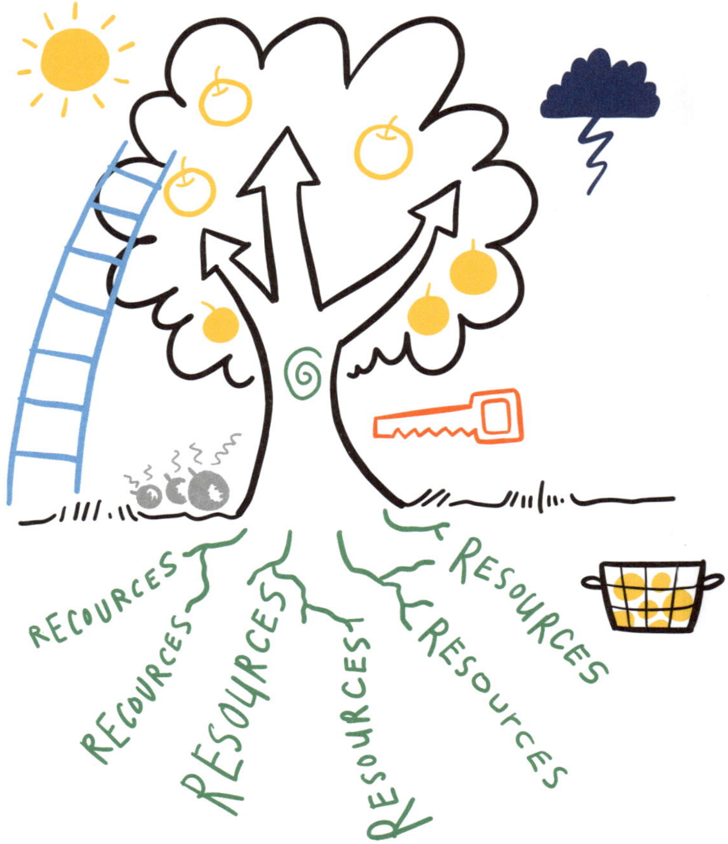

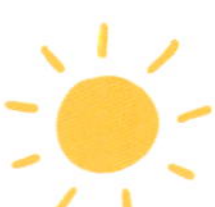 sun energy to grow

 bad weather threats we cannot control but we can anticipate

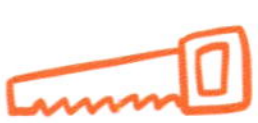 saw threats we can control

 high-hanging fruit outstanding products - to make them takes a lot of effort

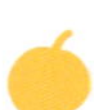 low-hanging fruit easy products (cash cows)

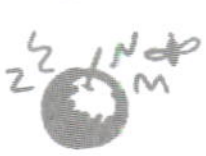 rotting fruit products that waste time and money

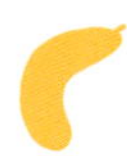 banana are we focussing on the right product?

 core our purpose

 branch one of our strategy pillars

 ladder what do we need to reach our goals?

 basket how do we want to market?

You can challenge yourself to think about the tree metaphor and growth and see what other metaphors you can think of. To get the ball rolling (there's another metaphor!): growth rings within a tree trunk, growing seedlings, roots, a hammock between two trees (relax!), Tarzan, a palm tree (relax again!), a tree through the seasons, etc. Let your brain associate freely and see what fits your story best.

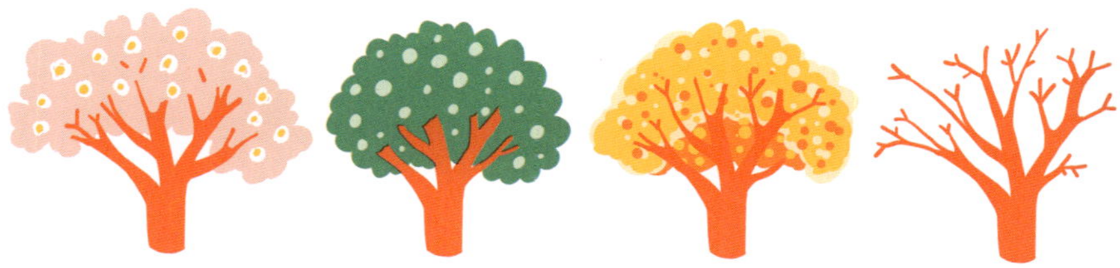

Each color represents a different aspect of the project we want to grow

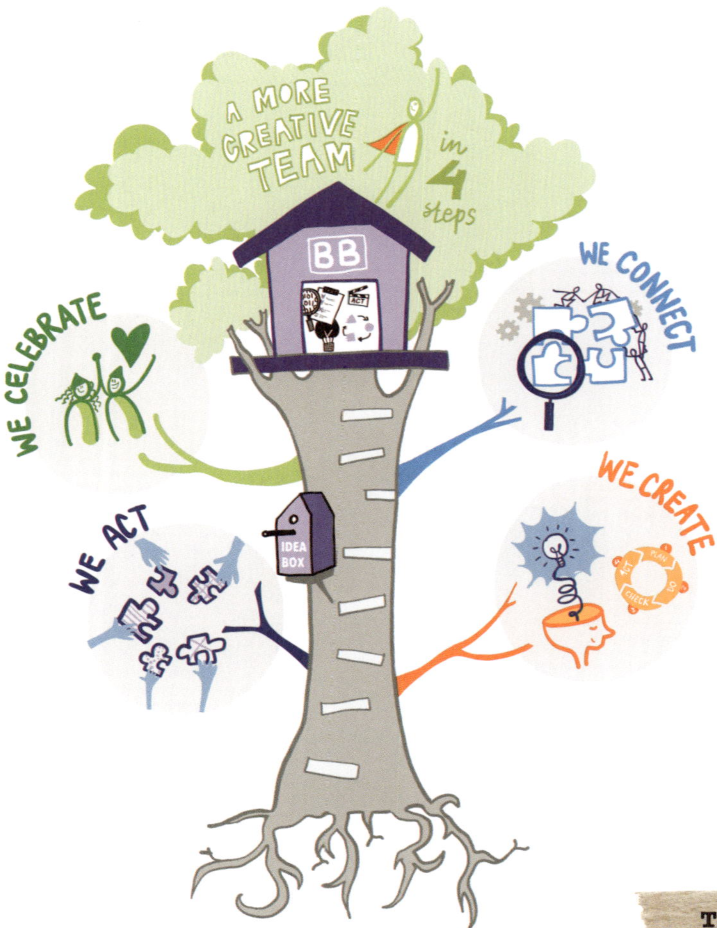

Instead of the tree we can also focus on a tree house or bird houses.

Do you often pick a visual or picture from the internet? And do you create or build your story around it? How cool it would be to create a metaphor yourself and build it around your own story and then support it with your own visuals?

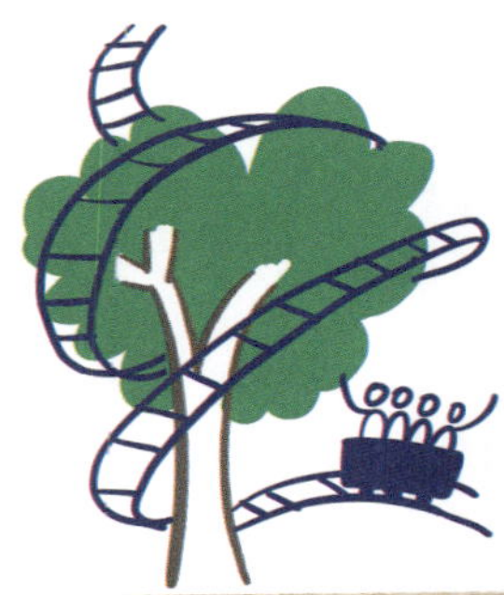

TIP Avoid using double metaphors! This may confuse the audience and does not benefit the outline of the story.

Here are some visualizations we have made in the past. These ones are richer than the obvious roadmaps that we also draw a lot :)

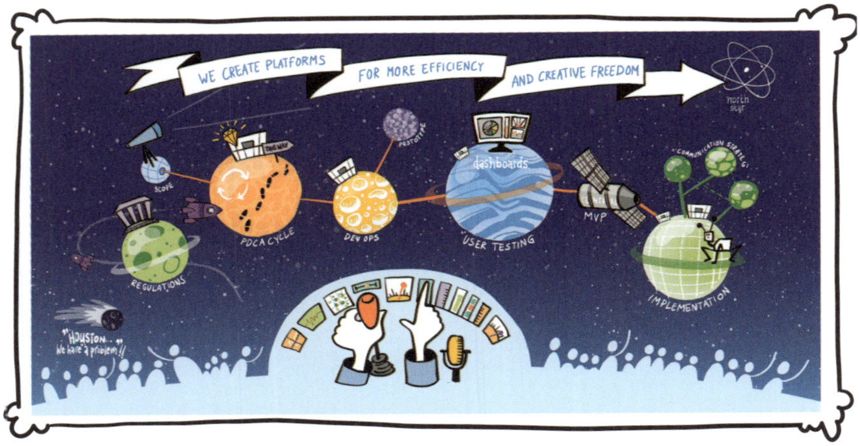

Data governance to be in control of master data, focussed on steps.

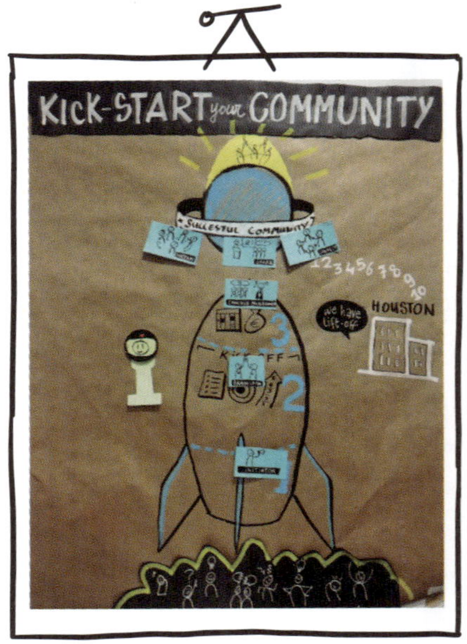

A plan with a three-phase process to kickstart the community.

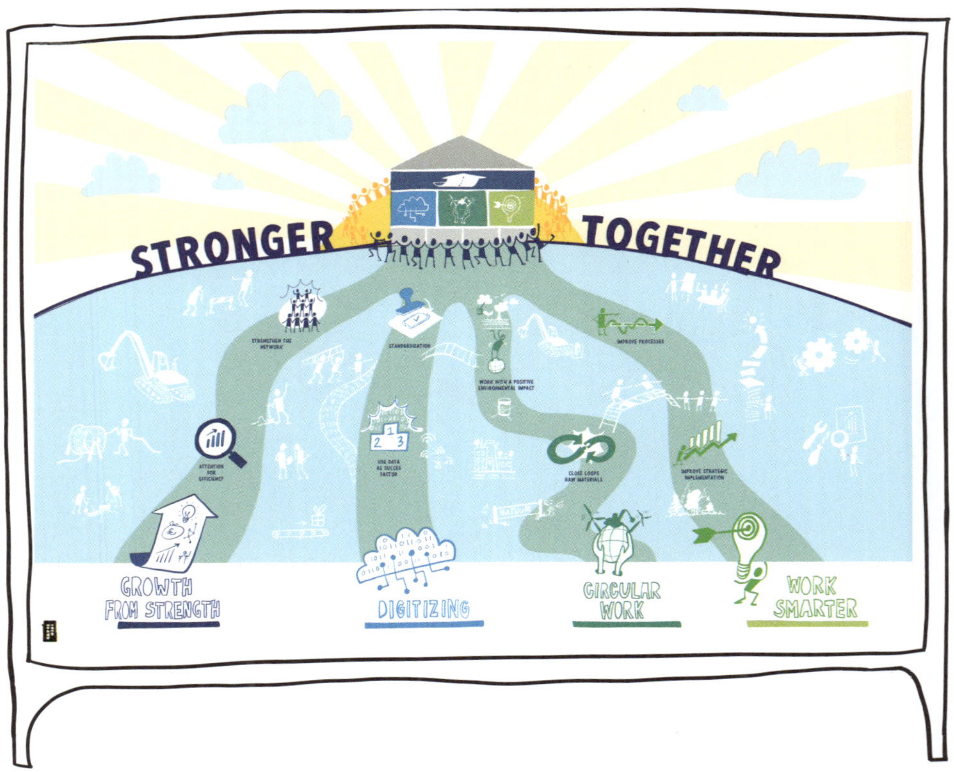

The challenges we want to tackle, divided into four subjects, on our way to a better future.

HOW TO TELL THE STORY?

You can have a great metaphor, but for it to make an impact you need to explain it using either text or speech. If your accompanying story doesn't match or strengthen your visual, it will be lost on your audience. Here are some elements to pay attention to during your story or presentation to ensure it has maximum impact.

Use your story and how it is built up to underpin your picture's visual hierarchy. Start with what is drawn boldest or what stands out first.

- Start with a fun anecdote (make it your own) and introduce the relationship between the information and the metaphor.
- Keep it short and sweet. The visualizations already speak volumes.
- Tell as much as possible from memory and follow a clear story structure.
- Make sure everything you cover in your visual is explained in your story. Otherwise, an unfinished feeling will linger in your audience's mind and get in the way as you want to move forward.
- Close with a catchy phrase, question or call to action.

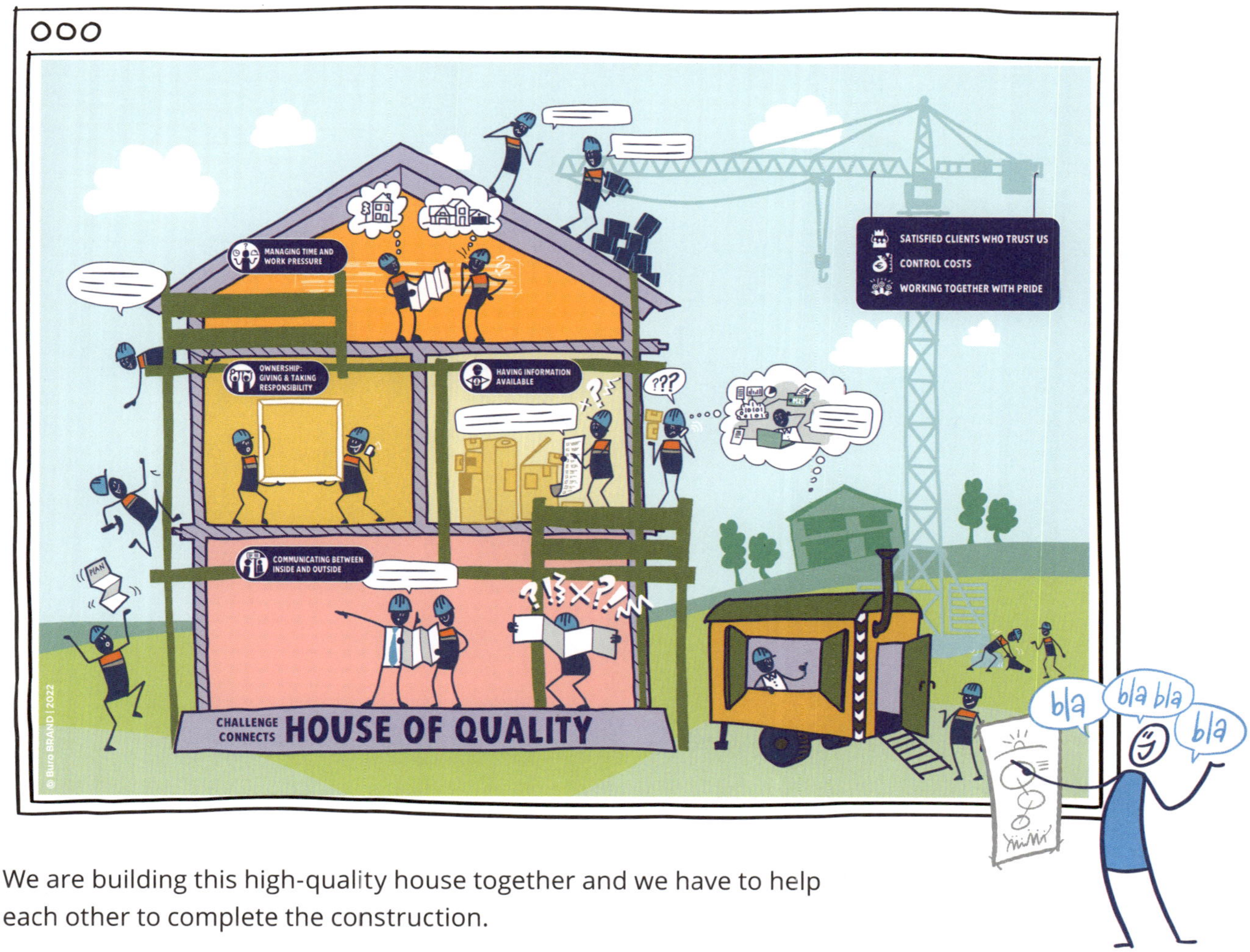

We are building this high-quality house together and we have to help each other to complete the construction.

7.2 METAPHOR HUNTING

We all know the famous SWOT analyses. But it's way more fun if you apply a metaphor! We love our Harry Potter-styled frame on the right, but it can also work with other metaphors. It's actually an easy way to get familiar with using metaphors or push yourself to try new ones!

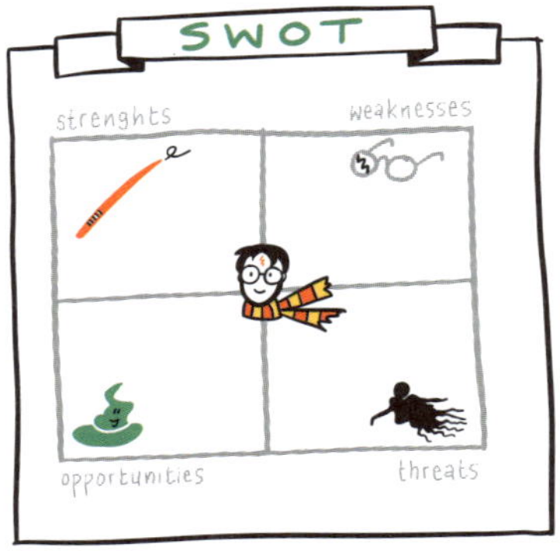

Think of what could be used as a subject for the S (strengths), W (weaknesses), O (opportunities) and T (threats) for the given metaphors below. In the last column, add your favorite TV-show, sport, movie, supermarket or whatever metaphor you like.

	Luke Skywalker (Star Wars)	Titanic	Barbie	
S	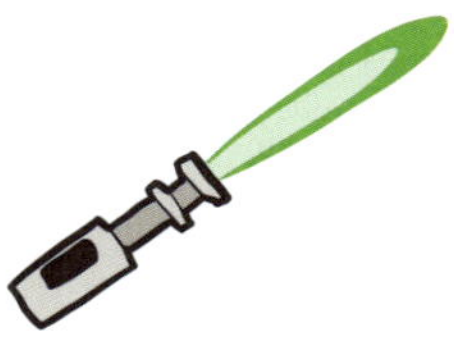			
W			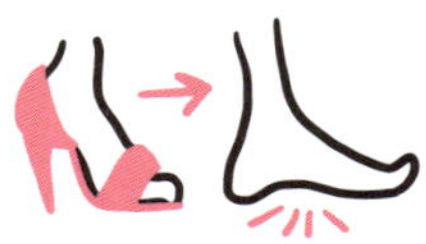	
O				
T		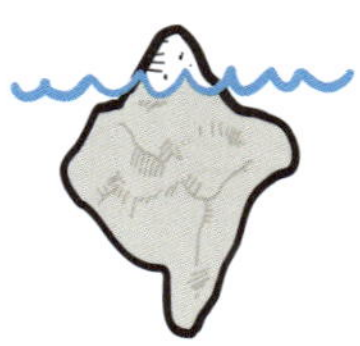		

creative	out of the box	square	home	dog	wagging tail
result-oriented	goal	ball	tennis	net	obstacle
...					
...					
...					
...					
...					

Another exercise to get your creative juices flowing! Think of some of your core qualities and write them on the left. Associate freely from that word, on to the next, as the example on the first row shows. You can't go wrong, they're YOUR associations.

TIP Somewhere around the 4th column there are probably some useful metaphors that you could use to describe or present yourself!

7.3 ASSIGNMENT: INTRODUCE YOURSELF

How cool is it to be able to introduce yourself with an image that people will remember you by?

Let's make sure your team, colleagues or clients know who you are. First, think of what you want to express about yourself. What kind of information do you want your audience know about you?

Second, think of a metaphor; are you the spider in a web, a guide or a problem solver?

Do you have any hobbies, or something that really sums you up? What metaphors popped up in the association exercise, is there anything you could explore further?

Dive into this as you did with the SWOT analysis. Before fully drawing it on a separate piece of paper, make a rough sketch on the right page and make sure you link the characteristics of your metaphor to the information about yourself.

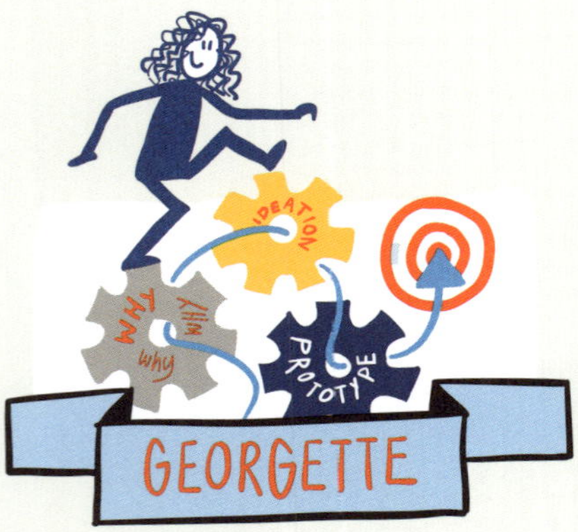

well-oiled machine

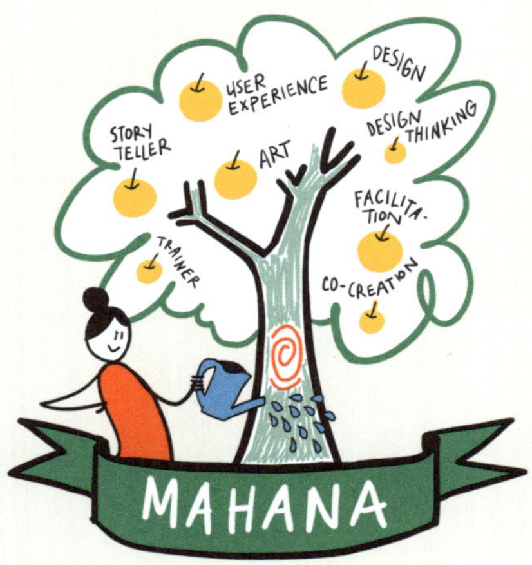

growing tree

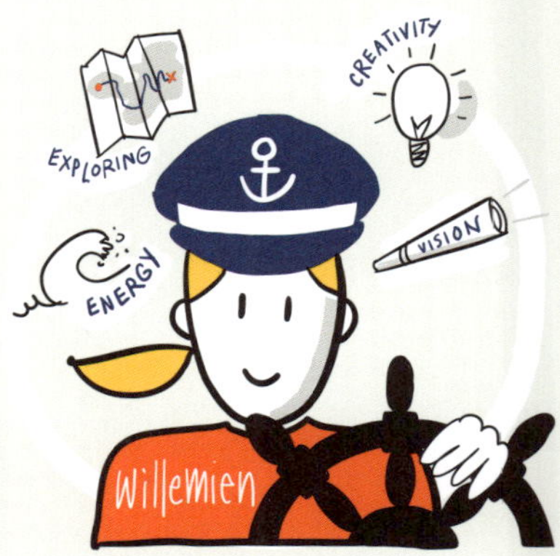

sailing

TIP You can draw yourself combined with the metaphor, but it's also possible to focus fully on the metaphor itself.

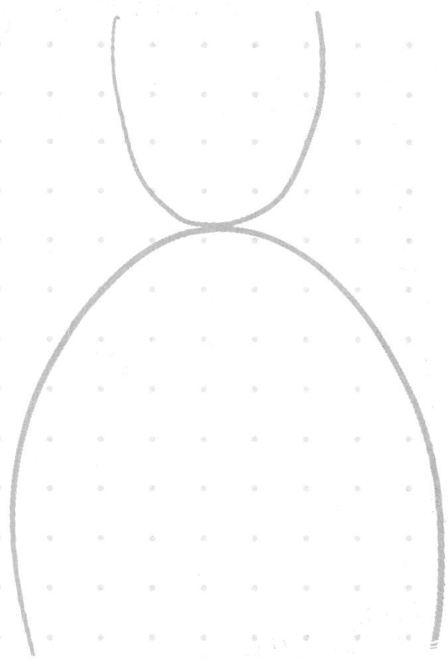

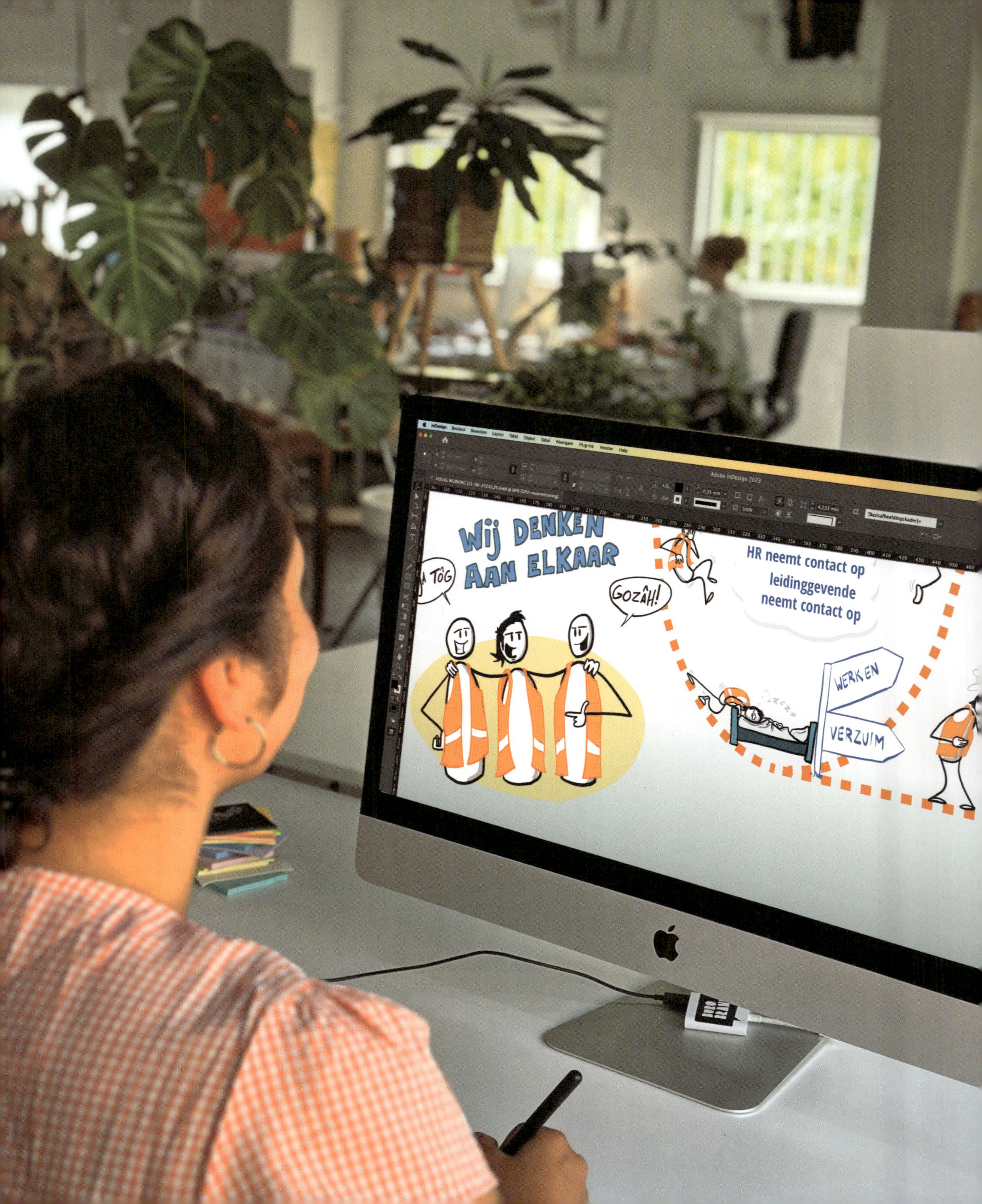
Wij DENKEN
AAN ELKAAR
GOZÂH!
HR neemt contact op
leidinggevende
neemt contact op
WERKEN
VERZUIM

8. VISUAL DESIGNER

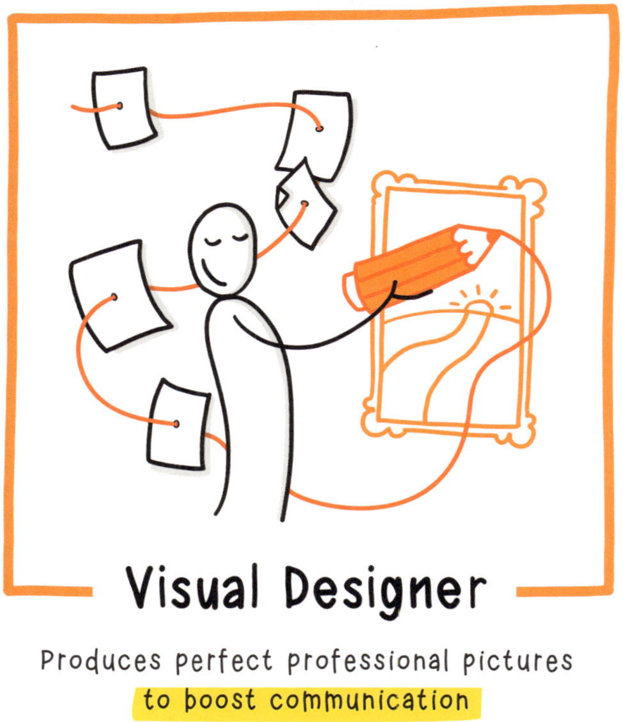

A Visual Designer uses Visual Thinking to develop concepts and conceptual ideas into cool, sleek expressions. Her focus is on the design and the small details of a visualization that make a big difference; illustrations, infographics and animations. They have the power to 'do' and 'make' things. They are able to visualize and therefore communicate anything, including their own plans, dreams and ambitions.

As you can see, drawing skills and knowledge about visualizations are important for this Visual Thinking Type. To highlight and practice just one thing, let's practice drawing people!

This is a great skill when, for example, you want to portray people taking part in a meeting, when drawing a visual with real characters, or when you want to portray someone with a specific job or demographic. When drawing people, it's best to use a unique or recognizable illustration style. And a great way to discover your unique style is by drawing people!

WHAT YOU WILL LEARN

8.1 O-heads and U-heads
8.2 Clothing and accessories
8.3 Assignment: Portraits

8.1 O-HEADS AND U-HEADS

Drawing a portrait sounds harder than it really is! You just have to cut down on details. No nose, lose the wrinkles and forget about the eyelashes.

- Start with a big O or U, depending the hairdo
- Look for the parting in the hair; this is your starting point for the rest of the hair
- Draw either the outline or some of the hair strands (not too many!)
- Add eyes, ears, a mouth, a beard or glasses if needed...

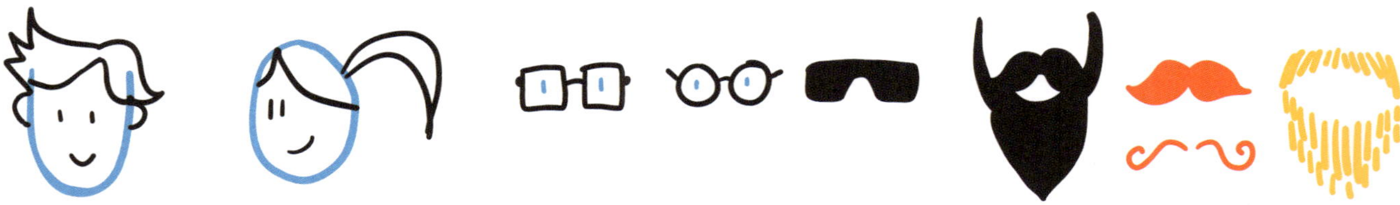

Practice makes perfect, so finish the portraits below. Step by step we make it harder for you by leaving out more details.

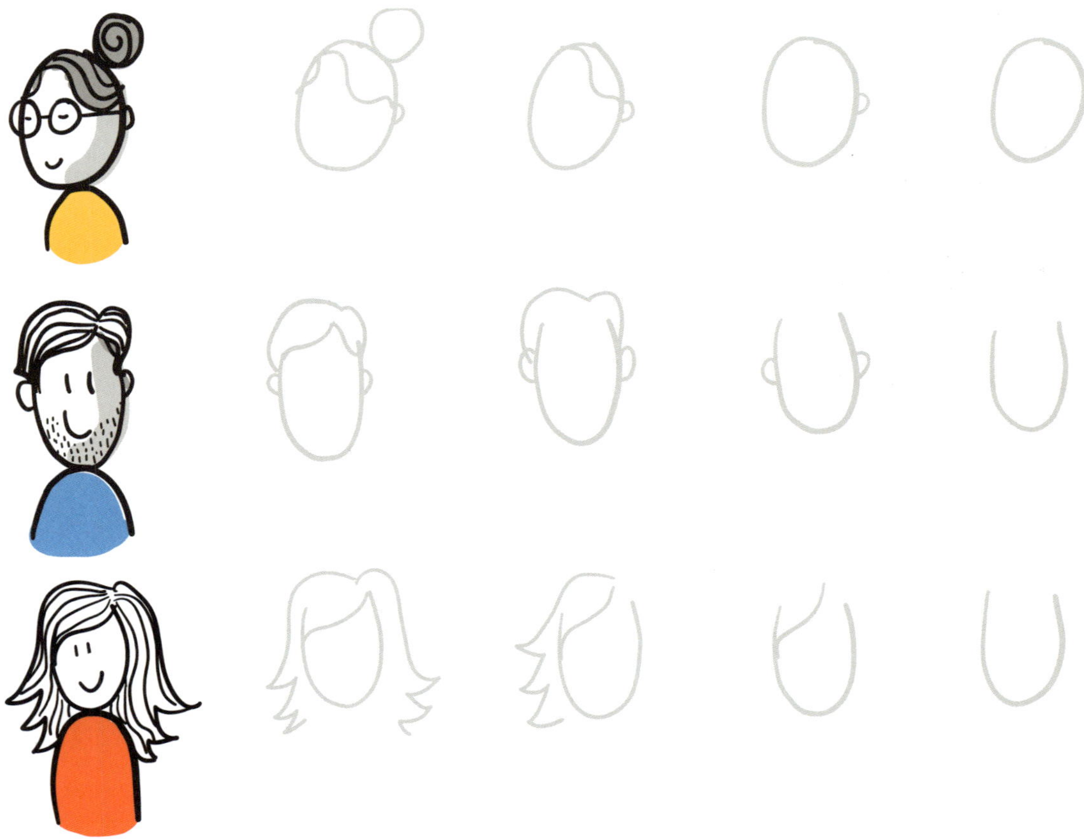

Copy the hairdo below

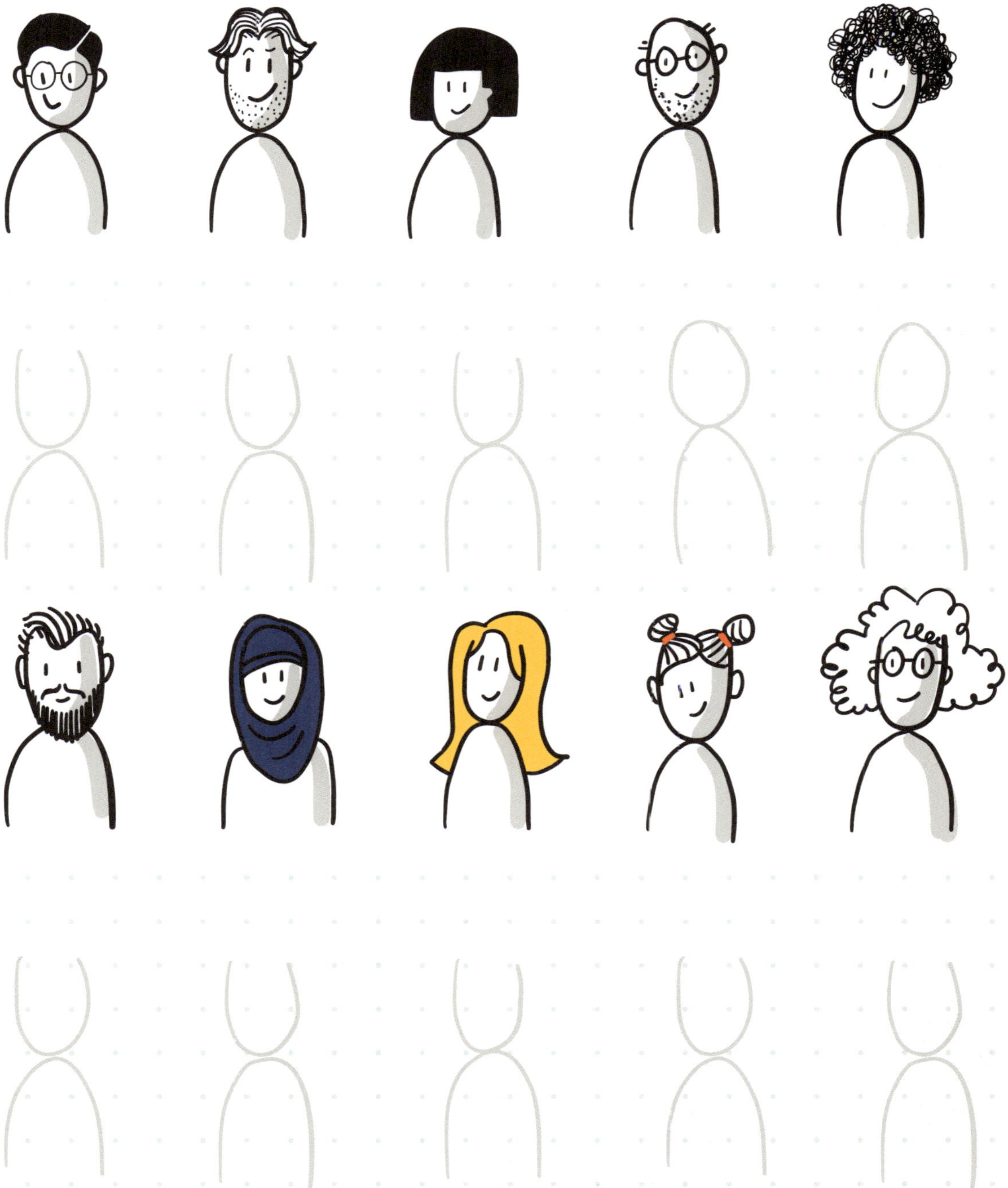

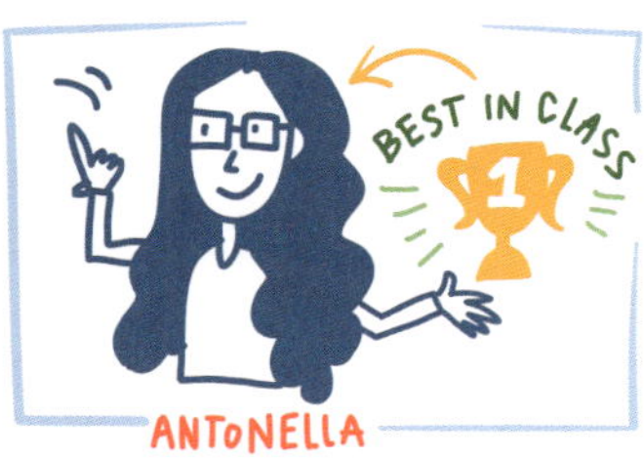

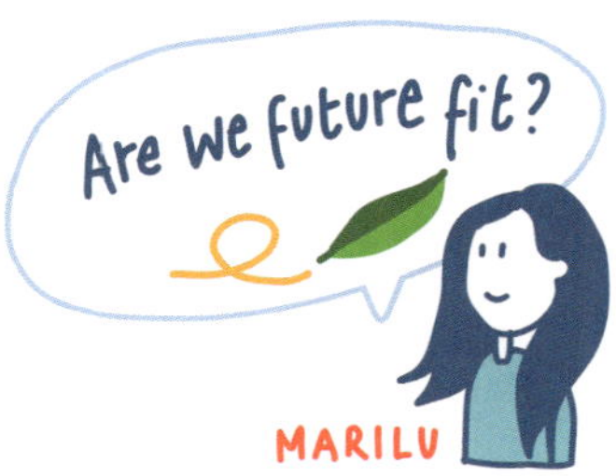

TIP Practice your portraits by sitting somewhere and drawing the people around you.

8.2 CLOTHING AND ACCESSORIES

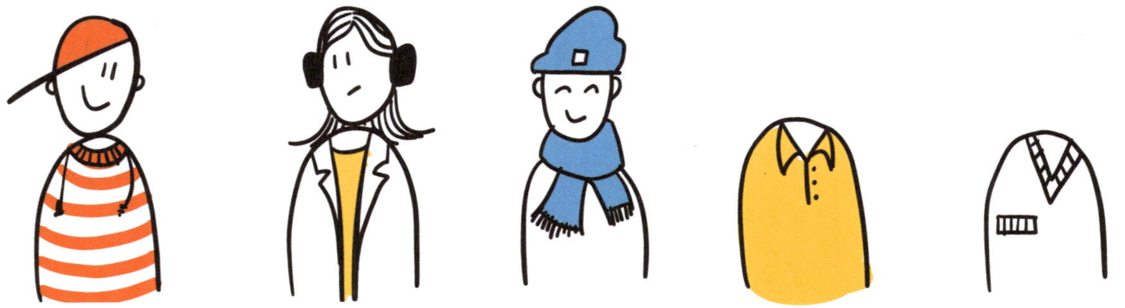

Copy these outfits and add some different heads and faces

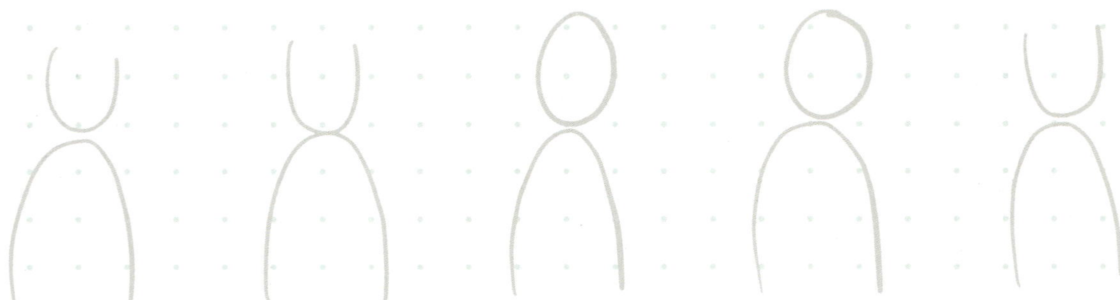

Copy these outfits

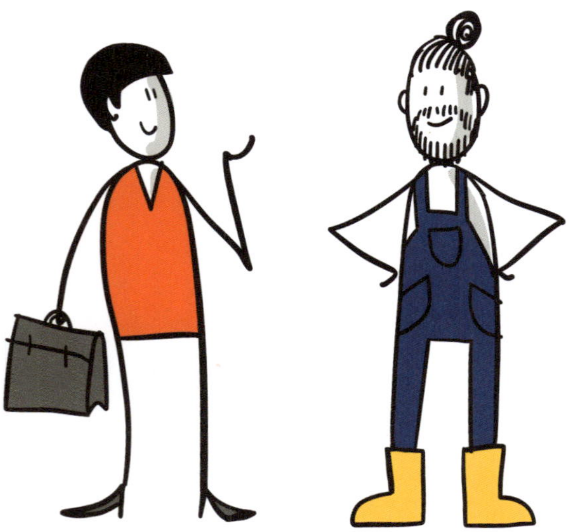

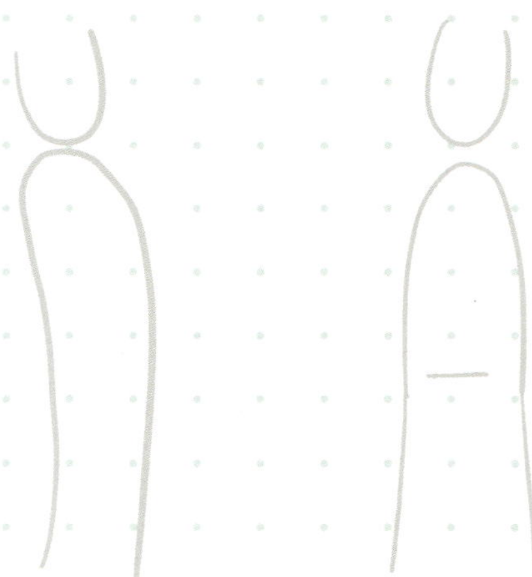

When drawing people going places, it is good to know how to portray jobs in a simple way. As you can see, there are several ways to do it. It's all about clichés and exaggeration! You can either portray their outfits, or explain what they do with icons, for example in their bodies.

Can you give the empty people outlines the missing elements to visually explain their job?

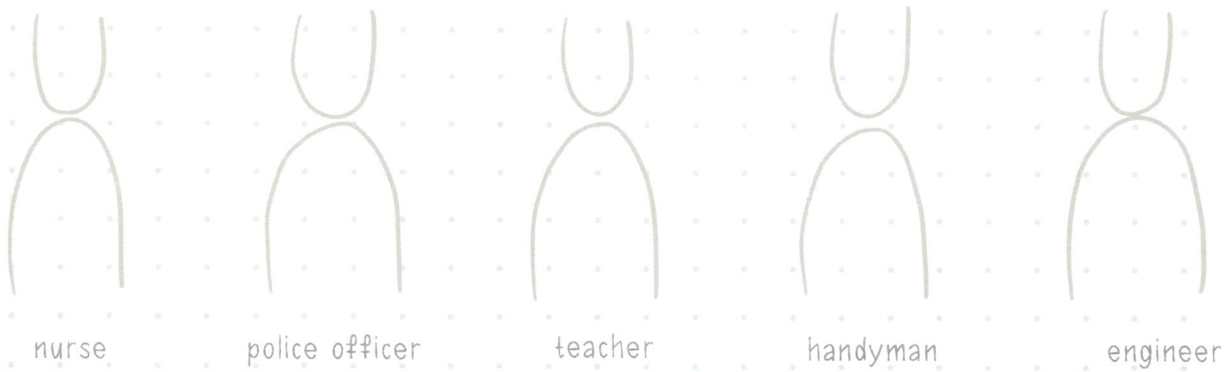

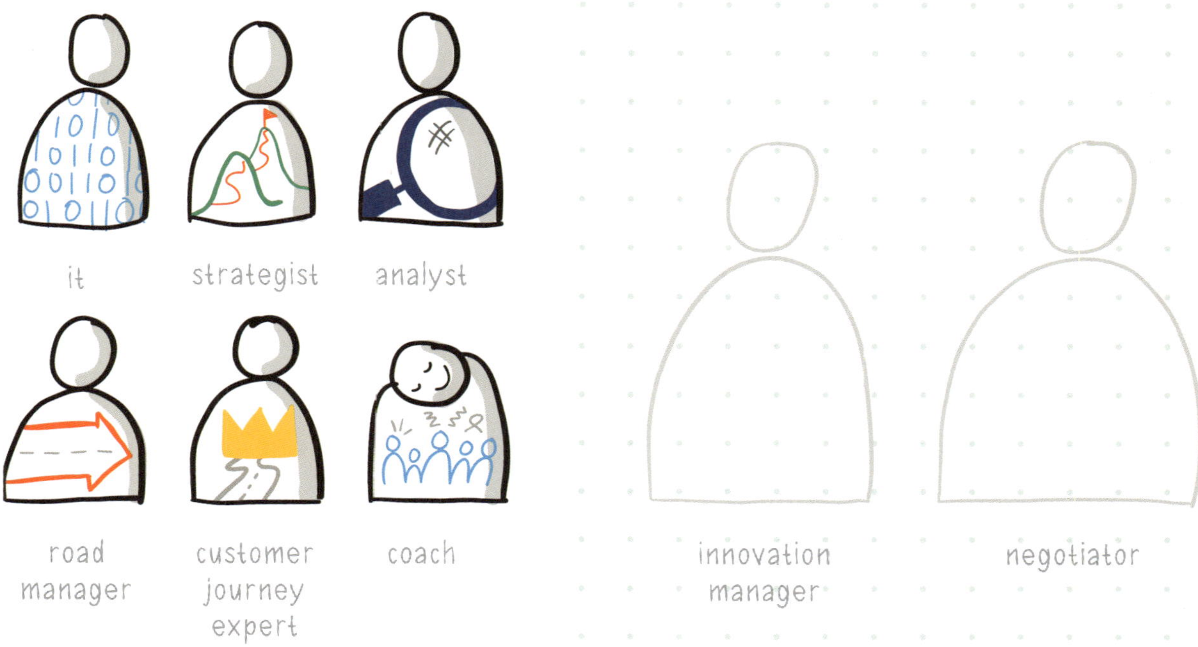

CREATE YOUR OWN STYLE!

Experiment with different ways to draw a character to find one you like and can always fall back on!

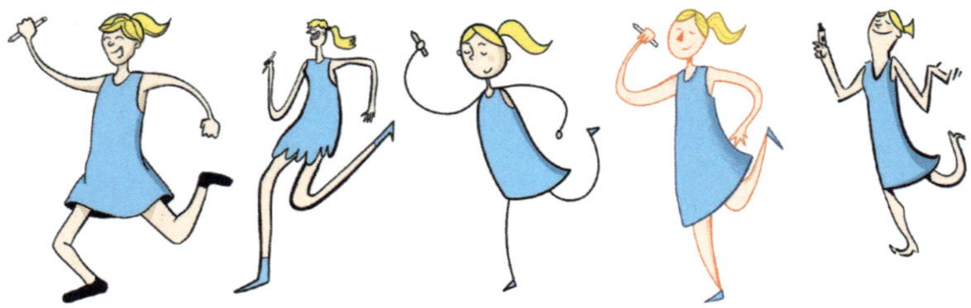

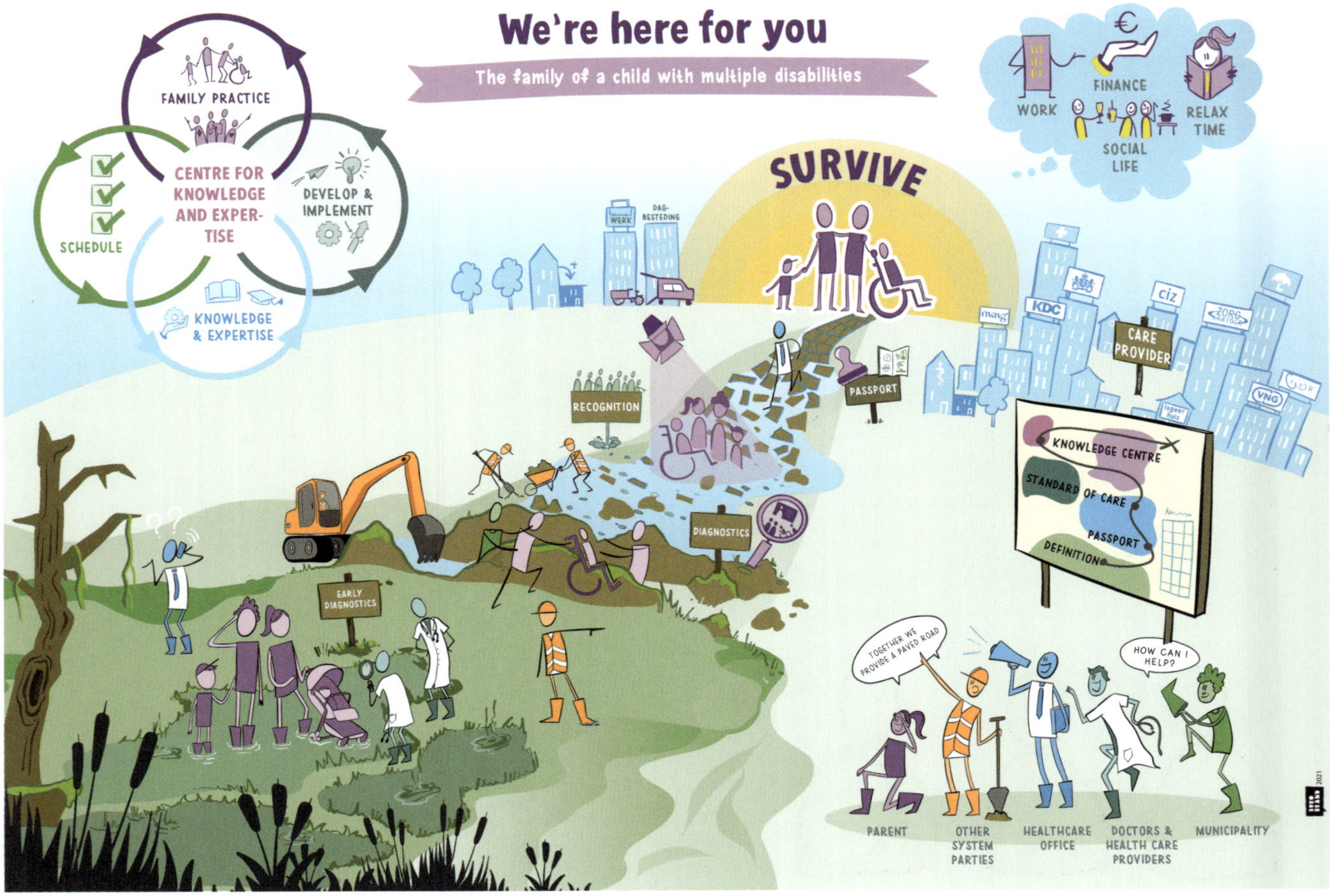

This is a large visual in which multiple layers of information come together to paint an overarching picture.

This Praatplaat shows a road that at the beginning (the "as-is" situation) is swampy, strewn with rocks and bumps, but slowly becomes passable. On the horizon (the "to-be" situation) is the relaxed family who have found their way through the warren of government rules and services for living with and caring for a multi-handicapped child.

The purple people are the family. Other people are stakeholders helping search for good care and support.

8.3 ASSIGNMENT: PORTRAITS

Next time you get together with your colleagues, try drawing them as a fun way to start the meeting. Of course, you can draw any other group of people, but whoever you choose: don't be afraid to show them your portraits! Don't be too hard on yourself, push through any insecurities and pay attention to the details that make people recognizable, e.g. their hairdo, shape of their glasses or what they wear.

TIP If you are in a meeting and have a list of projects or tasks shown somewhere, draw and cut out portraits that function as avatars. Everybody can put their own avatar next to the task they want to work on, have ideas for or consider important.

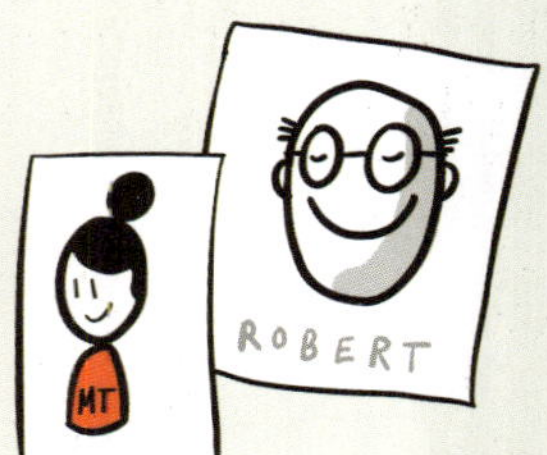

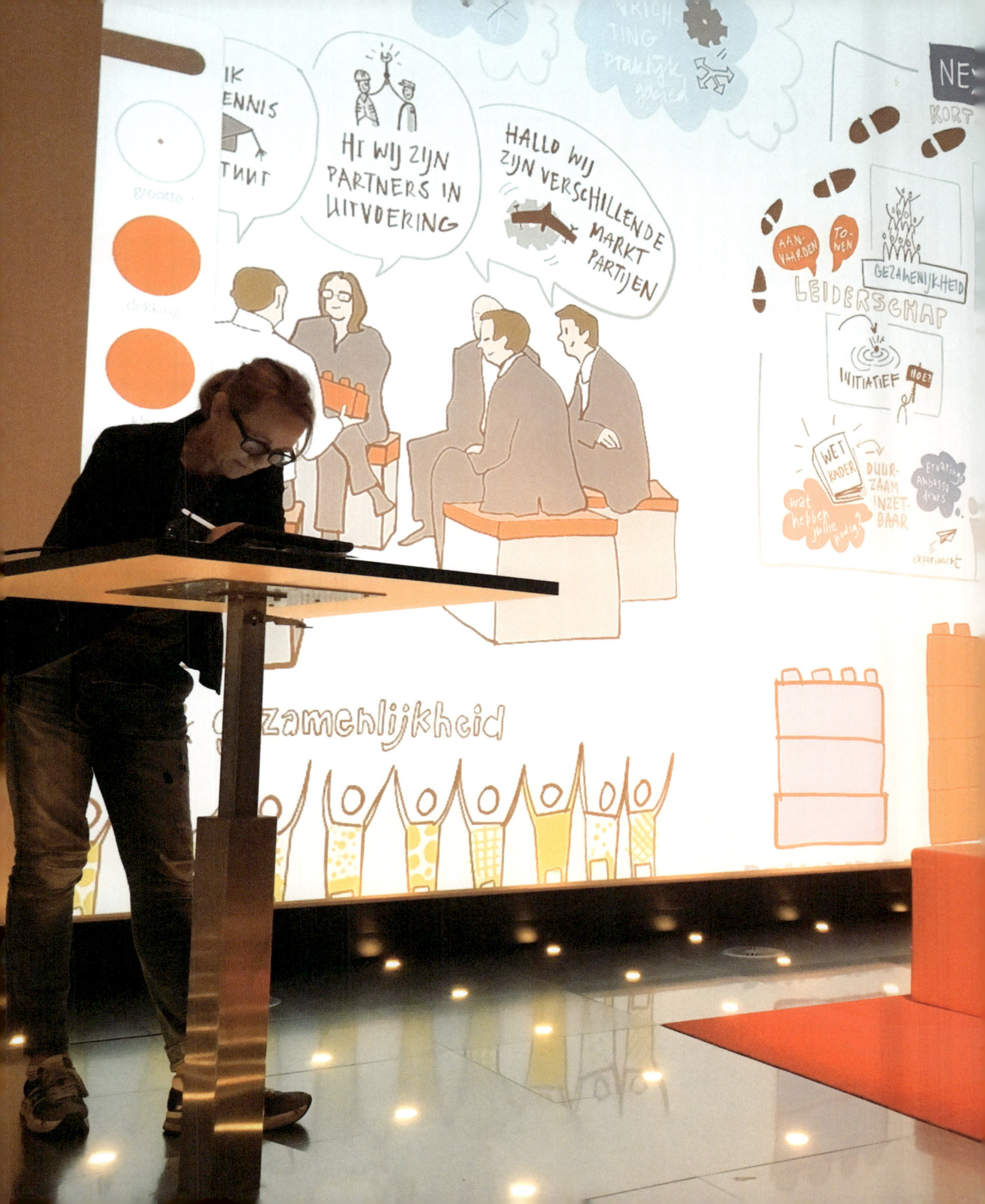
grootte
dekking
HI WIJ ZIJN PARTNERS IN UITVOERING
HALLO WIJ ZIJN VERSCHILLENDE MARKT PARTIJEN
KORT
AAN-VAARDEN
TO-NEN
GEZAMENLIJKHEID
LEIDERSCHAP
INITIATIEF
HOE?
WET KADER
DUUR-ZAAM INZET-BAAR
wat hebben jullie nodig?
Ervarings Ambassa deurs
experiment
zamenlijkheid

9. VISUAL REPORTER

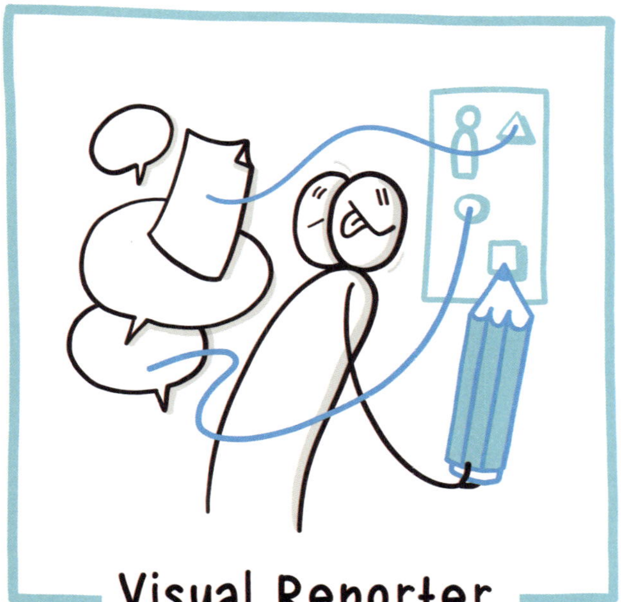

A Visual Reporter uses Visual Thinking to get to the core of a story, to summarize it and/or better understand it. Their focus is on translating text into (an) image. Think of developing appropriate icons, visual minutes and finding the perfect balance between text and image. They often work in communications, or need to communicate things regularly. They use visuals to help with their presentations, as their audience loves them to present things in a clear and 'to the point' manner. This helps people – including themselves – to get things done.

As you can see, when working on a larger canvas, it is important to pay close attention to the layout. You want to help people 'read' the overall image by providing a clear visual hierarchy. And you probably cannot draw everything, so your handwriting is also important. These are all subjects we practice in this chapter! It is also vital to have an extensive icon library at hand and know all about containers and dividers. Being a good listener/reader and being able to recognize key points are also what makes a good Visual Reporter. Combining all these elements will allow you to make summaries, visual notes and to-the-point illustrations.

WHAT YOU WILL LEARN

9.1 VISUAL HIERARCHY

You've already been introduced to the concept of visual hierarchy. In this chapter, we take the idea beyond a single illustration, and look at how to create visual hierarchy in situations where you have multiple illustrations and information components vying for attention. You make it much easier for your audience if you add visual hierarchy. Because we want people who look at your drawing to be able to instantly "read" it. It helps your viewers to see the big picture and the order within that picture before breaking it down into smaller components.

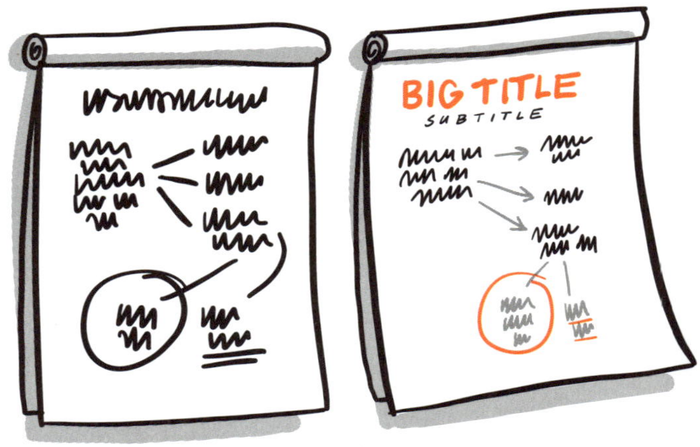

what usually happens — what we want

Circle the drawing that is the most eye-catching of the two: that's the one that stands at a higher level in the visual hierarchy.

TIP One color and thickness makes the drawing difficult to break down and "read". Vary your colors and thicknesses.

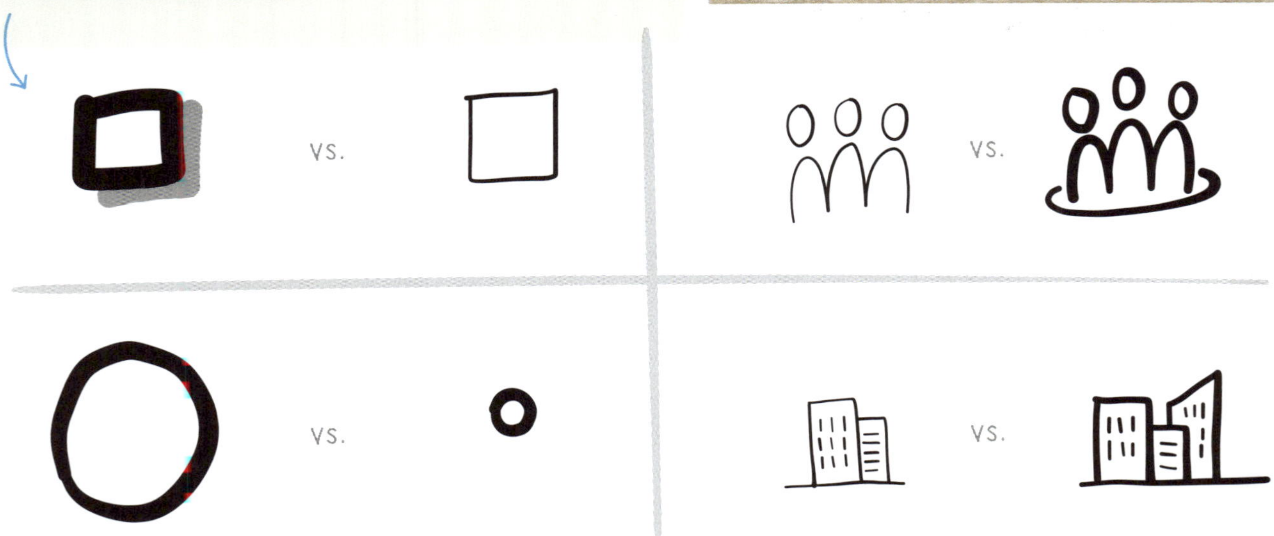

Which parts are interesting for your target group? How will you highlight it? You can use bold colors, or thicker black to make those parts stand out, or keep things light or gray. By varying in color and thickness, you can shift attention towards one piece of information or another. You have the power to decide which pieces of information are (more) important.

Try to make this poster easy to read for investors who want to know about the outcome and impact of this study.

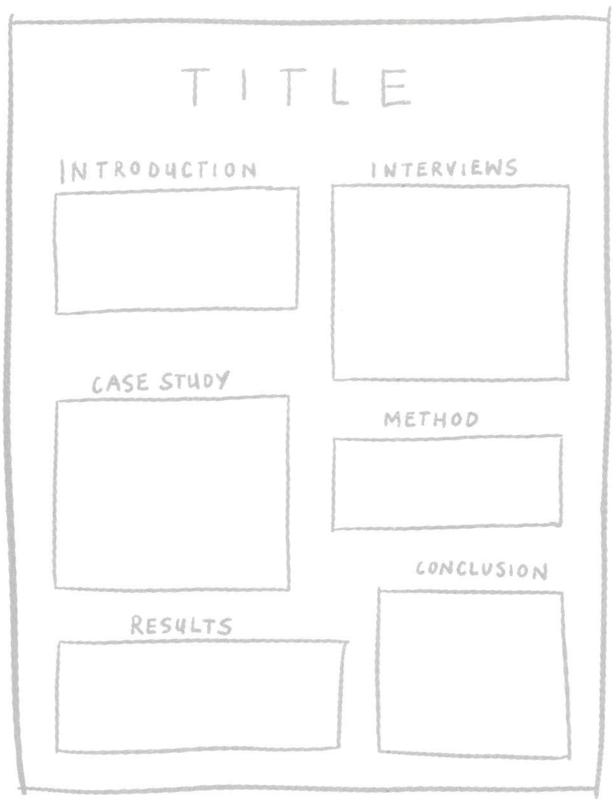

Try to make this poster easy to read for researchers trying to replicate the study.

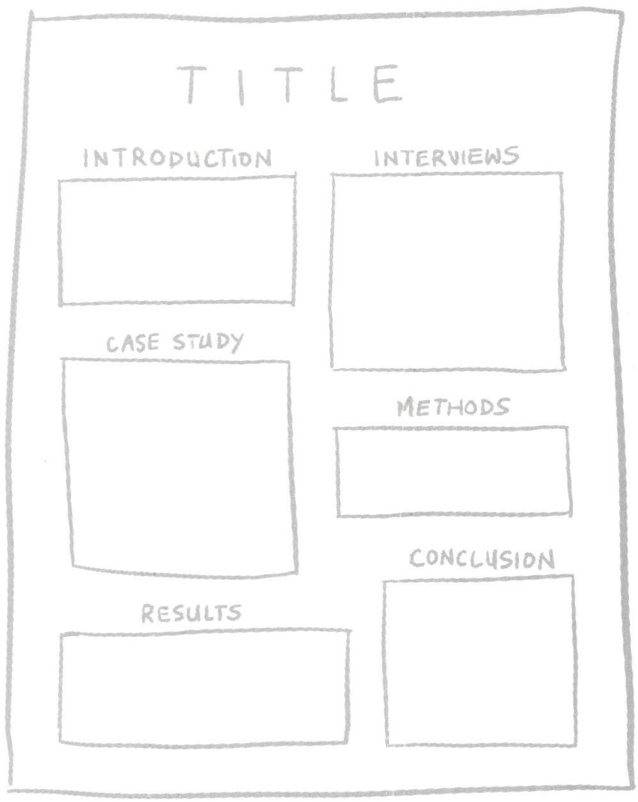

9.2 LAYOUT

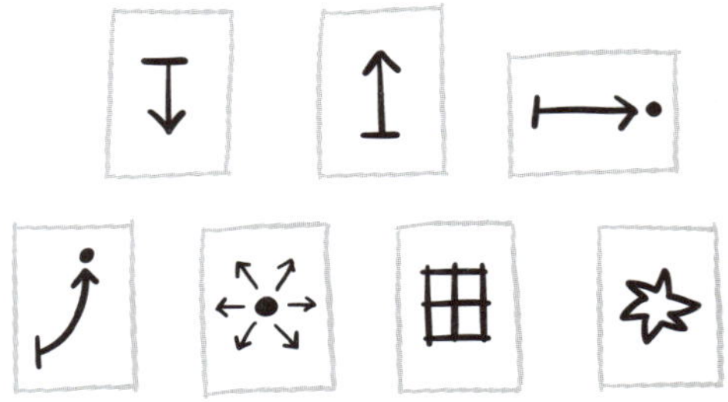

An easy to read poster needs a good layout. Are you making a summary? Or explaining a project's process? Each has layouts which fit better, or don't fit at all. You can often figure this out beforehand, based on the agenda of a meeting or the goal of a presentation.
There is a lot to learn about layouts and good composition, much more than we can squeeze onto these two pages! But this is a great place to start.

TIP Most layouts work their way back to these underlying plans. If you get to know them, you'll be able to take your layouts to the next level.

What layouts would you use for these situations?
Pick your favorite and copy it, or think of something yourself.

workshop or meeting agenda

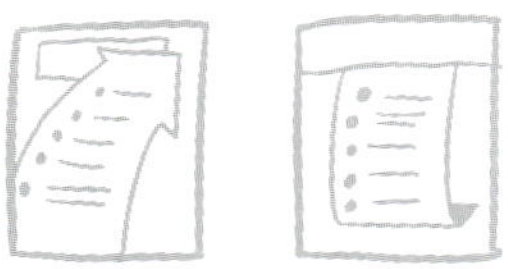

results of an employee satis-faction survey

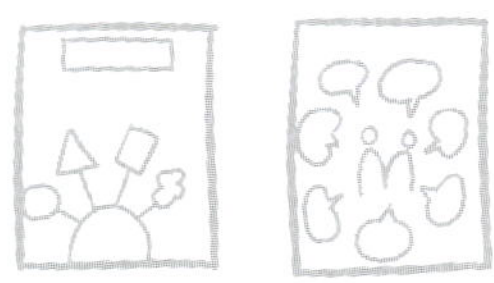

comparison of candidates for a vacancy

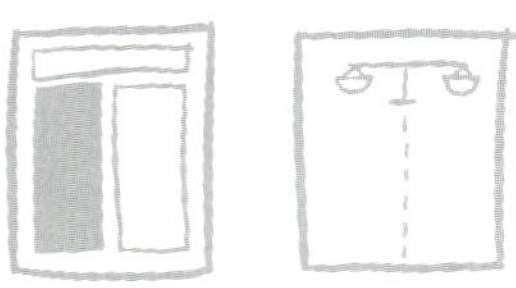

project plan

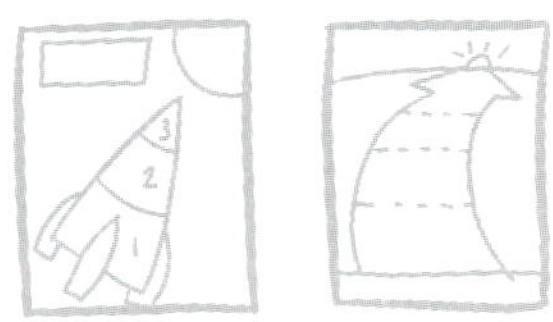

Imagine, you want to present your plan of approach for a project, including the goal that you're working towards. You need at least three steps to get there. What kind of layout could you use? Draw it below.

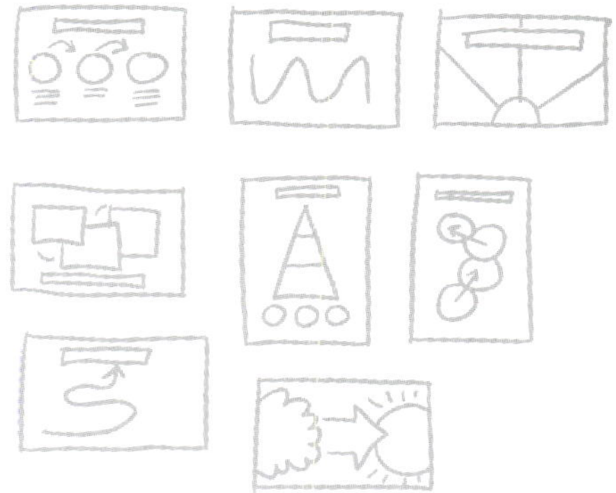

TIP You can test how your story fits in a layout by making small thumbnail sketches such as shown above.

Something went wrong in the drawings. Can you redraw the visual, so the layout feels more balanced, or logical?

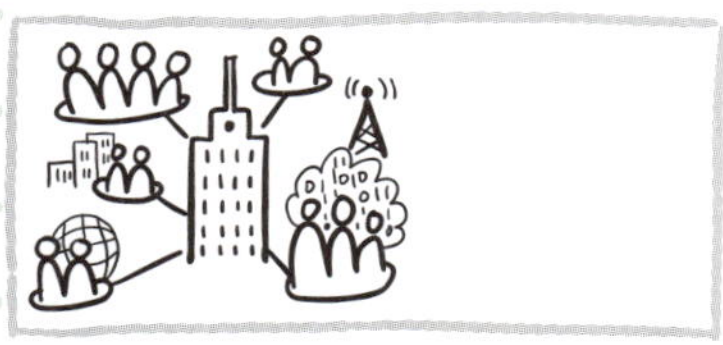

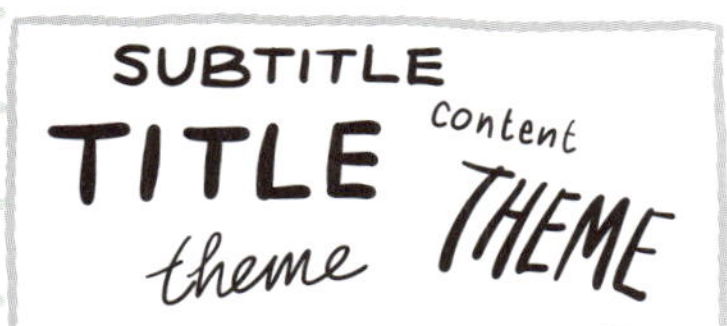

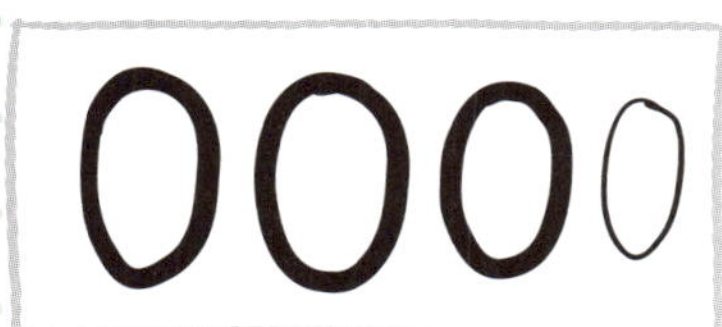

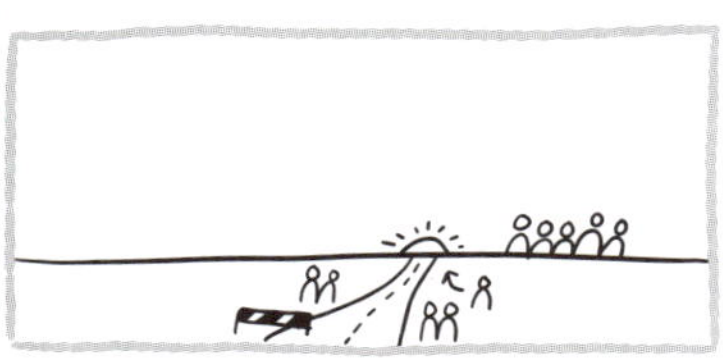

TIP Not only changing the layout can help with creating balance and hierarchy, also the thickness and color can help.

9.3 TYPOGRAPHY

Working visually is really powerful, even when you write! You can communicate visually with your texts too. If you have to write something, make sure it looks good and is easy to read. You can create visual hierarchy by varying your typography.

For example, pick a bold letter for titles, and pick a more subtle type of letter for content and details. Outline letters work well for titles. They're big, grab people's attention and you can easily make them even more eye-catching, for example, by adding color, shadow, or tracing the entire word.

Trace the outside of the alphabet to get a feel for the letters. Afterwards, draw the whole outline alphabet yourself without the help of the gray letters!

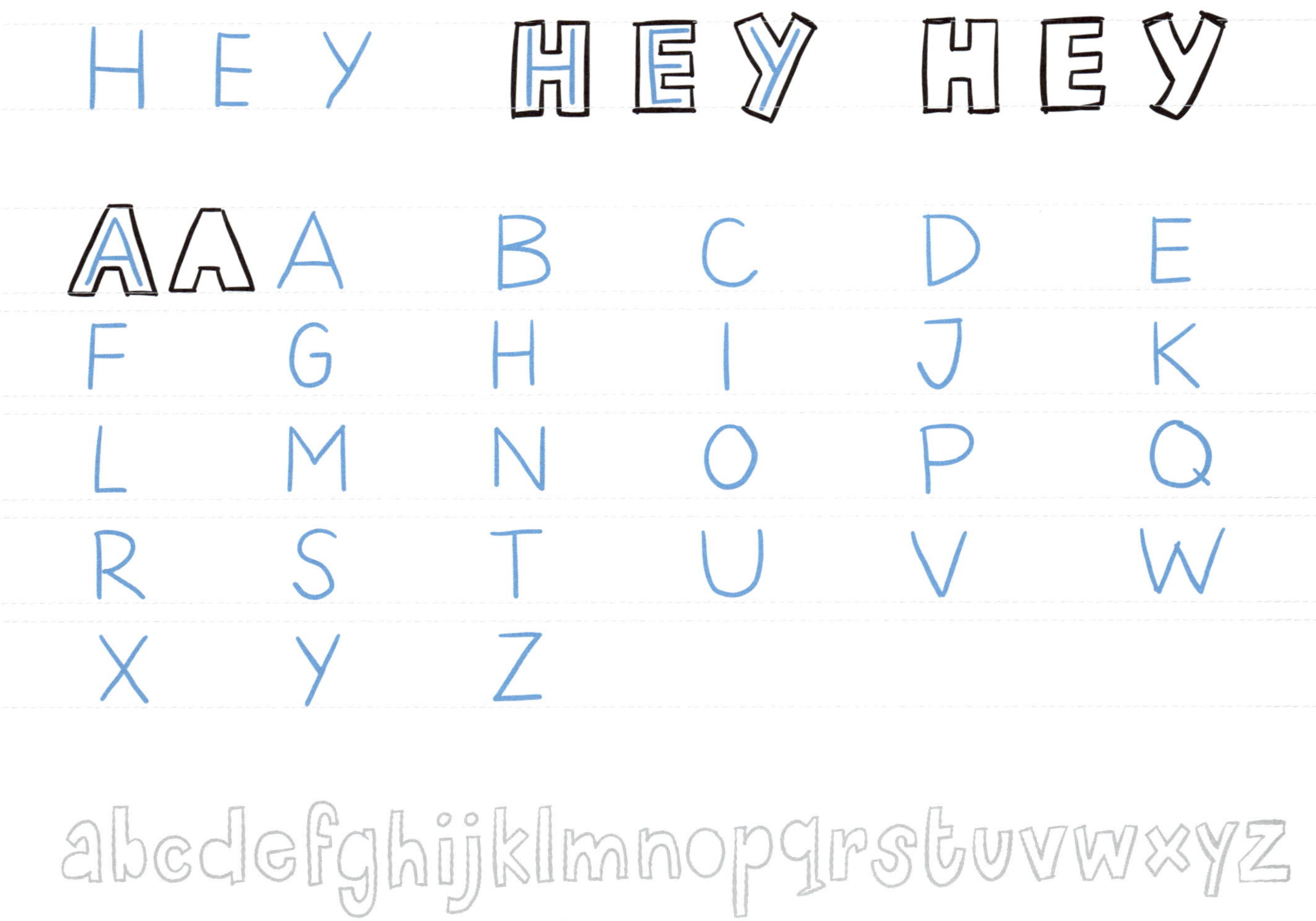

Trace and decorate the titles below. Draw a striking title by adding shadows, extra outlines, colors or other elements. Be creative!

MY NAME

TITLE

LOOK!

TOP

GEORGE

TITLE

TIP Don't be afraid to add a little colour to your letters. Want your title to stand out? Try brightly colored shading!

Take a look at Willemien's day-to-day notebook. You can see she uses a lot of text (and typography styles) to make sure she can use it as a reference later.

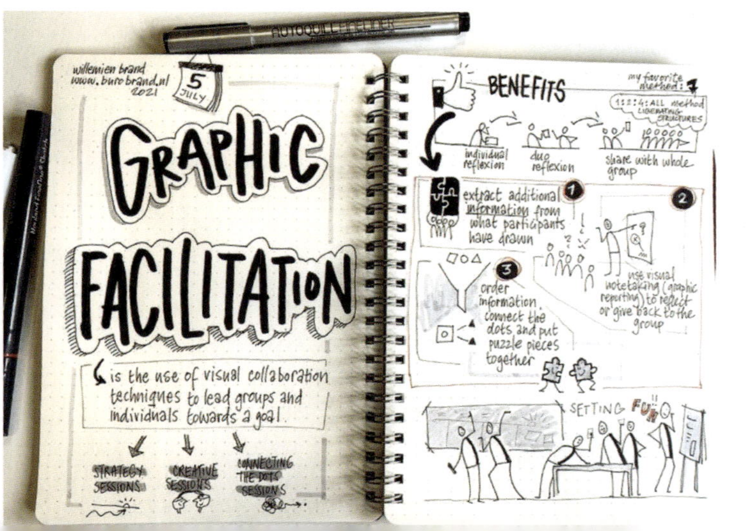

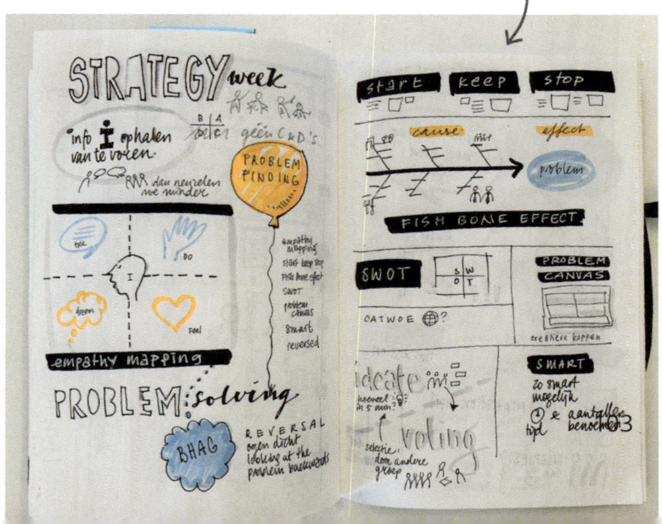

There are lots of options for eye-cathing titles. Here are some more!
Copy them, have fun and play around with big and bold letters.

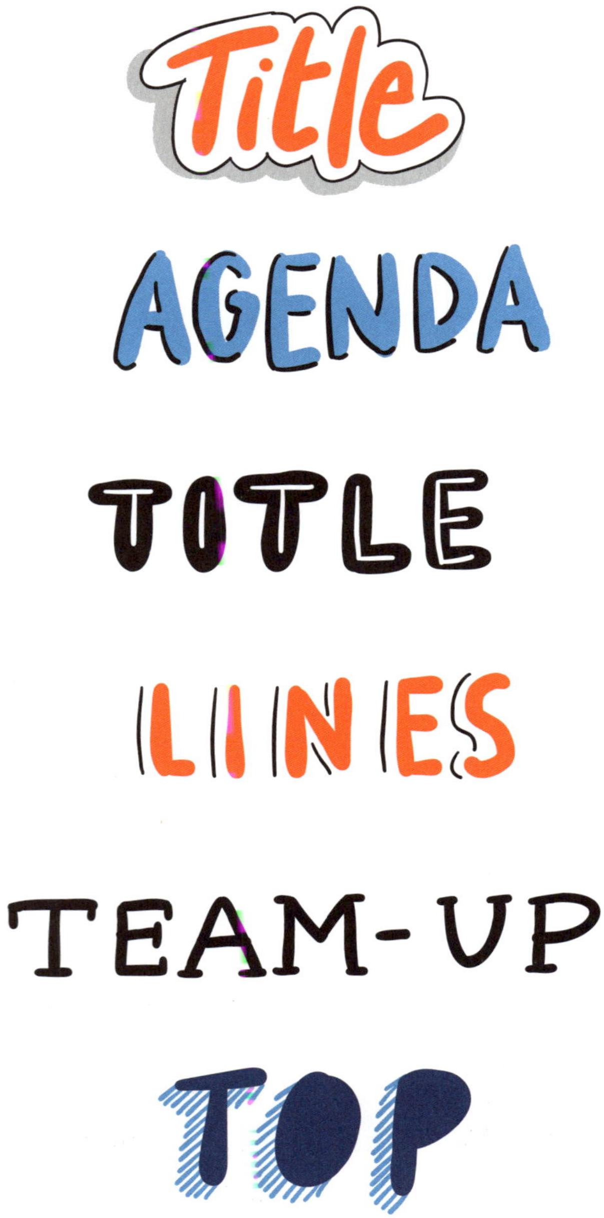

If you use text in your drawing it will probably be either for titles, subtitles or key words (for categories or themes, for example). Sometimes a different type of information can be emphasized by using another style of handwriting, for example a quote.

TIP First draw in black and then you can write in white.

This handwritten typography works great for quotes, especially when you use it in combination with speech balloons.

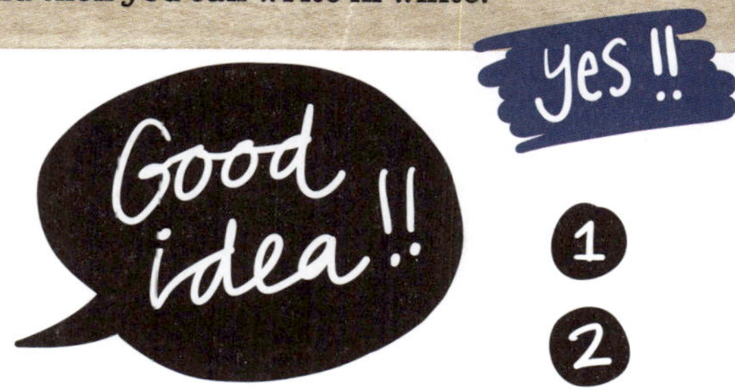

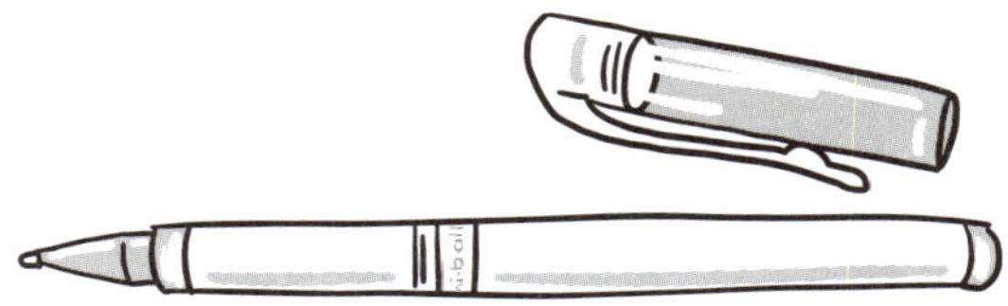

hello
handwriting
h e l l o

Try it yourself and see if you can still write in your oldskool handwriting!

There are several ways to make an outstanding title or subtitle. Make a black marked square and use a white marker.

HEADER
or SUBTITLE

TIP You could also use a piece of brownpaper or a colored paper.

We draw most letters in two steps. Take a good look at the example of the 'n', on the left. Now try it yourself with the whole alphabet. First, try to 'draw' it. Go slowly! Once you have mastered it, try to (almost) speed up to your normal handwriting pace.

TIP Keep all vertical lines at the same angle.

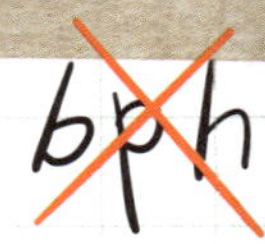

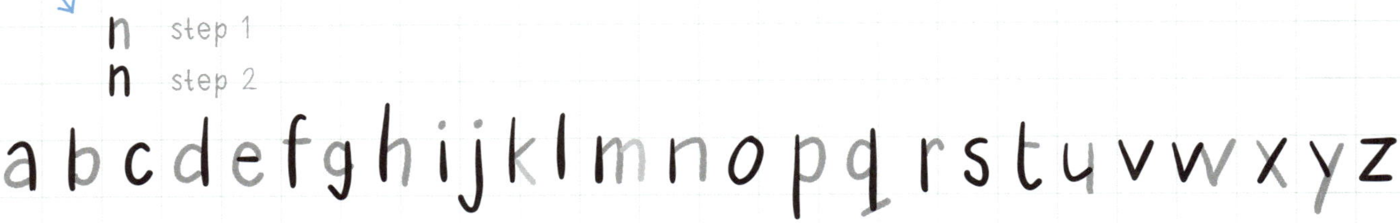

Use this area to try out some combinations of typographies. Lay some ground rules for yourself, and make a typography plan to distinguish different 'levels' of information with typographies.

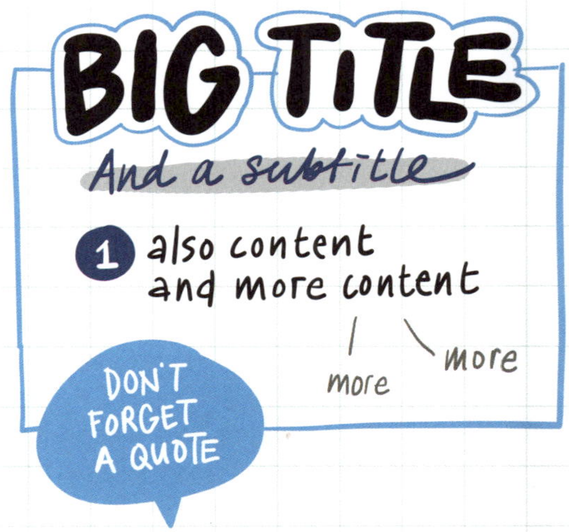

TIP Choose a look for: titles, a subtitle, content and perhaps even something unexpected, such as a quote.

9.4 ASSIGNMENT: VISUAL AGENDA

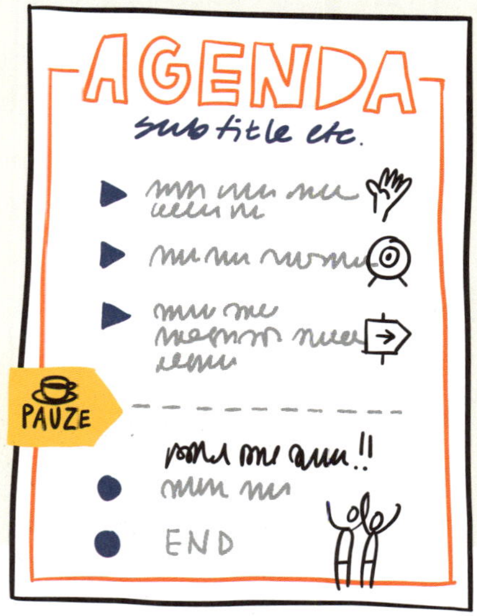

Can you (re)make the agenda for one of your meetings? Think of the layout and hierarchy of your typographies. What does your title look like? Is there a coffee break? Will there be follow-up steps? Bring it all together using drawings and text. You could leave some empty spaces and fill these in with (visual) notes during the meeting itself!

Sketch your first ideas here. Draw/write the final one on big piece of flipchart paper so everyone can see it!

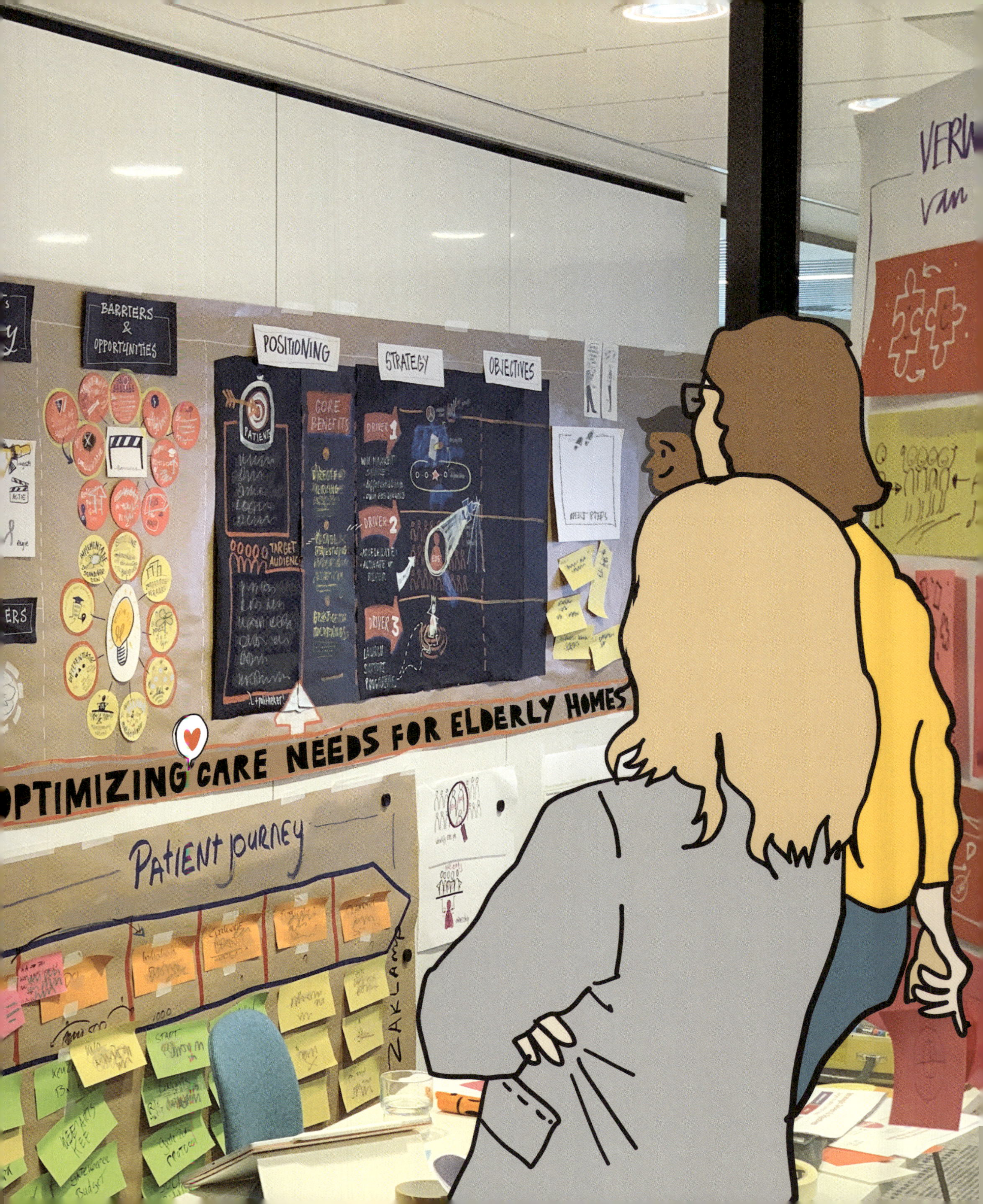
BARRIERS & OPPORTUNITIES
POSITIONING
STRATEGY
OBJECTIVES
CORE BENEFITS
DRIVER 1
DRIVER 2
DRIVER 3
TARGET AUDIENCE
PTIMIZING CARE NEEDS FOR ELDERLY HOMES
Patient journey
ZAKLAMP
van

10. VISUAL CO-CREATOR

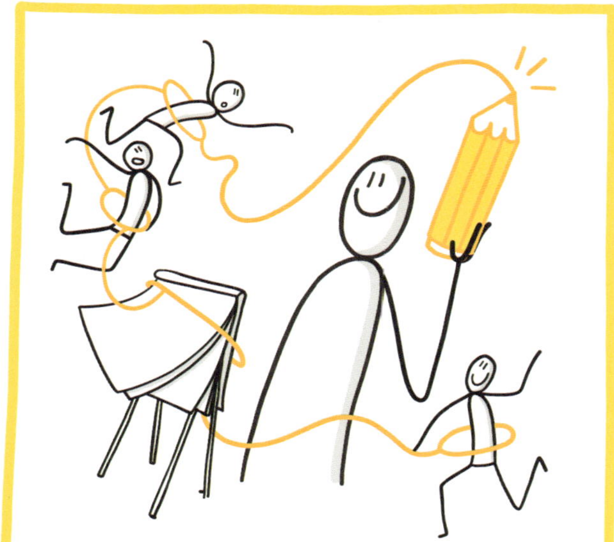

Visual Co-creator

Uses visual tools and templates to spark creativity and engagement

A Visual Co-Creator uses Visual Thinking to take steps in a process together with others and to give everyone a voice. Their focus is on working in group contexts and on applying visual methods together. This could be setting up creative sessions or applying visual working methods with others. They often operate in the context of change management, to engage people and help them experience the desired change. They are very successful in enabling a modern form of leadership or coaching, that gives people room to express their creativity and problem-solving abilities.

Often Visual Co-Creators know something about different design methods such as Design Thinking. As you can see, facilitation skills are important for this Visual Thinking type. Besides that, creativity and visualization skills are vital.

To focus on just one of the many things you can do and draw, let's practice drawing frames and containers! Using these frames and containers, you can create your own visual working forms and templates. You can show people what you want to do, give guidance and activate people. Use the visuals from this chapter to make this happen!

WHAT YOU WILL LEARN

10.1 Containers
10.2 Frames
10.3 Assignment: Design a template

10.1 CONTAINERS

Accentuate an element (text or visual) by placing it in a container. One of the most commonly used is a mile marker next to a (road) map that indicates where we are chronologically on our journey.

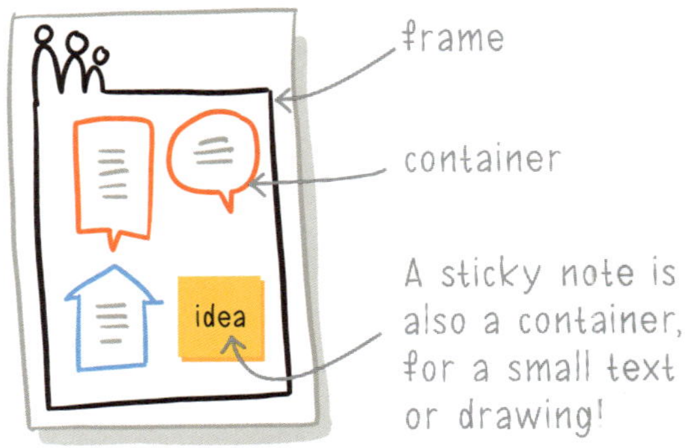

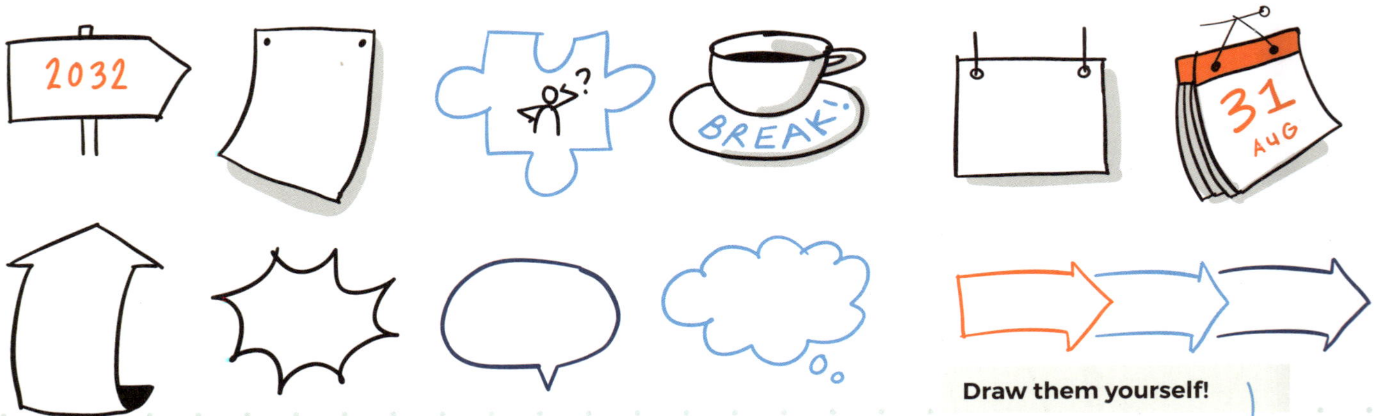

Draw them yourself!

Banners can be great containers for titles or attractive visuals in their own right. Even better; you can make an entire template out of them! We will show you some 'how to draw' examples and variations.

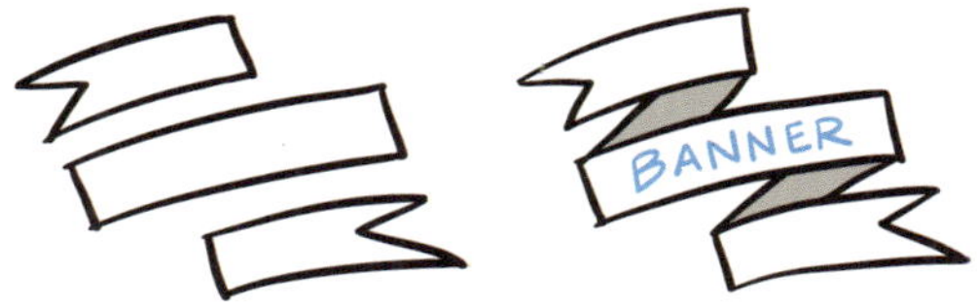

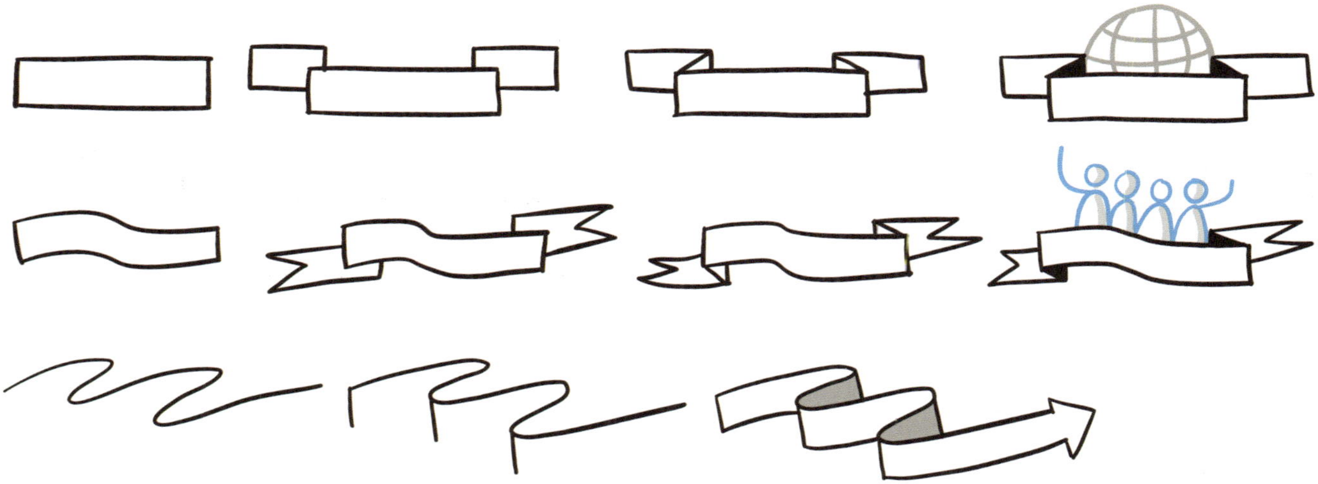

Draw them yourself!

TIP Write the title first so you can make sure the banner is the right size!

Banners are used a lot on brown paper walls to show ideas, steps, time-based plans and for appealing titles, of course!

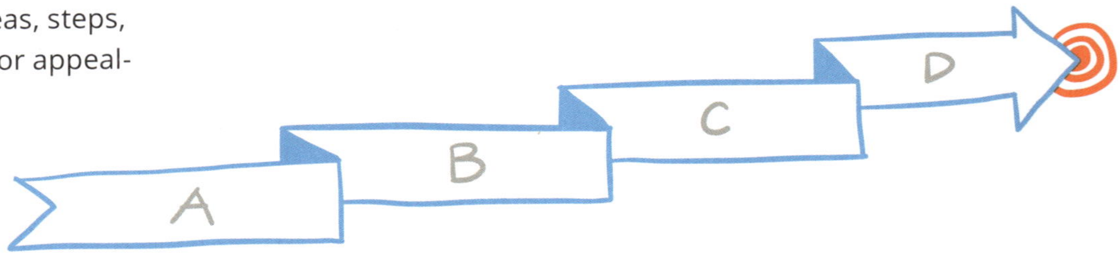

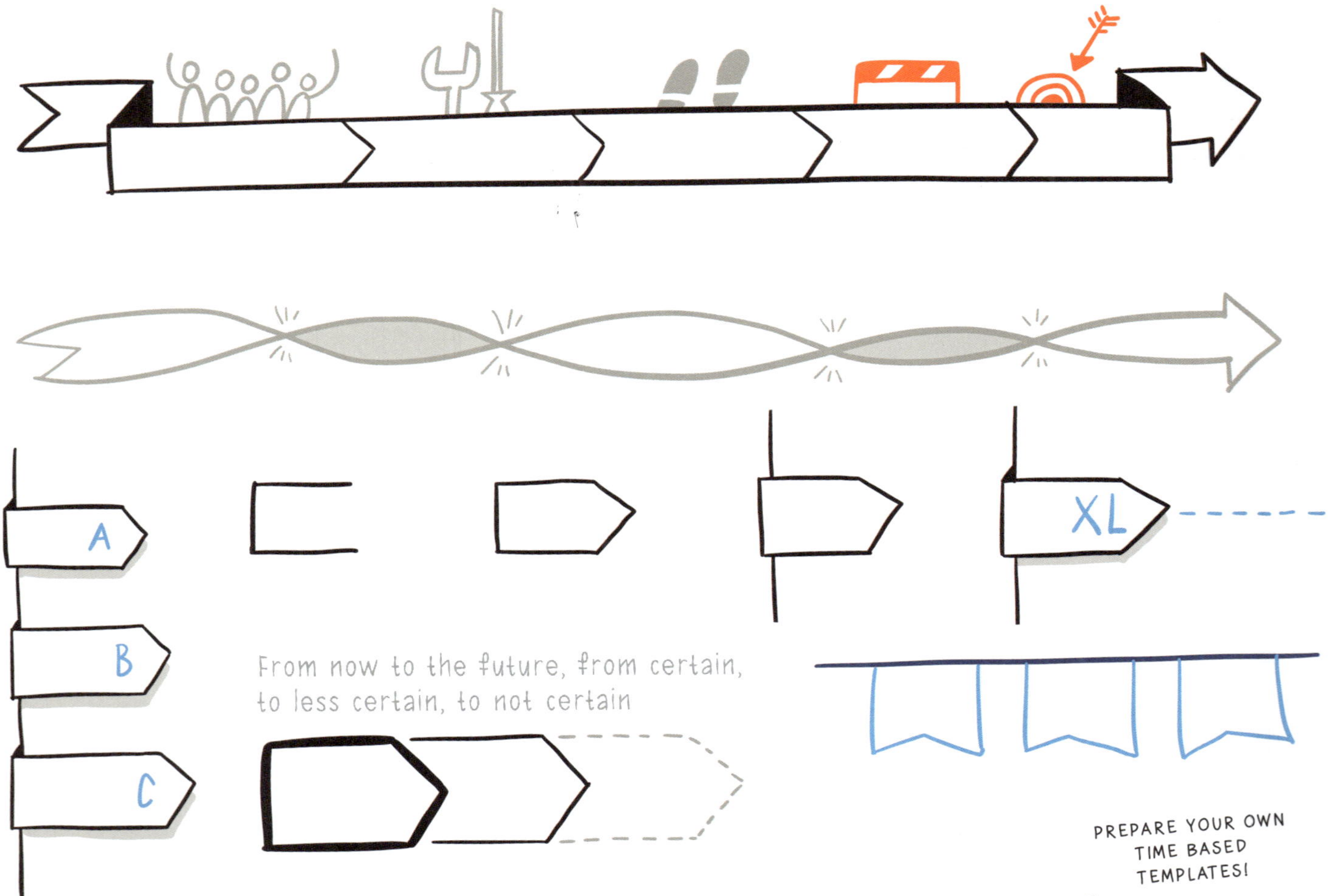

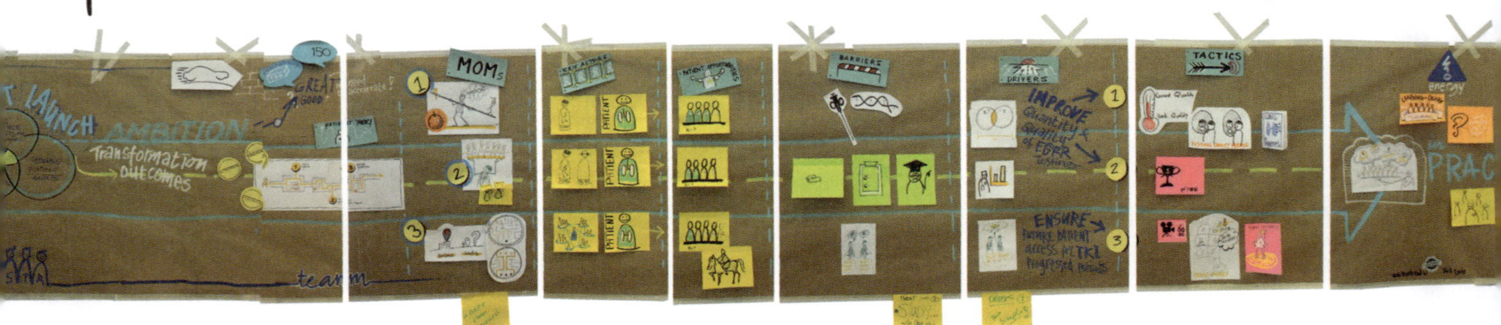

Copy the drawings you like or see if you can come up with your own design!

10.2 FRAMES

We use frames to merge content (mulitple elements) in our drawings. A frame says: everything within this frame is about one particular subject. It can either be a big rectangle around the entire drawing as we often do (like here on this pages) or you can blow up a container and use it as a frame.

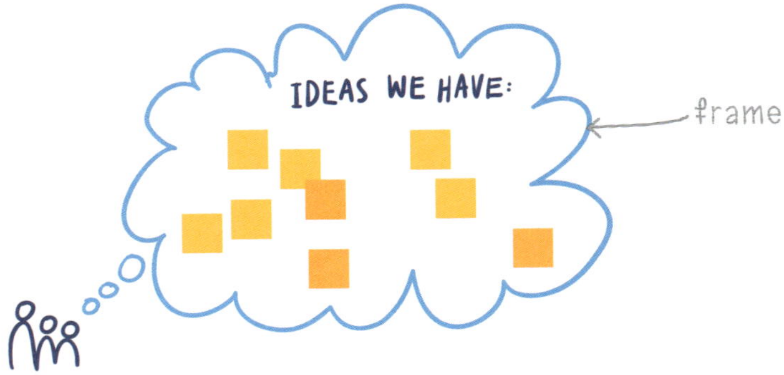

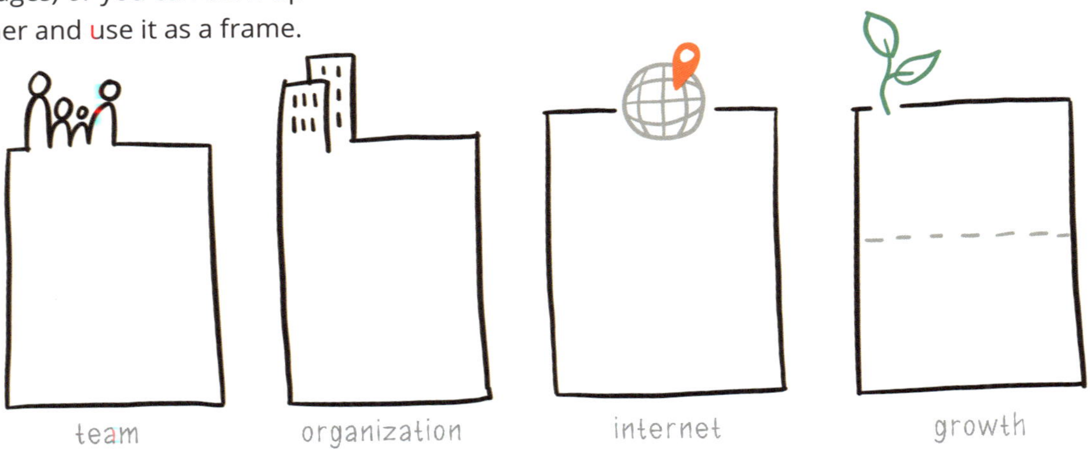

Draw them yourself!

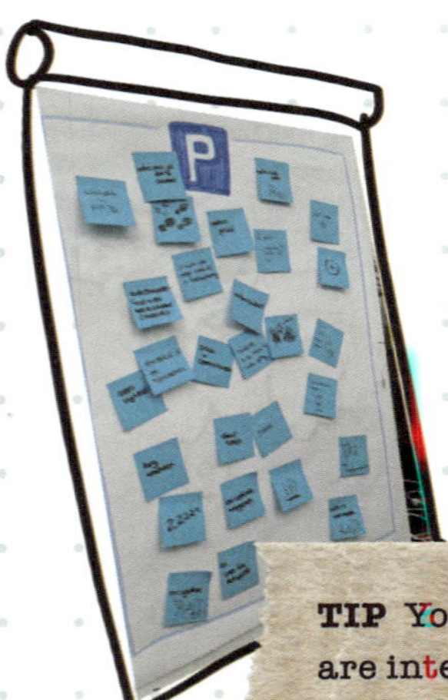

TIP You can use a flip to 'park' things people say in a meeting that are interesting or useful, but not relevant to the current discussion.

Create your own frames! Think of a subject or icon to visualize and incorporate it into your frame.

TIP Use words to define your frames!

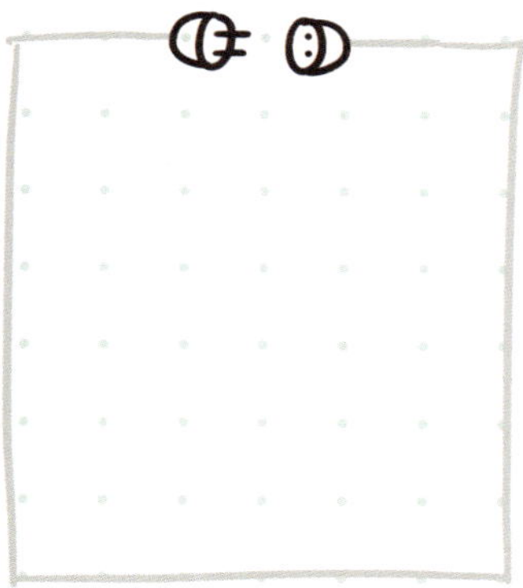

connect

goals

finance

action

to do

next steps

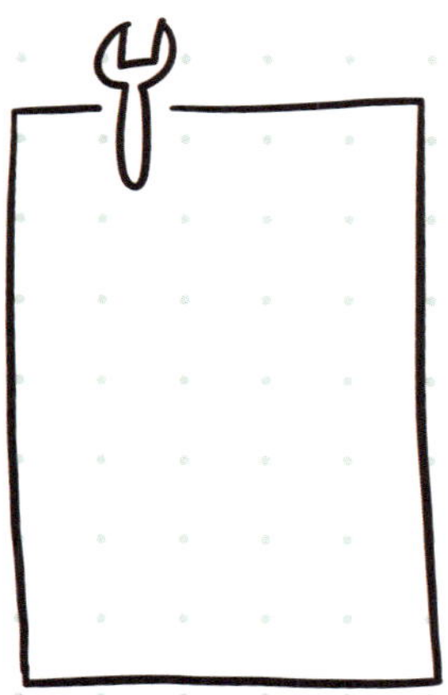

....

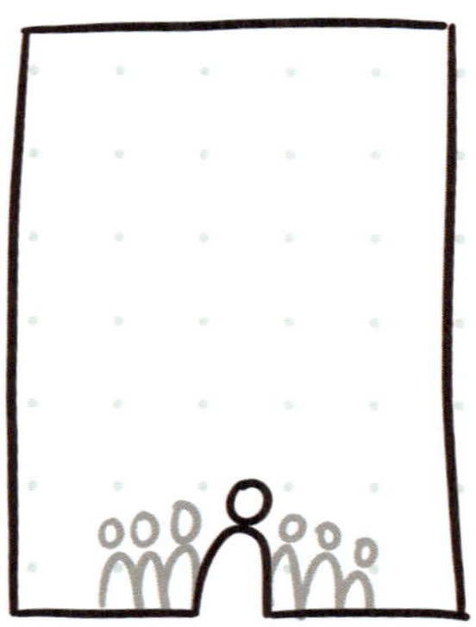

....

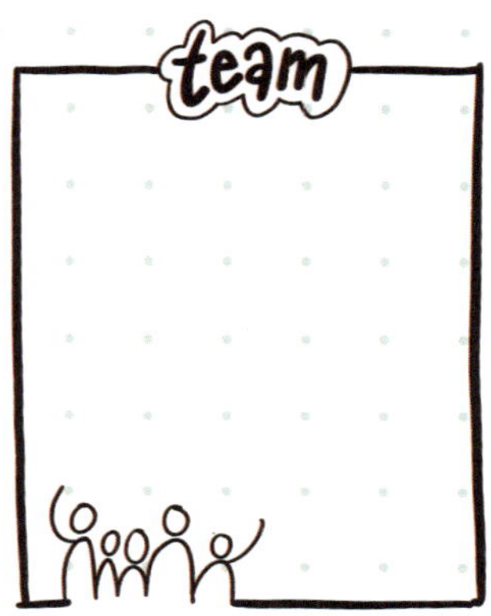

....

You can either frame your content afterwards, or you can use frames and containers to create a structure to work with beforehand. In that case we use the drawing as a template or canvas that you can use during meetings, share with colleagues or use for yourself.

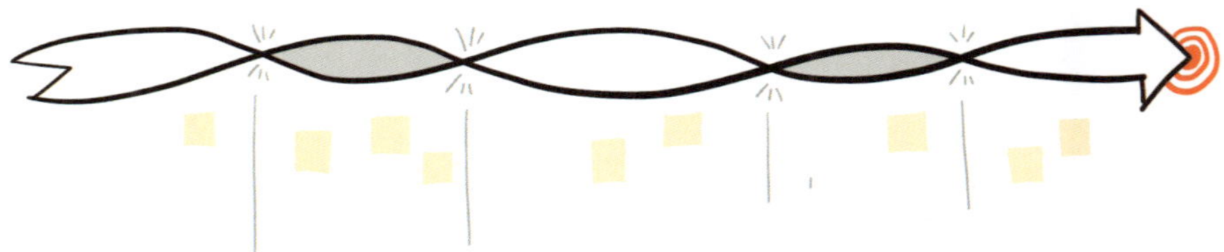

As you can see in some of our examples, you can use lines to divide your visual into different parts. It's a great way to organize the input within a frame or container.

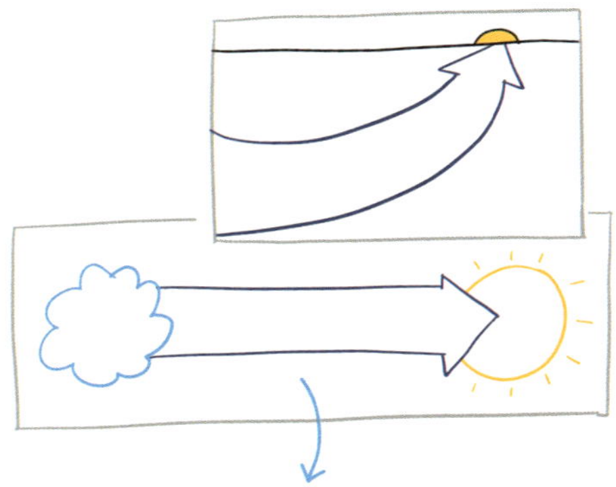

Divide the two roadmaps into four parts and label them Q1, Q2, Q3 and Q4.

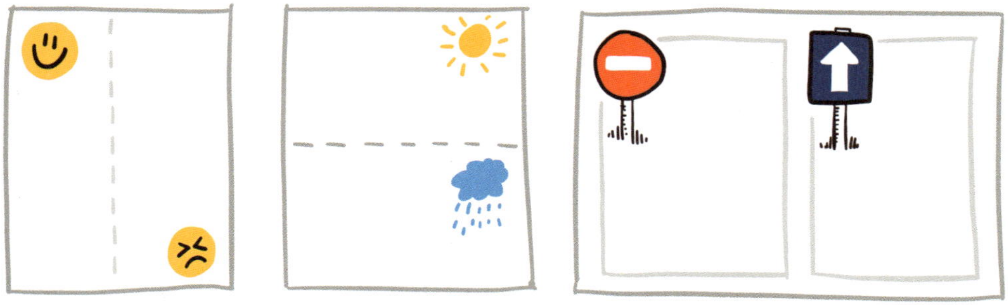

Design a template. Think up as many ways as possible to make a template designs or visuals to gather input that is 'positive' or 'good,' and 'negative' or 'bad'. We've already made a start for you!

Divide and conquer. Imagine you are working on a project with the themes "time", "budget" and "quality". Think up creative and fun ways to create a template (with frames and/or containers) to gather input on these three topics.

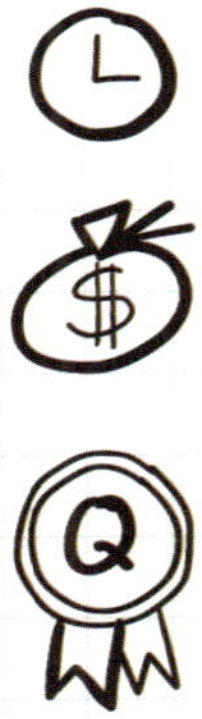

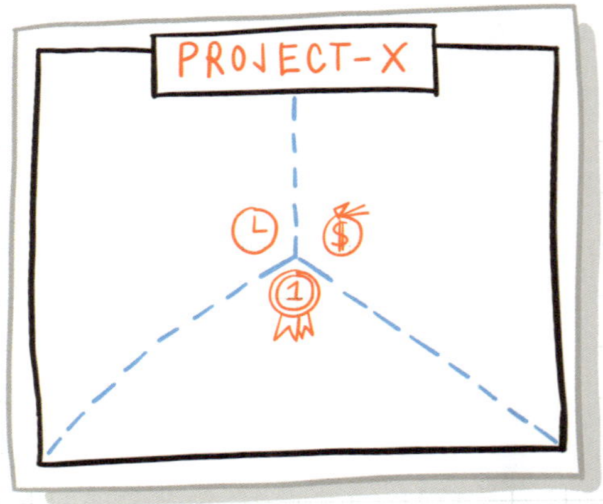

example

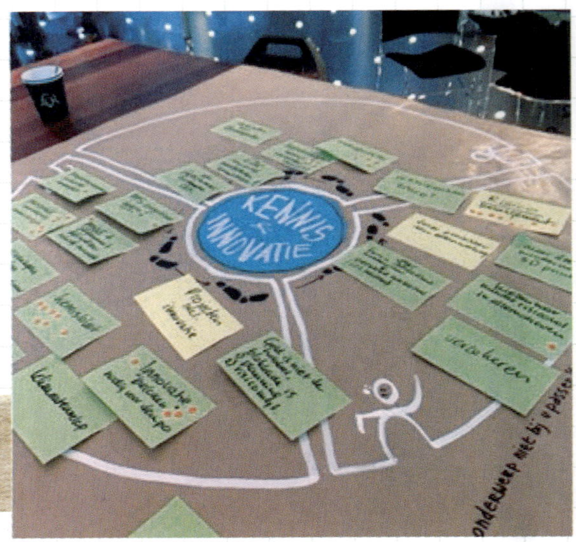

TIP A round template is fun and different when participants can walk freely between (high) tables.

10.3 ASSIGNMENT: DESIGN A TEMPLATE

If you can draw containers, frames, dividers, titles and other basic elements, you are ready to create your very own brown paper wall! Think big! Design a template that you can use at work, for example a team planning meeting. What is the overall objective? What are the steps to success? What is the timeframe? Who is responsible?

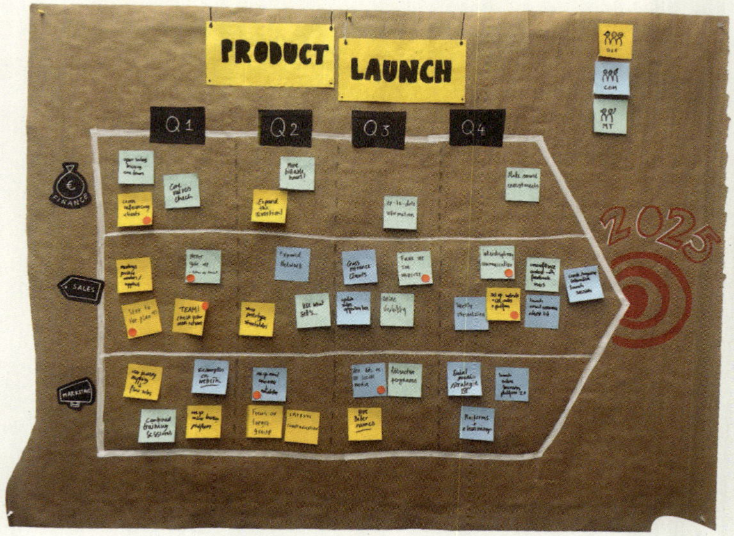

Take it step by step. Which subjects do you want to include? How many are there? This will determine the number of spaces you need. What type of template layout can you think of with that number of subjects? Make some sketches below. Once you have the sketch, take a big piece of paper to draw out the template. Think of icons for each of the subjects and make eye-catching titles.

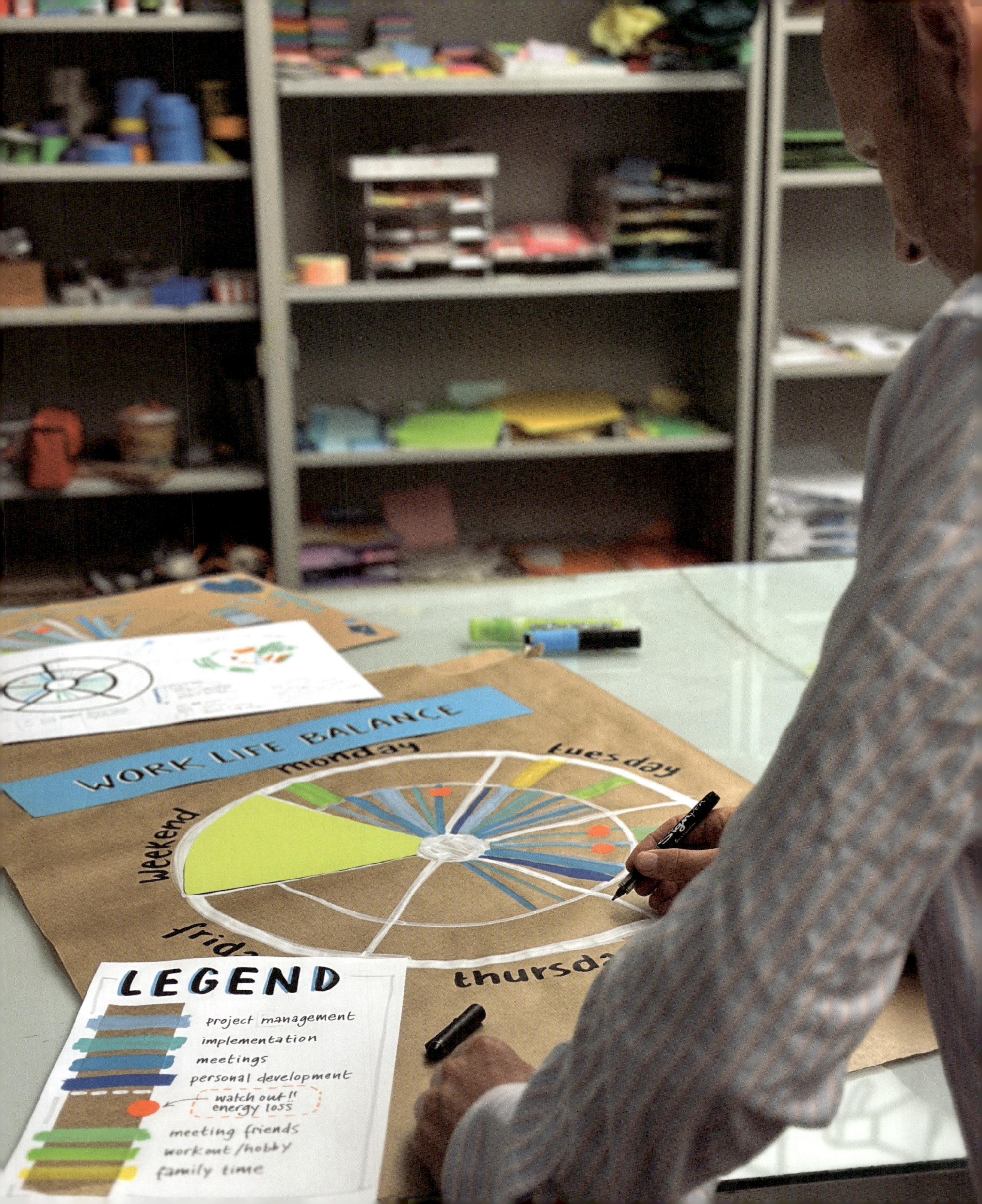
WORK LIFE BALANCE
monday
tuesday
weekend
friday
thursday
LEGEND
project management
implementation
meetings
personal development
watch out!! energy loss
meeting friends
workout / hobby
family time

11. VISUAL ANALYST

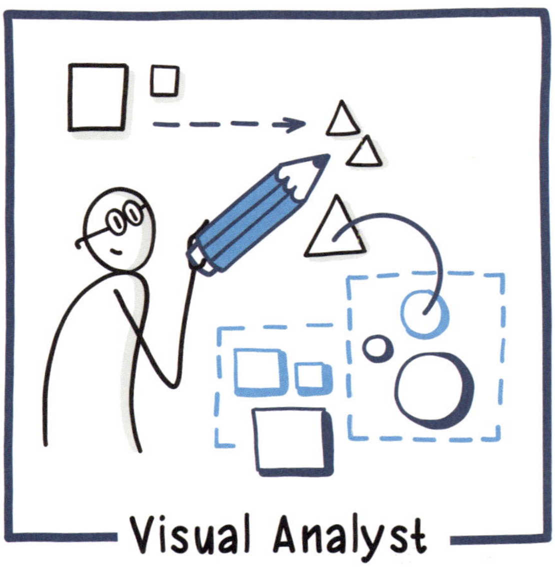

Dissects (complex) information visually to connect the dots

A Visual Analyst uses Visual Thinking to gain a clear overview of and insight into complex processes. Their focus is on the analytical application of Visual Thinking, and the use of visual structures to organize text or information.

They often use their skills to analyze data and gather insight. They are great with complex information and love to clarify topics, either for themselves or for others.

As you can see, this Visual Thinking Type is expert in creating logical (visual) structures. Adding meaning to your text or visual with, among other things, colors, lines, patterns and shapes is a great talent to develop. In this chapter we get acquainted with these skills, especially a simple but impactful one: using color. We challenge you to think about this by making a data visualization.

nce you learn to use visual elements and rules to break down complex information, you will develop a better understanding of visual communication and data visualization. You can use this for yourself when trying to gain insights and you can make it easier for people to get a grip on the information at hand.

WHAT YOU WILL LEARN

11.1 Color coding
11.2 Network
11.3 Assignment: Data visualisation

11.1 COLOR CODING

Color can convey information, but you can also use color to add meaning to information.
For example:

- Each color carries its own type of content (i.e. how many people, what they do, how they relate to one another, see 11.2).
- A seperate color is used for each theme.
- Color is used to say something about the (visual) hierarchy (i.e. if you have a cluster of sticky notes, create a 'main' sticky note in a different color).

This makes a sheet full of information more readable and easy to break down into clusters. Look out for / Benefit from certain color associations, for example red (hot) and blue (cold). Don't use extra colors when it makes sense to use colors from the same color range (sequential). Only use extra colors when there are seperate categories that need to be highlighted.

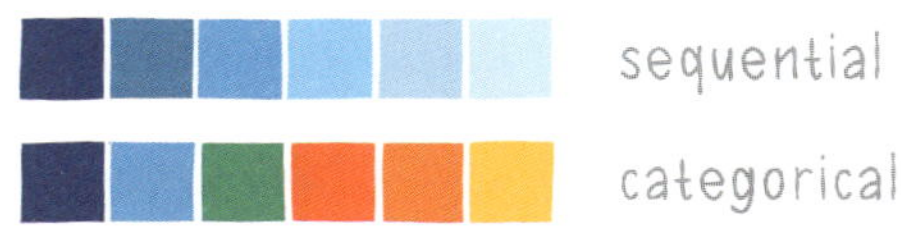

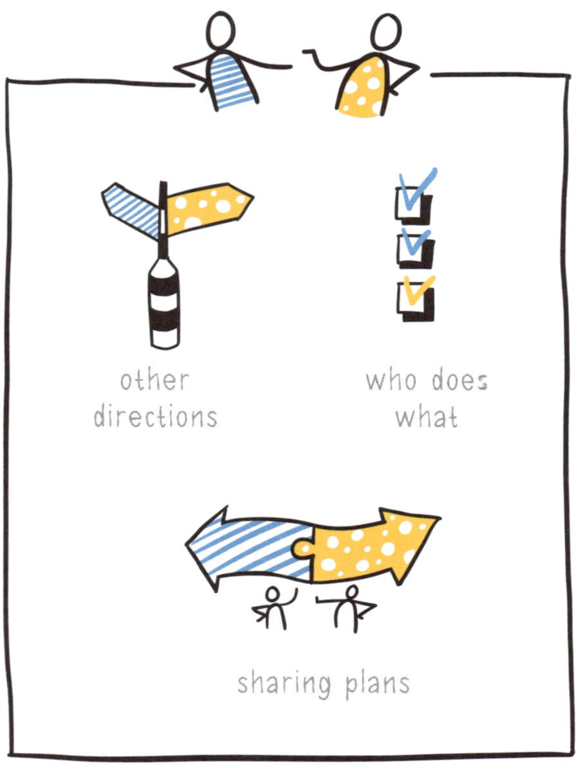

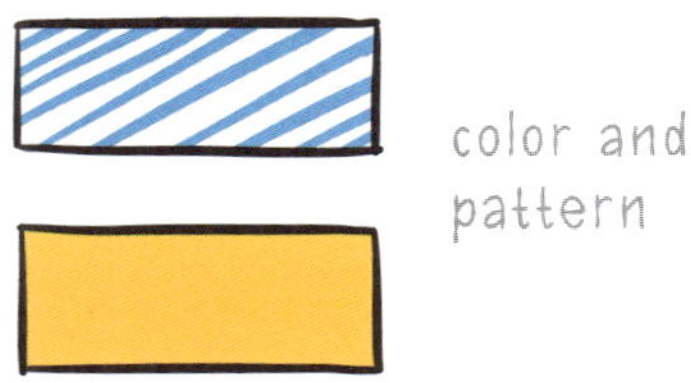

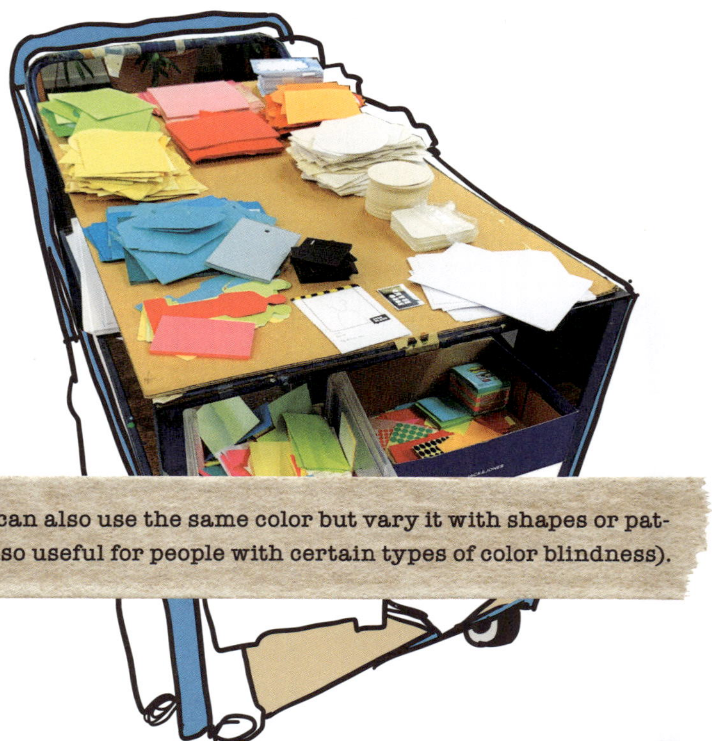

TIP You can also use the same color but vary it with shapes or patterns. (Also useful for people with certain types of color blindness).

I use color (and/or patterns) to visually show who walks my dog Ollie on what days. In the weekends I do it myself. Monday and Friday Patricia walks the dog. On Friday her daughter joins her. Tuesdays and Thursday (every other week) Carl walks the dog. Wednesdays I walk the dog, every other week I do Thursday too. Can you make the legend and give Ollie the right colors?

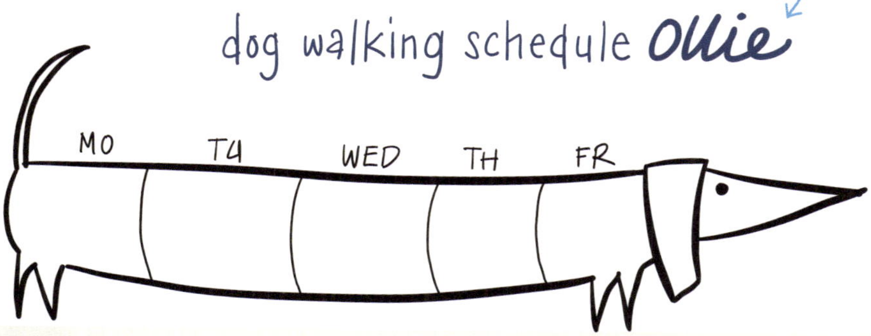

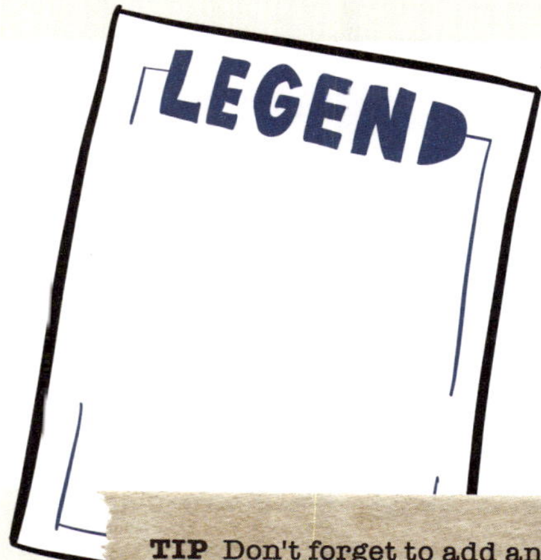

TIP Don't forget to add an legend! See the next page for an example.

In the exercise above you already have the data/information, but you can also collect your own data! Below, keep track of the following data.

color	keep a score when, at work, you:
	use a visual to present/explain something
	see somebody else use a visual
	think 'this would be better with a visual'
	read the slide that is shared instead of listening to that person
	see people talking but struggling to make themselves understood

Like this!

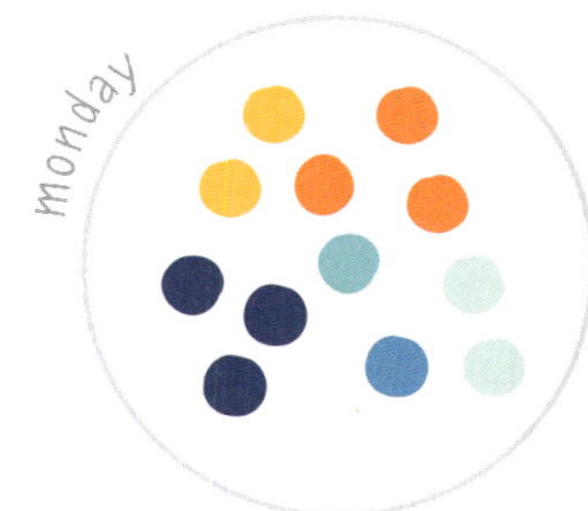

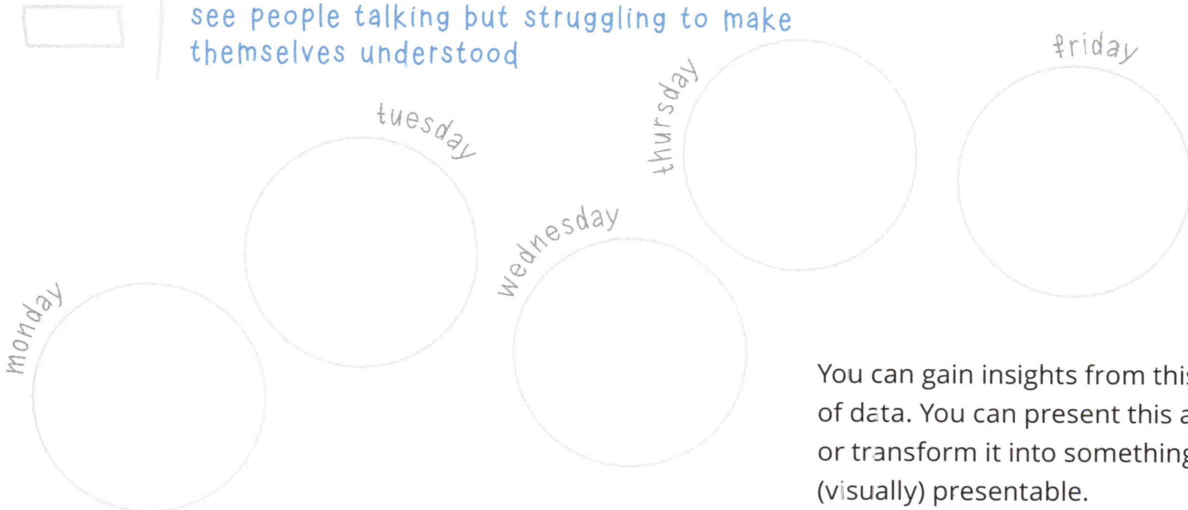

You can gain insights from this collection of data. You can present this as-is or transform it into something more (visually) presentable.

11.2 NETWORK

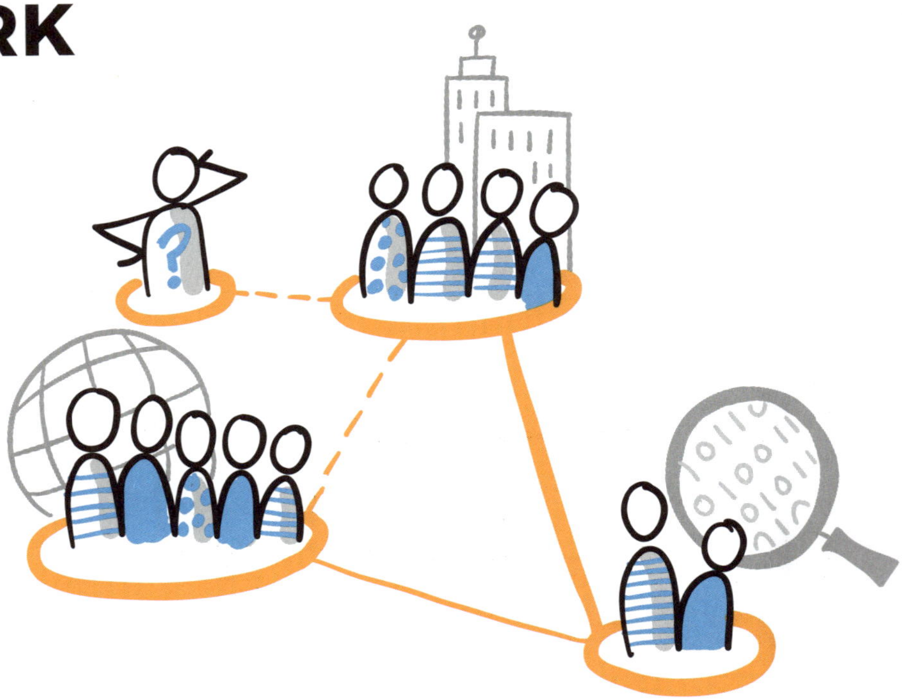

With only a few icons and the ability to draw people, you can create an overview of structures and networks. You don't even need this, but it does make the visual more appealing and fun to look at. You instantly know we're talking about actual people.

For the network drawing on the right, see the rules it's made up of below. Each layer of information has its own color, and patterns and linework are used too. It's a great example of figurative drawing combined with non-figurative visual techniques.

number of teams and team members

how the teams relate to each other (see lines)

roles of the people (see patterns)

what the teams do (icons)

project manager

it-specialist

intern

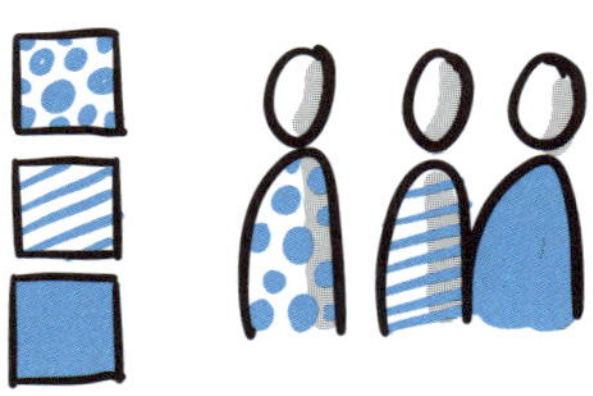

collaborate a lot

collaborate regularly

collaborate sometimes

On the right page, make your own network! Draw a schematic overview of your team and how it relates to other teams in your company (or outside of it). Optionally, you could do this with your friends and family as the subject.

Try to squeeze in as much information as possible, without it becoming cluttered and unclear. Don't forget to use (at least) color to keep it organized.

11.3 ASSIGNMENT: DATA VISUALIZATION

Challenge yourself to make a data visualization presenting your calendar for the week!

First, write down what kind of activities you do at work, (or private life). This is your basic dataset.

Categorize them, sketch out your idea for the visualization, and plan how you will insert your information. You might want to use a chart or table as the underlying structure. Use color and pattern appropriately!

Finally, make an index to help your audience understand the visualization. Let's go!

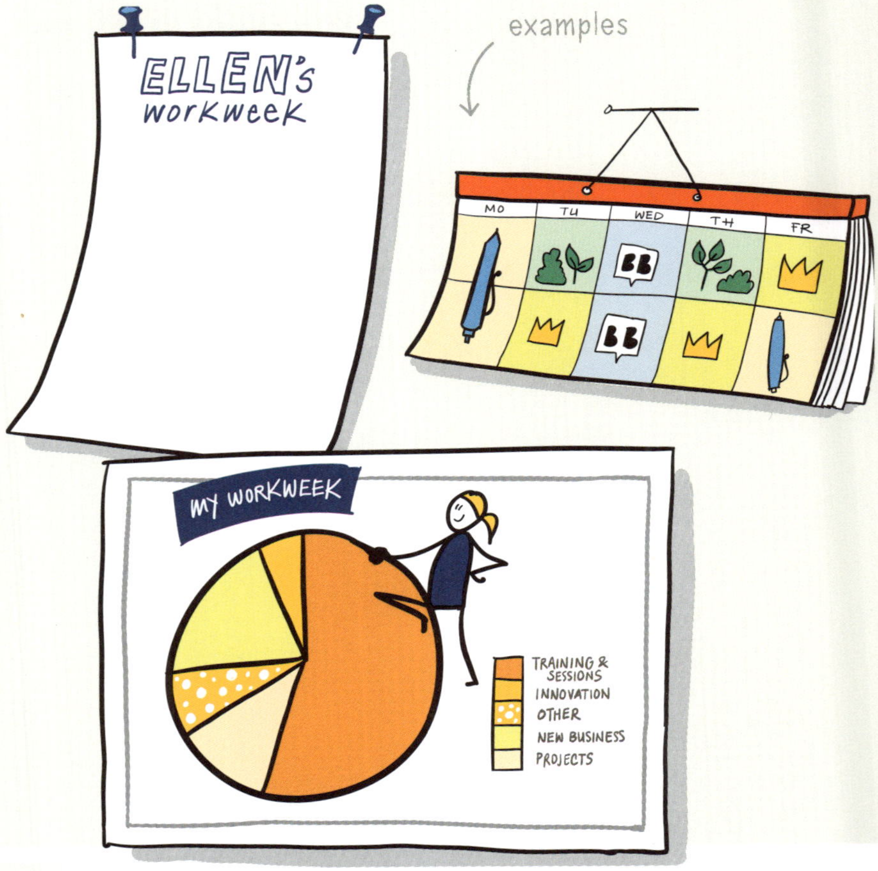

Prepare your visual: what activities do you want to include?

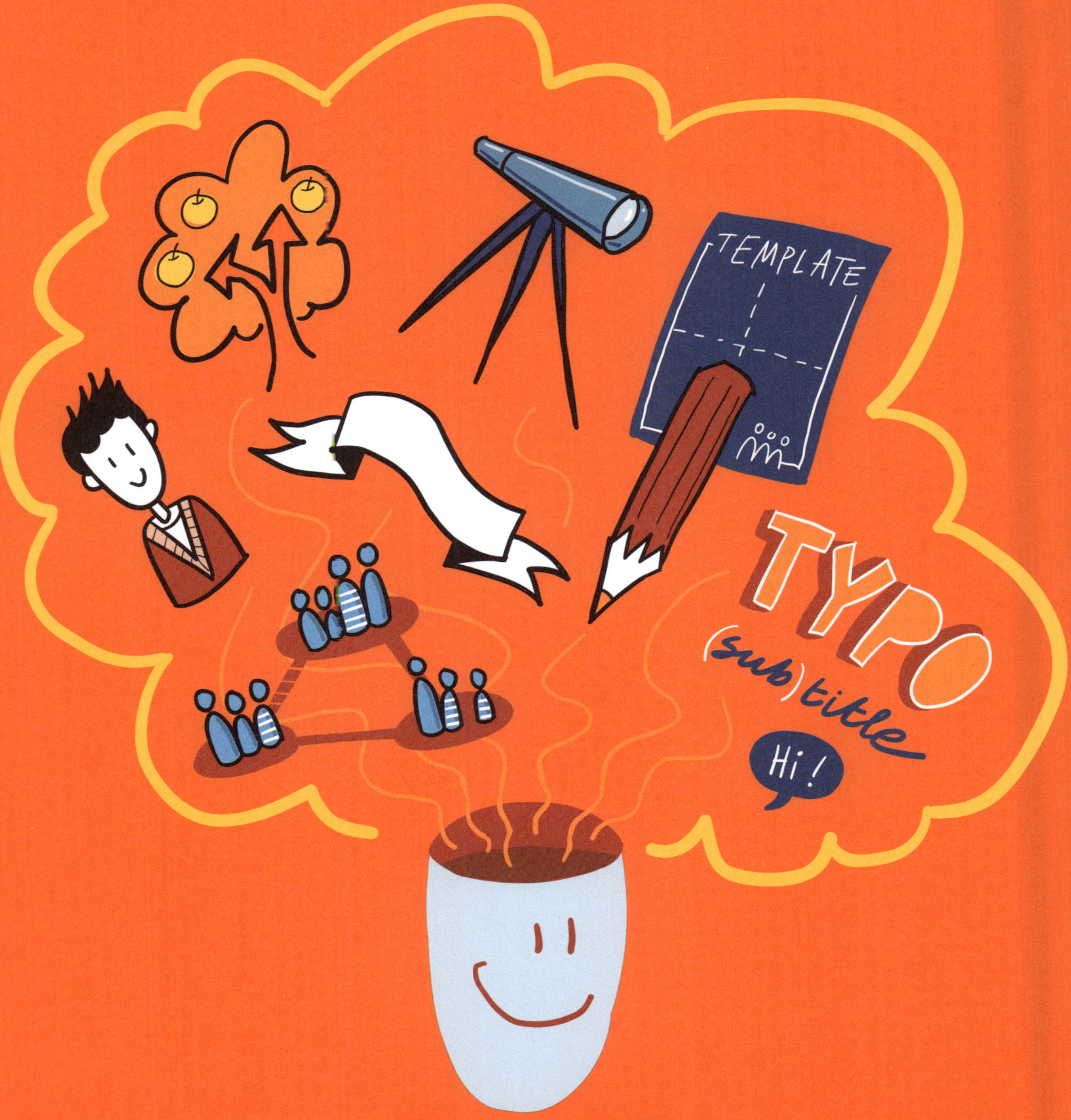

MAKING IDEAS HAPPEN

12. BRINGING IT TOGETHER

In the previous chapters we talked about Buro BRAND's Five Visual Thinking Types©. We did some specific drawing exercises that fit those types, but these exercises are useful for more than just one type! That's because you aren't bound to only one.

The Buro BRAND's Five Visual Thinking Types© can be interchangeable when you're working. Think of them as specific hats you wear as you need them when applying Visual Thinking.

For example, if you're making a hand-drawn infographic: First you consider the information you want to bring across. Maybe you want to dive into it in a creative session with your team, so everybody is in line with the goal. This would make you the Visual Co-Creator type at that moment.

WHAT YOU WILL LEARN

Perhaps you want a metaphor for the story, or you want to think about how you can make the story as visual and tangible as possible. For this you use your Visual Storyteller type powers.

But what should you and shouldn't you show? What's important and what are unnecessary details? How would you visualize this in a clear and to-the-point way? Put on your Visual Reporter type 'hat' to figure this out.

Make some sketches, see how it all comes together and visualize your story. Grab people's attention with a clear visual hierarchy and reading direction. That's a task for the Visual Designer type. Of course you also need to think about logical structures, the use of color and consistency throughout the drawing. So somewhere within this process it's a good idea to put your Visual Analyst type 'hat' on.

As you might've guessed, this chapter is about bringing together all our types. We ask you to put all the Buro BRAND's Five Visual Thinking Types© to work and complete a final assignment. But before you get to work, let's first give you a few, final tips!

12.1 CHUNKS AND CLUSTERS

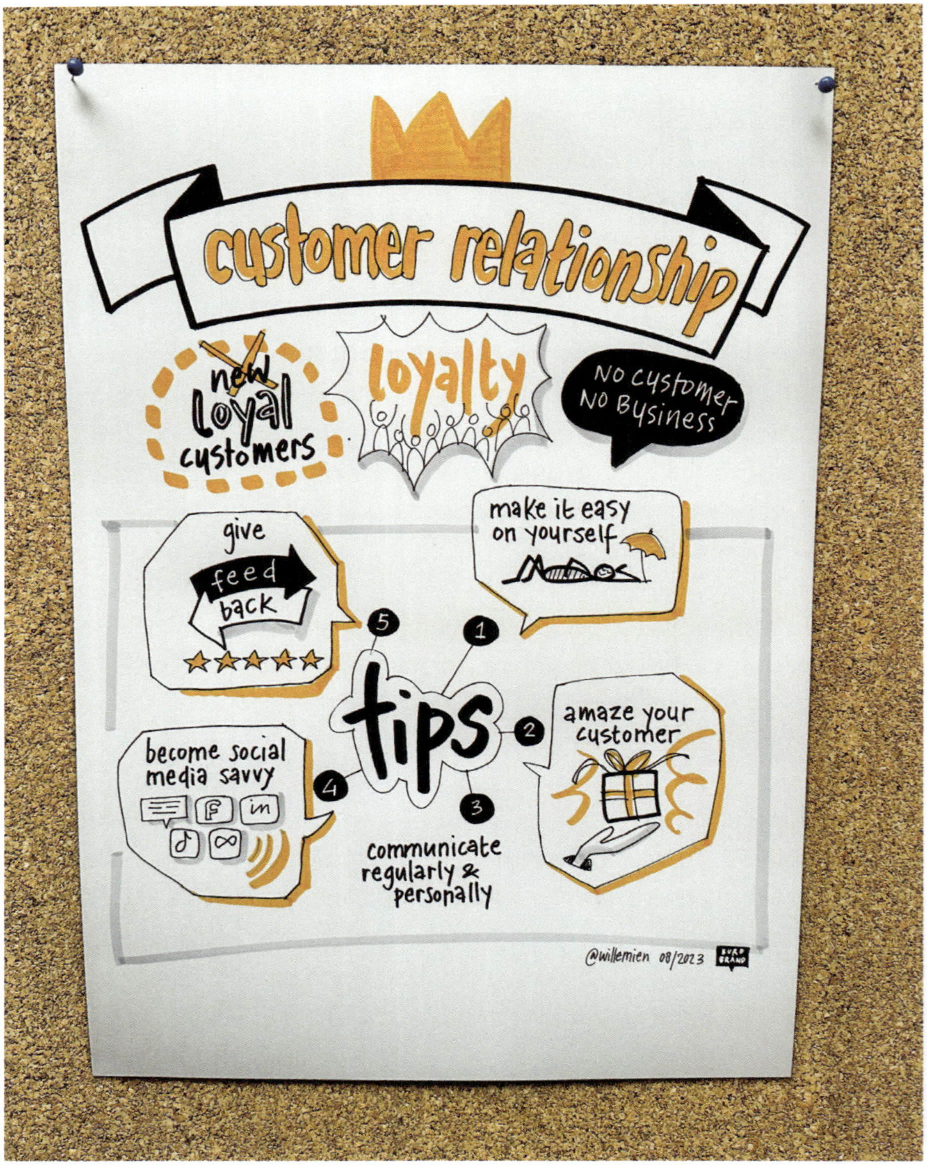

When you want to communicate something, you first have to work out what exactly it is that you want to express.

Break down your story into chunks. Small pieces of information, often combined with a visual or a popping title and, if possible, combined in a container.

There are several ways you can design chunks.

Look at all these chunks, they're all clearly visualized within their own container.

The tips are in a text balloon and the three results or forms of impact have their own type of container.
Even the title has a banner shaped container!

The five tips are all accompanied with a short description and a descriptive illustration.

TIP This is a good example of how to divide your information into readable chunks!

TIP There are multiple ways to design your chunks! Did you know they are are also great as a guideline on how to use sticky notes!

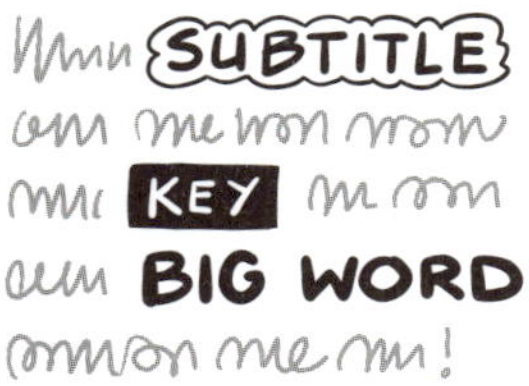

with only text (in a visual way)

with text and small icons

with a combined icon and a title (optionally some keywords)

Decide for yourself what best fits your chunks. Do you prefer to use text, or do you want to avoid words altogether? Everyone has their own preference and style. There's no right or wrong.

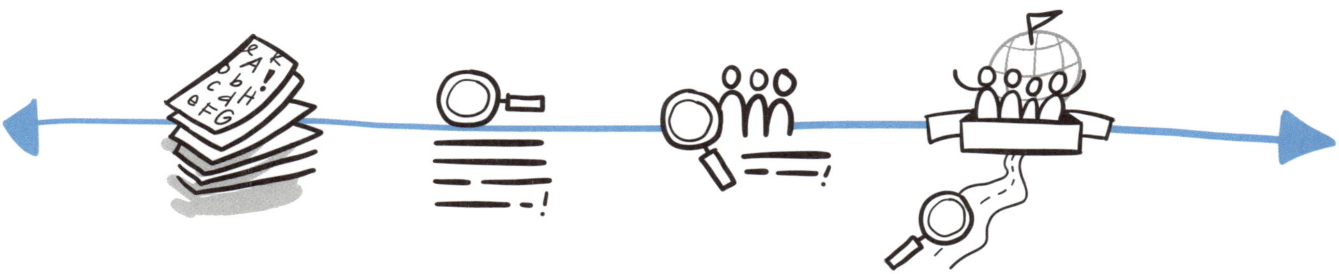

Once you know the separate chunks of information that tell your story, decide what sequence makes most sense.
Which chunks belong together and which stand alone?

Combined with the lay-outs from Chapter 9, you can conjure up a strong and balanced composition. We check to see if our visuals feel balanced left to right, top to bottom. Symmetry is, of course, an easy way to achieve this. But you don't always need to be symmetrical. You can also create balance using colors, text and illustrations.

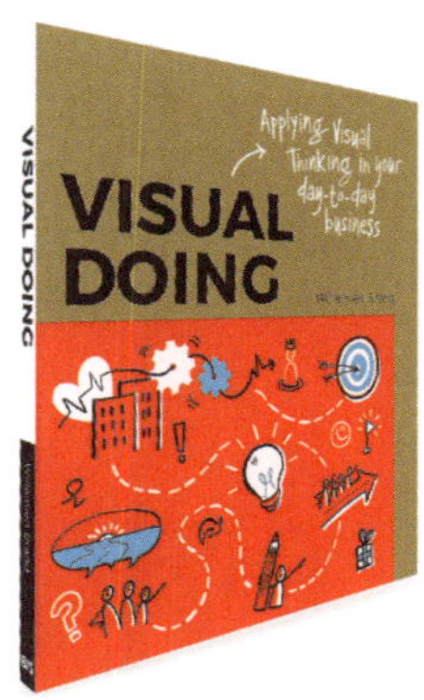

TIP Look at chapter 2 of our Visual Doing book for more information on how to create a visual.

12.2 FINAL ASSIGNMENT

It's time to tie together everything you have learnt so far about Visual Thinking! You can use a metaphor, recognizable icons, typography, frames and containers and decide which colors you want to use.

Draw up your own mission statement! What's important to you? What is your main mission in your (working)life?

Start with the chunks, make some sketches and then draw the final visual on the page to the right.

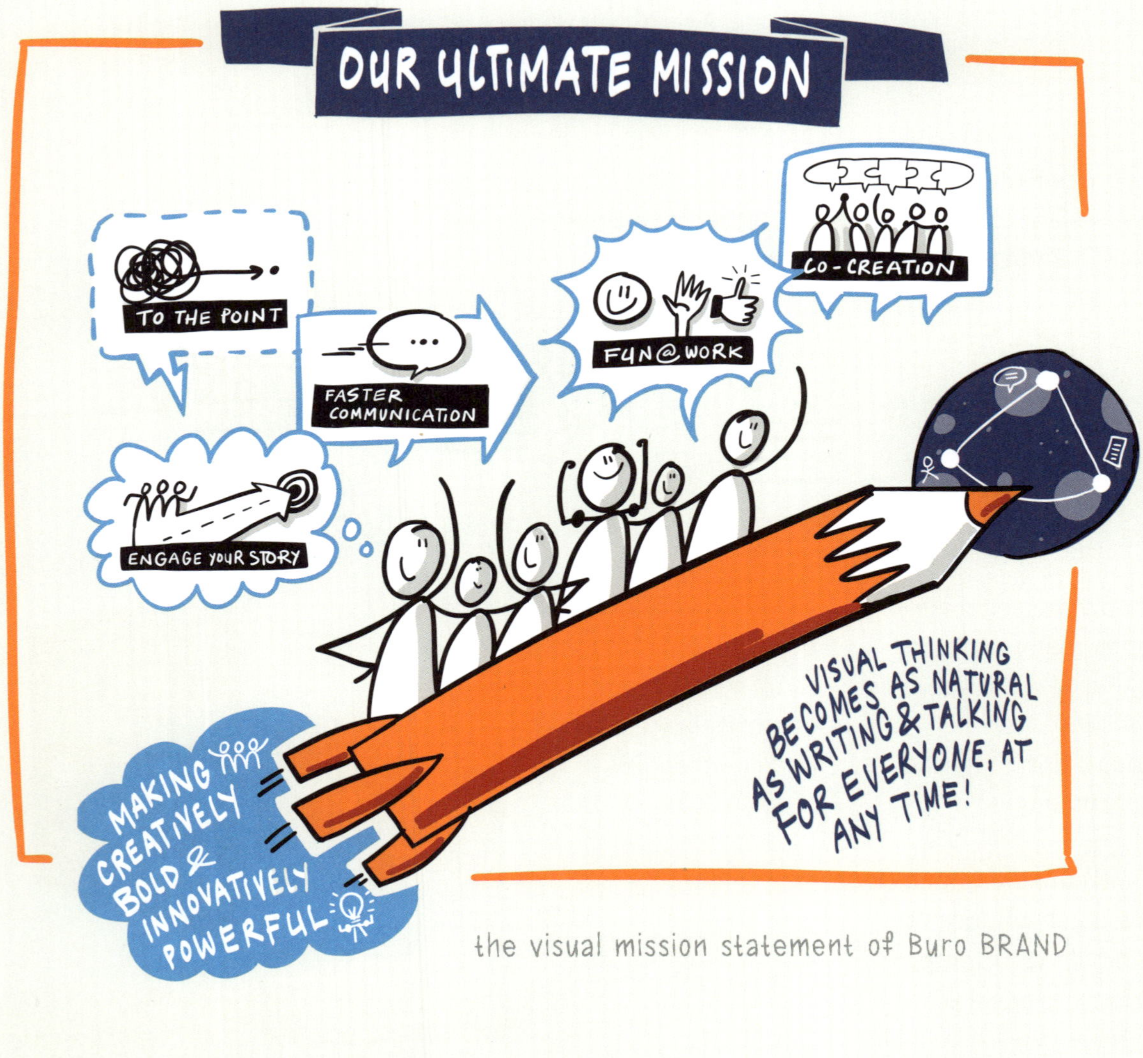

the visual mission statement of Buro BRAND

TIP Look back at how far you've come, from the first page to this final masterpiece! If you're critical of yourself put the book aside for a while. You'll likely apreciate it more when you look back at it in a few months.

CONQUER THE WORLD VISUALLY

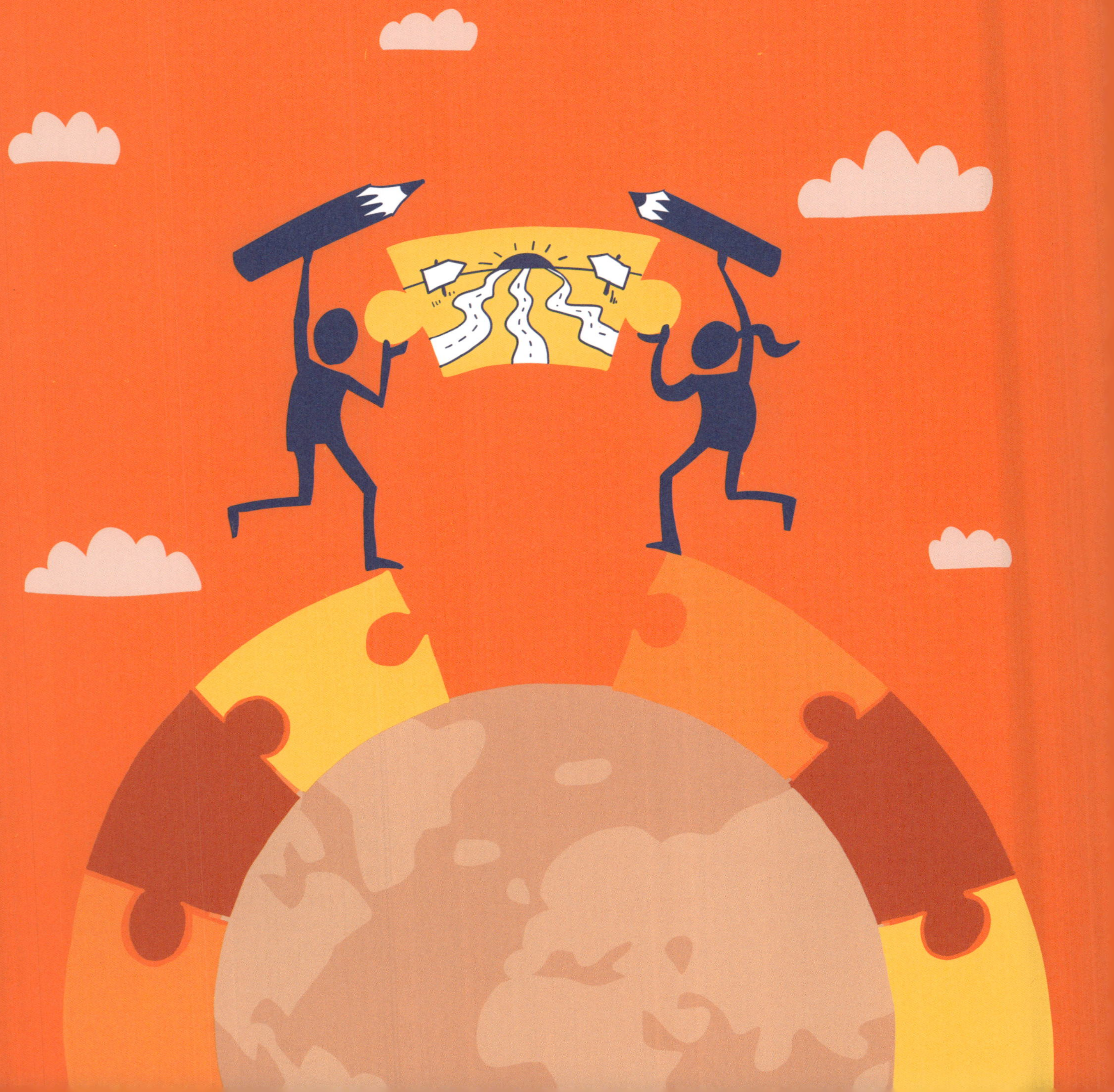

13. ALL GOOD THINGS END

You've made great progress! From drawing people, to things, to stories, now it's time to wrap things up.

In this final chapter we would like to give you some tips to keep you drawing after you finish this book. We'll offer some encouragement and inspiration to work more visually. And, of course, we would like to tell you something about ourselves and the other books we have published.

WHAT YOU WILL LEARN

13.1 Recap
13.2 Words of encouragement
13.3 Drawing in this digital era
13.4 About this book

13.1 RECAP

Congratulations, you have taken the plunge into the world of Business Drawing i.e. Visual Thinking and made your first successful attempts at communicating through visualization!

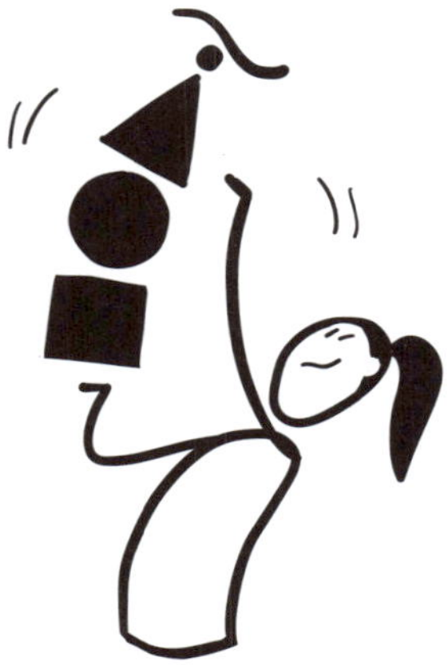

We started this book with some rules and basic shapes. We told you about the materials we use, and gave some general tips and tricks. We practiced drawing recognizable objects from a couple of basic shapes. And we looked at objects and things around us and tried to translate them into business drawings. You now possess the necessary skills and you've drummed up the courage to start drawing.

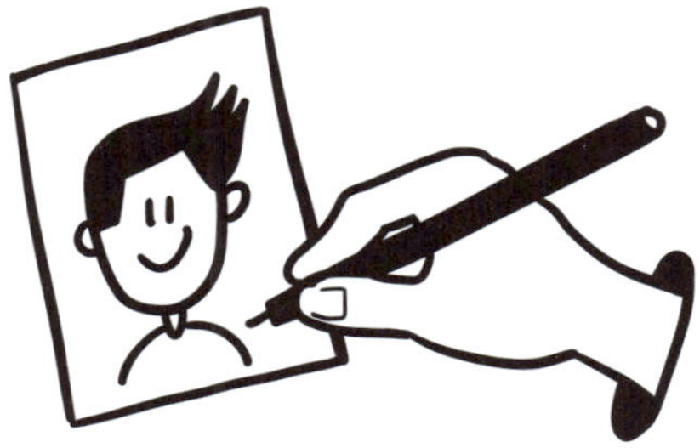

You should now have confidence in your skills at drawing people. We discussed common mistakes when drawing people and looked at interaction, emotion, expression lines and poses. By drawing a scene, we tapped into your creativity.

Next, it was time to beef up your Visual Vocabulary. That's why we covered basic icons. It's important in communicating with drawings to grow and develop your own visual vocabulary, or icon library.

The more icons you know, the easier and better you can express yourself visually. It's just like writing: The richer your vocabulary, the more elaborate and specific your stories become.

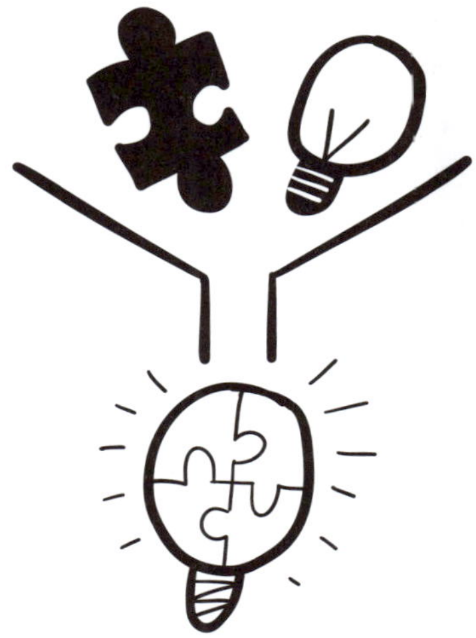

To turbocharge your icons, we taught you to combine them. Finding and using an appropriate icon is one thing, the magic really happens when you combine multiple icons to create images and visual metaphors. Icons are no longer general visuals, they become tailored to your story, enriched with your experience and knowledge. This is where your creativity really kicks in and you tap into the power of visual thinking.

BURO BRAND'S FIVE VISUAL THINKING TYPES

You got to know Buro BRAND's Five Visual Thinking Types©. Each one has its own strengths and opportunities, and hopefully you discovered which types fit you and your goals.

You've learned to use metaphors to tell inspiring stories and help your audience engage with and understand them. Instead of communicating separate pieces of information, a metaphor serves as the thread connecting all elements of your story. We practiced this Visual Storyteller skill by having you introduce yourself through a metaphor.

You can now draw people, behavior and actions. Not only do you how to draw a basic Buro BRAND figure, you can also join them together in groups, customize them, and create your own personal avatar. We brought out the Visual Designer in you by explaining layouts and enhancing your typography.

We wanted to give you the tools to help your audience easily differentiate between important information and minor details.

So we taught you to vary typographies and create visual hierarchy with lettering. That's something that comes in handy when you're working as a Visual Reporter, where sometimes information needs to be captured in text.

Sometimes, you want your audience to interact through your visuals. Perhaps you want to get feedback, interview someone, or properly organize the input you receive during a meeting. To do that, you've learned how to use and apply containers and frames. They help us structure information afterwards and prepare flip charts and templates beforehand. A very useful skill for a Visual Co-Creator.

To bring even more meaning and coherence to your visualizations, we looked at the power of color coding, patterns and linework. With just a few non-figurative shapes, you can structure and tell a story in a visual. These simple steps can make complex topics and information insightful and approachable. The first steps and skills for a Visual Analyst.

And finally, we challenged you with one last assignment where you channeled everything you did and learned in this book (and beyond) to create your own visual mission statement.

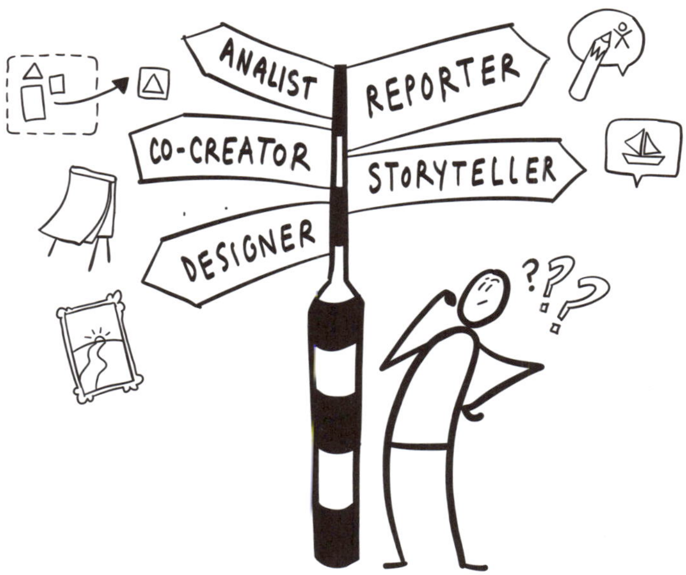

13.2 WORDS OF ENCOURAGEMENT

We can't leave you without some final words of encouragement. People are often hesitant about starting to use visuals. Don't be! Using visuals lets you communicate more clearly and powerfully. So here are some general tips, inspiration and encouragement to help you incorporate Visual Thinking into your day-to-day business.

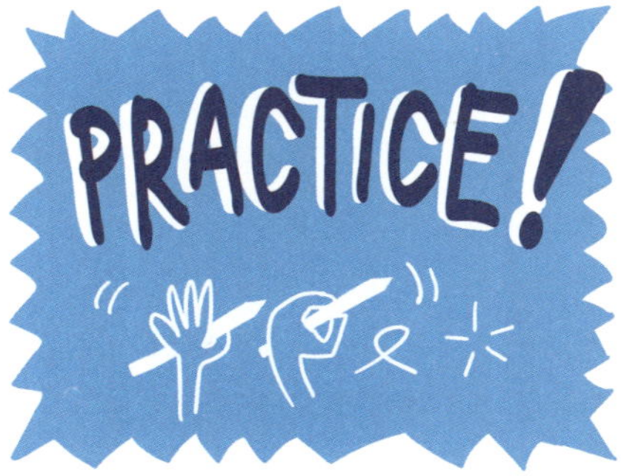

PRACTICE MAKES PROGRESSION

That brings us to our last and most important tip: Practice

To make the most of your drawing, practice, practice and then practice some more! Draw everything at least three times and copy, copy, copy everything you see, until you make it your own. You'll get better, your visual vocabulary will grow and so will your confidence.

Show your drawings to other people and get motivated by their positive reactions. We say: Dare and share!
Consider your drawings as prototypes. Adjust, dare and share again!

Remember, drawing is the same as speaking and writing; another powerful tool to make yourself clearly understood.

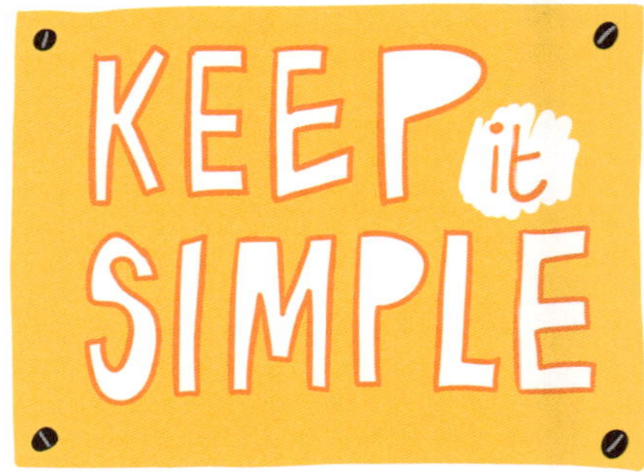

START SIMPLE

If you don't know where to start, keep it simple. Begin by replacing words with icons in your notebook and gradually build from there. Mark a bright idea with a light bulb, or if you're talking about an organization, draw a building with its logo.

Use a boring meeting or call to doodle icons about the subject being discussed. These could be your first visual notes!

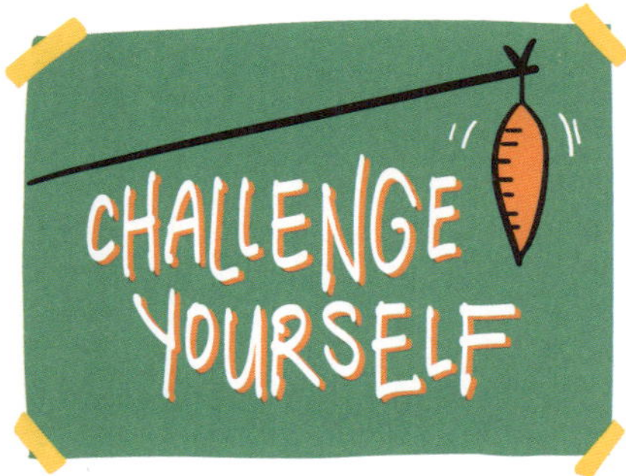

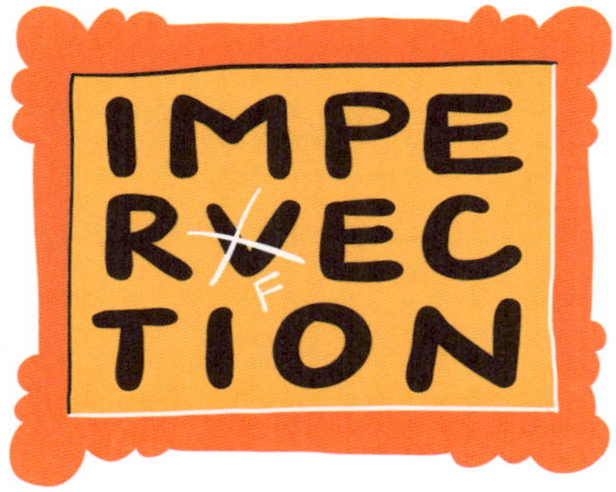

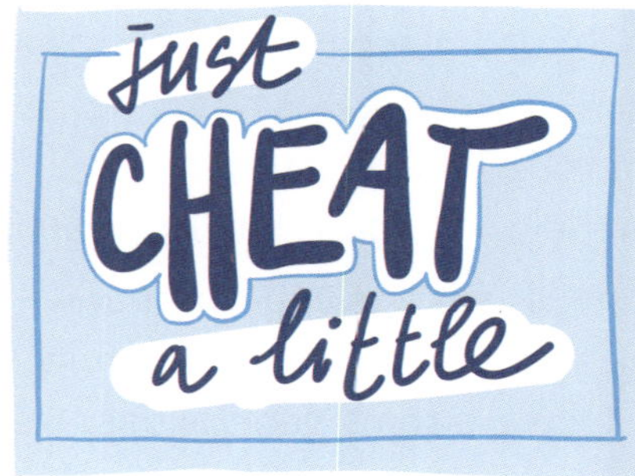

FIND TOPICS

You can also expand your own visual library. Every week, choose two words to visualize.

Find challenges that inspire you to draw. Why not make an infographic of your life story? You can also take part in (online) drawing challenges.

EMBRACE IMPERFECTION

You can even 'embrace' the imperfection, by placing extra emphasis on it. For example, if you've made an error in your drawing or text, draw an arrow pointing at it and write what it should have been.

Or draw two people discussing what the drawing actually represents. Sometimes an imperfection can be more memorable and generate feedback and fresh ideas.

BE PREPARED

Do you work a lot on flip charts, and are you excited to draw live? It can be scary to start drawing for an audience, so why not cheat just a little? Prepare your flips by lightly outlining what you plan to draw live. When the time comes, you just trace over the light lines with black.

After a while you will develop enough confidence to stop preparing the flips, and will only need to sketch beforehand on a separate piece of paper. Practicing and experience will give you the skill and courage to draw live and freehand.

TIP To practice drawing, why not create your own birthday cards for friends and family? They will value your personal touch far more than any shop-bought card!

Building on our general tips, advice and encouragement, let's finally drill down briefly into each of Buro BRAND's Five Visual Thinking Types©. Hopefully we can help you choose which one(s) to really focus on.

VISUAL STORYTELLER

To practice your Visual Storytelling skills: at your next presentation, replace snooze-inducing PowerPoint slides with a catchy metaphor. Use slides with an image that represents your story. Limit yourself to one sentence or a few key words of text per slide. Your audience will thank you!

VISUAL DESIGNER

Discover your own drawing style to become more fluent as a Visual Designer. Now you've mastered (we hope!) how to draw the Buro BRAND-style figure , see if you can adapt it to fit your style.

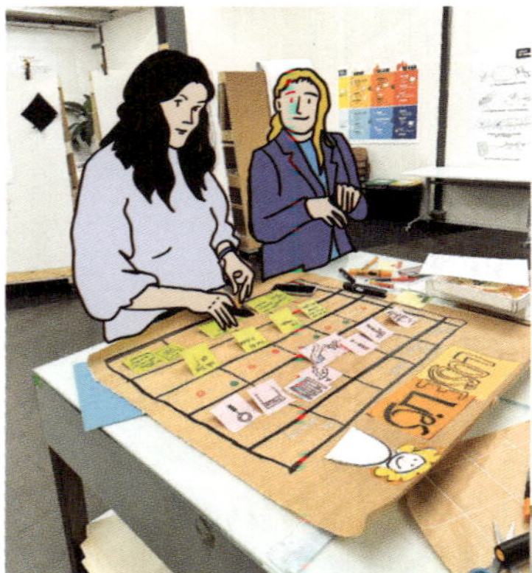

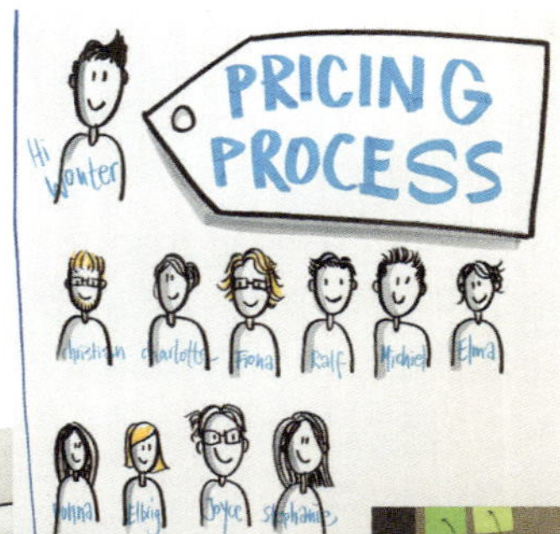

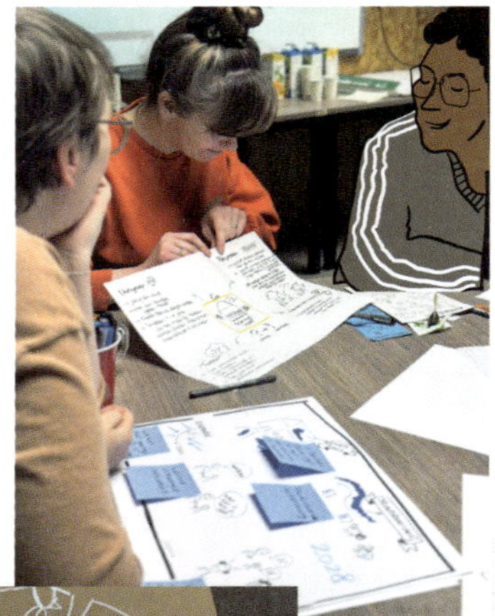

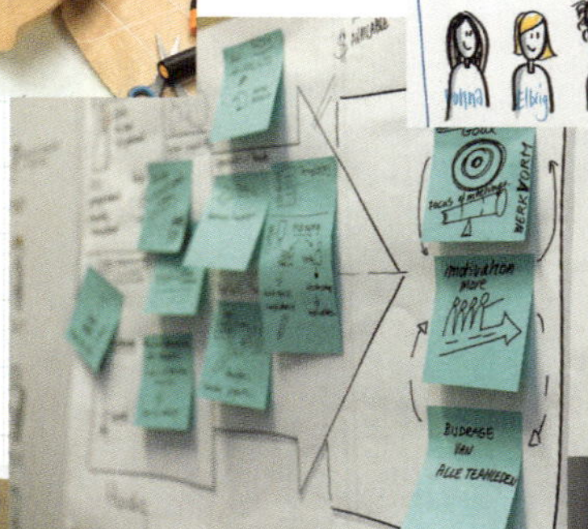

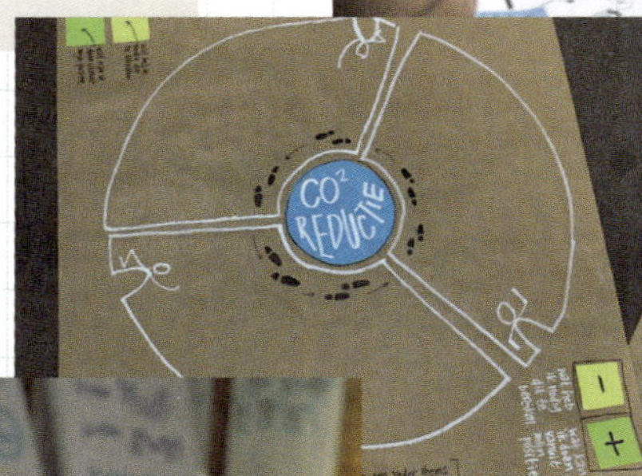

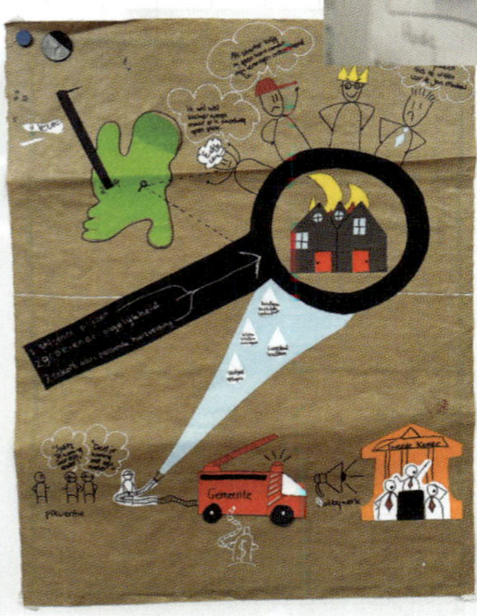

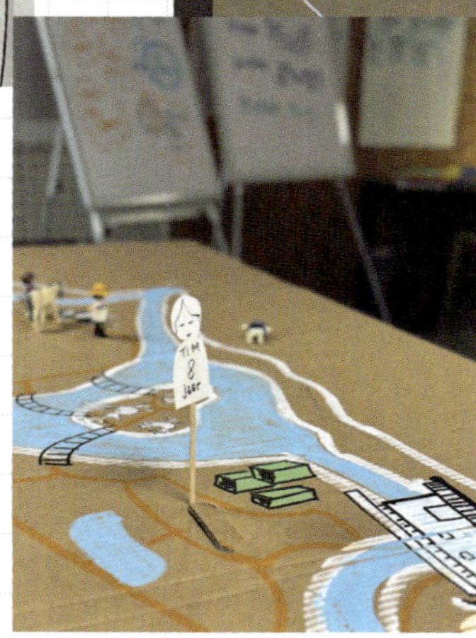

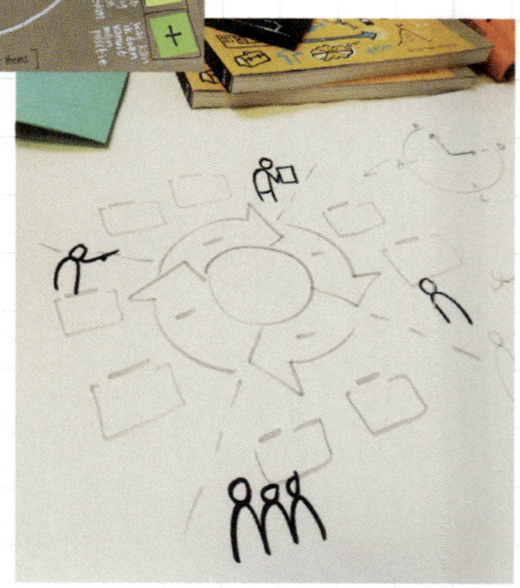

VISUAL REPORTER

Visual Reporting takes practice, so start small when making visual notes. It can help to make a personal typography plan. Choose two or three different typographies and decide when you'll use each one. Soon, you won't have to think twice about which typography to use. And when you've gotten used to applying those different typographies in your notes, put them in a container, draw a small icon next to it and continue from there by adding more and more drawings!

VISUAL CO-CREATOR

Make your moments of co-creation more visual. The next time you have a one on one meeting, or a clearly structured discussion, make a visual template for it. Plan ahead by making containers for the different parts of the meeting, so notes have a predefined spot. Visually label calls to action or outcomes. Amaze your colleagues with your meeting template, invite them to help fill it with sticky notes, and send photos to them afterwards as a visual summary of the meeting.

VISUAL ANALYST

An easy first step to being a Visual Analyst is color coding. You can apply this skill to mindmaps, data sets or sticky notes at brainstorming or planning meetings. Try imposing structure on a complex document or process you're working on. Link to the actual document with colors or icons and get a better grasp of the 'whole' instead of getting bogged down in details.

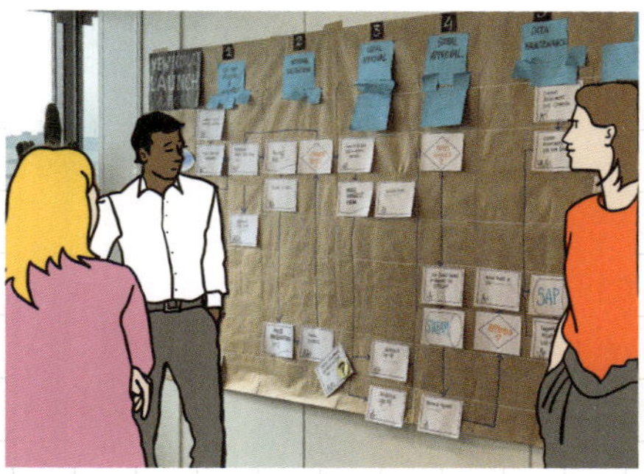

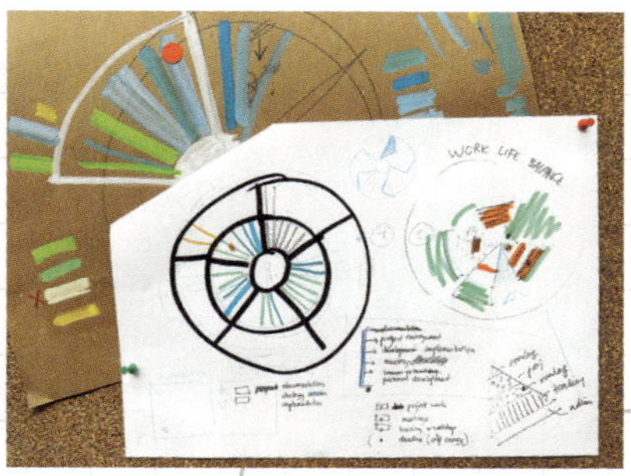

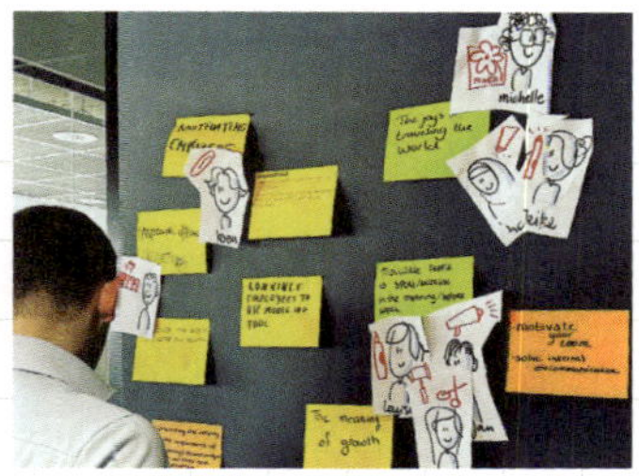

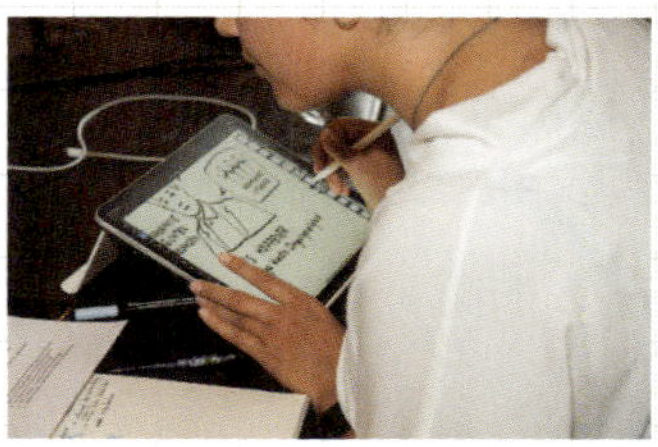

In this book you've gotten to know Buro BRAND's Five Visual Thinking Types©. Now it's time for you to discover which ones fit you best.

When you're ready to specialize in one or more of these types, go out there and learn it by doing or follow one of our training courses.

We hope you're inspired to practice and broaden your Visual Mind!

13.3 DRAWING IN THIS DIGITAL ERA

In this book you drew analog, with actual markers. There's no better way to get a feel for how drawing works and to build confidence. Even so, you might prefer making digital drawings, whether it's on an iPad, other tablet, a touchscreen computer or one of those more paper-like devices such as a Remarkable. They're all good options as long as you can use a (pressure sensitive) pencil.

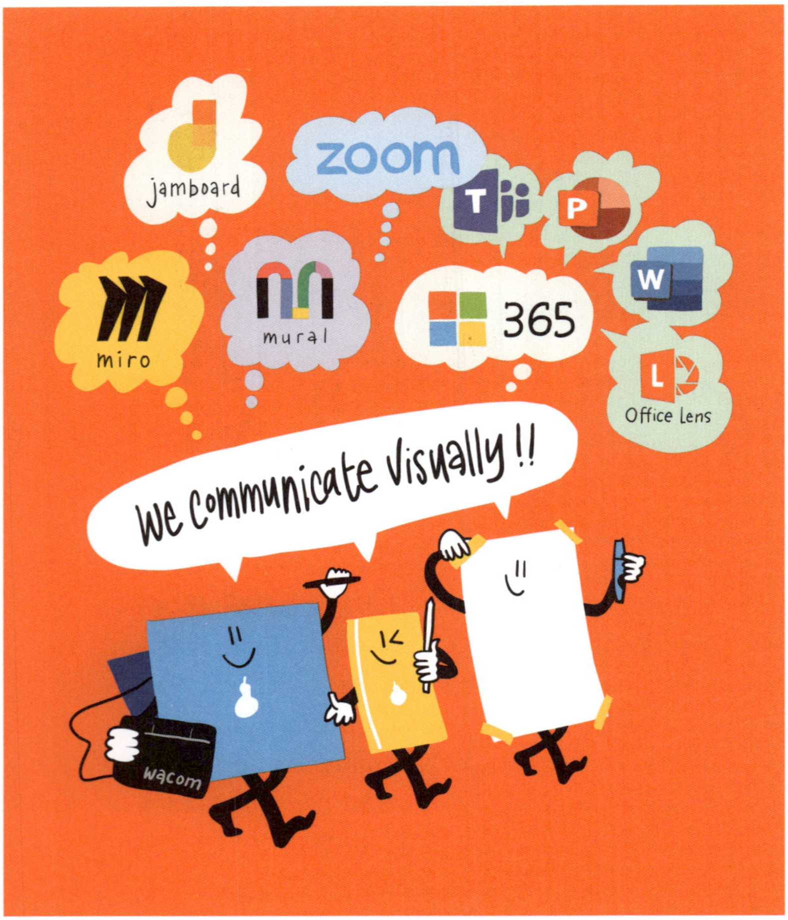

DIGITAL DRAWING

There are loads of different drawing programs and apps. We use a range including OneNote and PowerPoint, Miro and Mural, as well as actual (artistic) drawing apps such as ProCreate and Adobe Fresco.

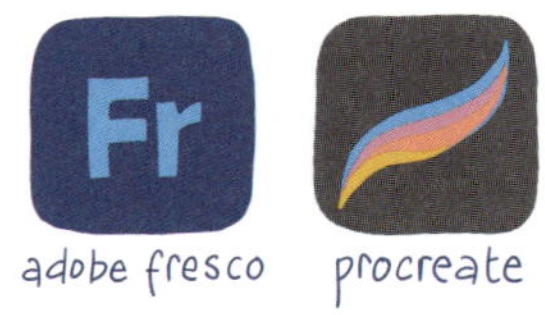

Working on our iPads gives us the freedom to continue our drawings on the computer or to instantly upload them to PowerPoint or e-mail. And don't forget digital meetings. We log in with our iPads so we can share our screen, explain something or draw along. Zoom or Teams whiteboard is great for that as well!

TIP Try out different tools, and see which one works well for you (or which one doesn't).

ANALOG DRAWING

For those that like to stick with paper, We get it! It gives you some much-needed screen downtime. We love to draw on paper when we're trying to understand something, want to impose structure or ideate.

When you've drawn something you're really happy with on paper, you want to share it with others!

Mostly you want to share it digitally. You can simply take a photo with your phone. Don't forget to adjust the brightness and contrast and make sure you have good lighting and no shadows.

Alternatively, you can scan your drawing as you would with a (text) document. It's easy with your phone and your drawings will look brighter, whiter, and more professional. Just use the 'scan document' functionality on your phone, maybe in your notes app, or download an app like Adobe Scan.

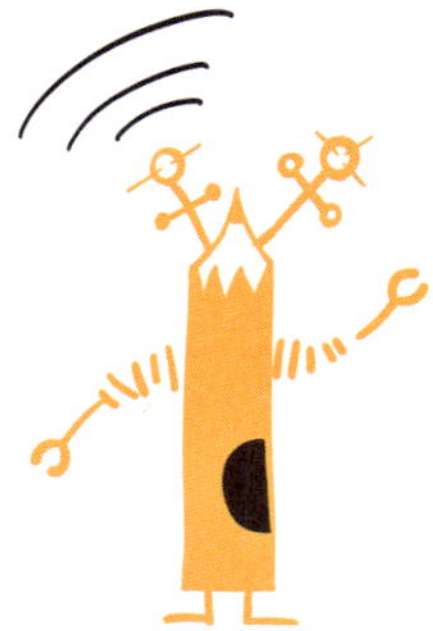

A.I.

We can't ignore recent developments in technology and the ongoing debate over AI-generated art. The controversy basically boils down to a clash between those who embrace its innovative potential and others who defend traditional artistic values. Supporters highlight AI's ability to analyze vast data and produce intricate creations. Critics, however, worry about eroding the human touch and emotional depth in art, raising concerns about authenticity, authorship, and fair compensation. As AI-generated art challenges established norms, it prompts crucial discussions about art's essence, copyright, and the evolving relationship between technology and creativity.

We cannot predict what this technology will mean for accessibility of drawings and images, but it for sure will get easier to communicate visually. With tools such as DALL-E or Midjourney you can already create images you could never find online or make yourself.

With Stable Doodle you can have a little more control because you can make a sketch first. There is probably already something new that works even better.

The downside for us is that, as far as we know, you cannot stick to a certain style, or create images following your company's brand guidelines, yet.

But AI could be great to:

- brainstorm about visuals
- make mock-up visuals
- inspire visual notes
- create style or color proposals

Whether you love AI or hate it, it will change the way we work. Communication, collaboration and co-creation will only get more important. Therefore it is still very valuable to be able to pick up a marker and explain your ideas to someone. And as a bonus, visualizing skills and knowledge can only help you when using visual AI.

13.4 ABOUT THIS BOOK

WILLEMIEN BRAND

Willemien turned her passion for drawing and design into her life's work. After graduating with distinction from the prestigious Design Academy Eindhoven, she had an award-winning career as an industrial designer before founding the successful visual communication company Buro BRAND, based in the Netherlands.

The longer she worked in communication, the clearer it became to Willemien that drawing and visual thinking can break down complex problems, engage employees and build bridges. She never goes anywhere without a pen. In meetings her paper and tablet reveal strategy, plans and future actions. Now she shares her passion and skills with people and companies around the world as one of the leading figures in the visual communication revolution. Her primary Buro BRAND's Five Visual Thinking Types© are the Visual Co-Creator and Visual Reporter.

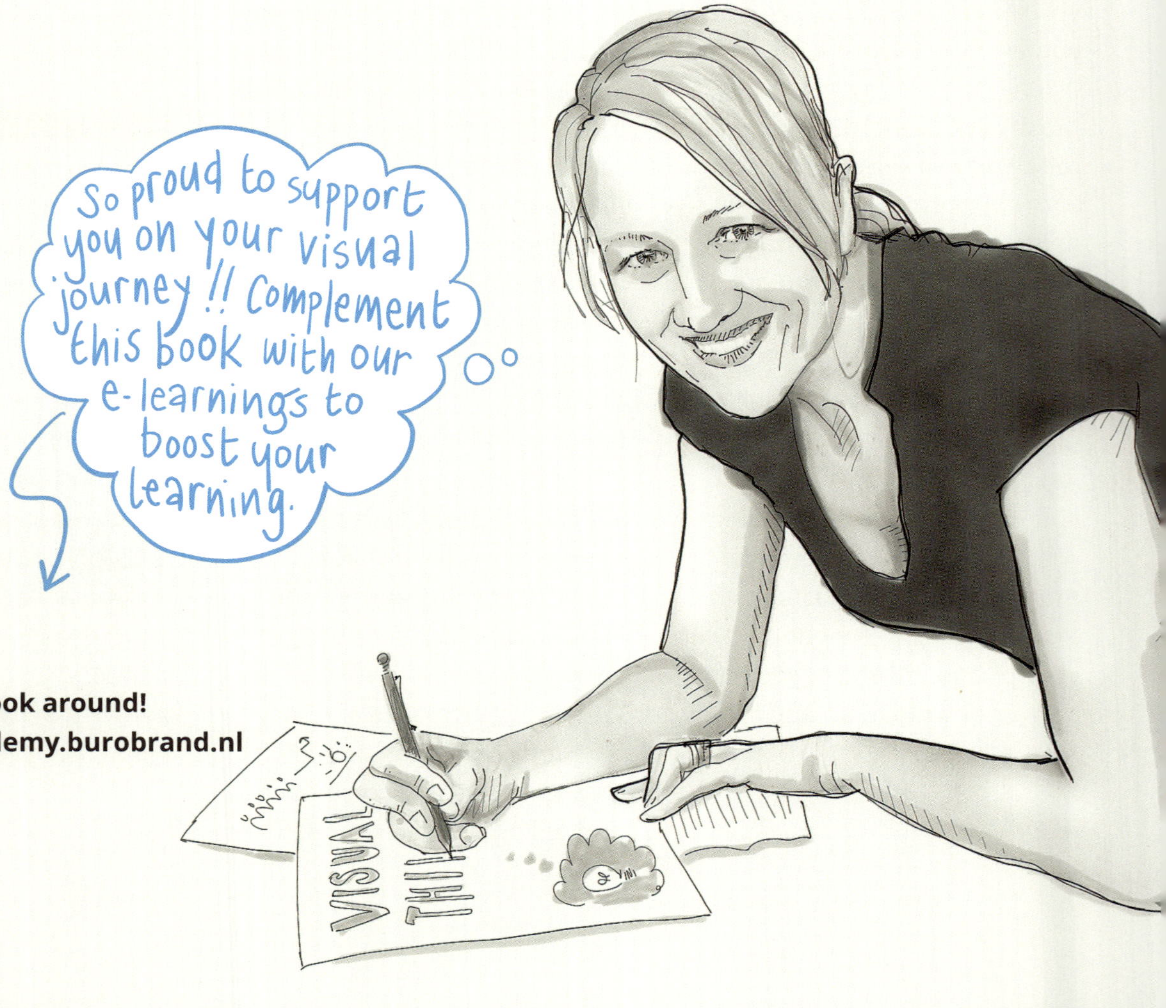

Come and take a look around!
visualthinkingacademy.burobrand.nl

GEORGETTE PARS

As program manager at Buro BRAND, certified Scrum Master and professional Visual Thinker with a background in design, Georgette helps people and organizations find structure and focus so new ideas can emerge. Georgette has always had an interest in communication and a keen eye for contradictions and misunderstandings. She discovered that it's hard to convey a crystal-clear, unambiguous message using only words. In business settings, it is such an important skill to be able to grab a pen and support your story with visuals! Her primary Buro BRAND's Five Visual Thinking Types© are the Visual Co-Creator and Visual Analyst.

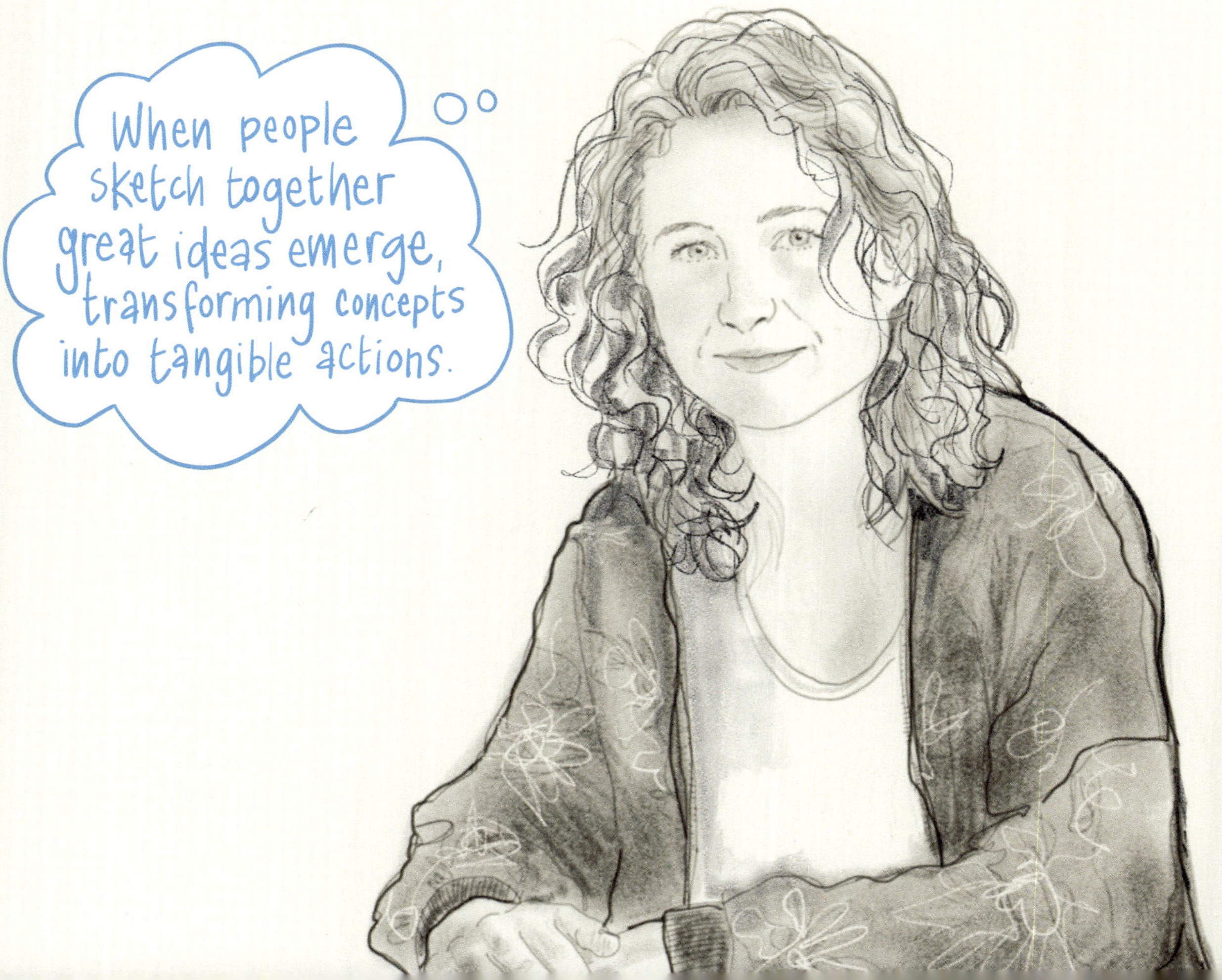

MAHANA TUIMAKA

She shines as visual facilitator at Buro BRAND, just like she shines on the rugby pitch. With a master's degree in Design for Interaction, she combines her knowledge of Design Thinking, and user interaction with Visual Thinking.

Mahana's a pro at leading creative sessions where she gets everyone involved and drawing. She's always been quick with brainstorming and communicating conceptual ideas. With the help of modern tools and digital drawing she can quickly translate fuzzy ideas into clear visuals. She's a top-notch Visual Thinker, specializing in storytelling, capturing moments visually, and working with others to create impactful visuals.

Her primary Buro BRAND's Five Visual Thinking Types© are the Visual Storyteller, Visual Reporter and Visual Co-Creator.

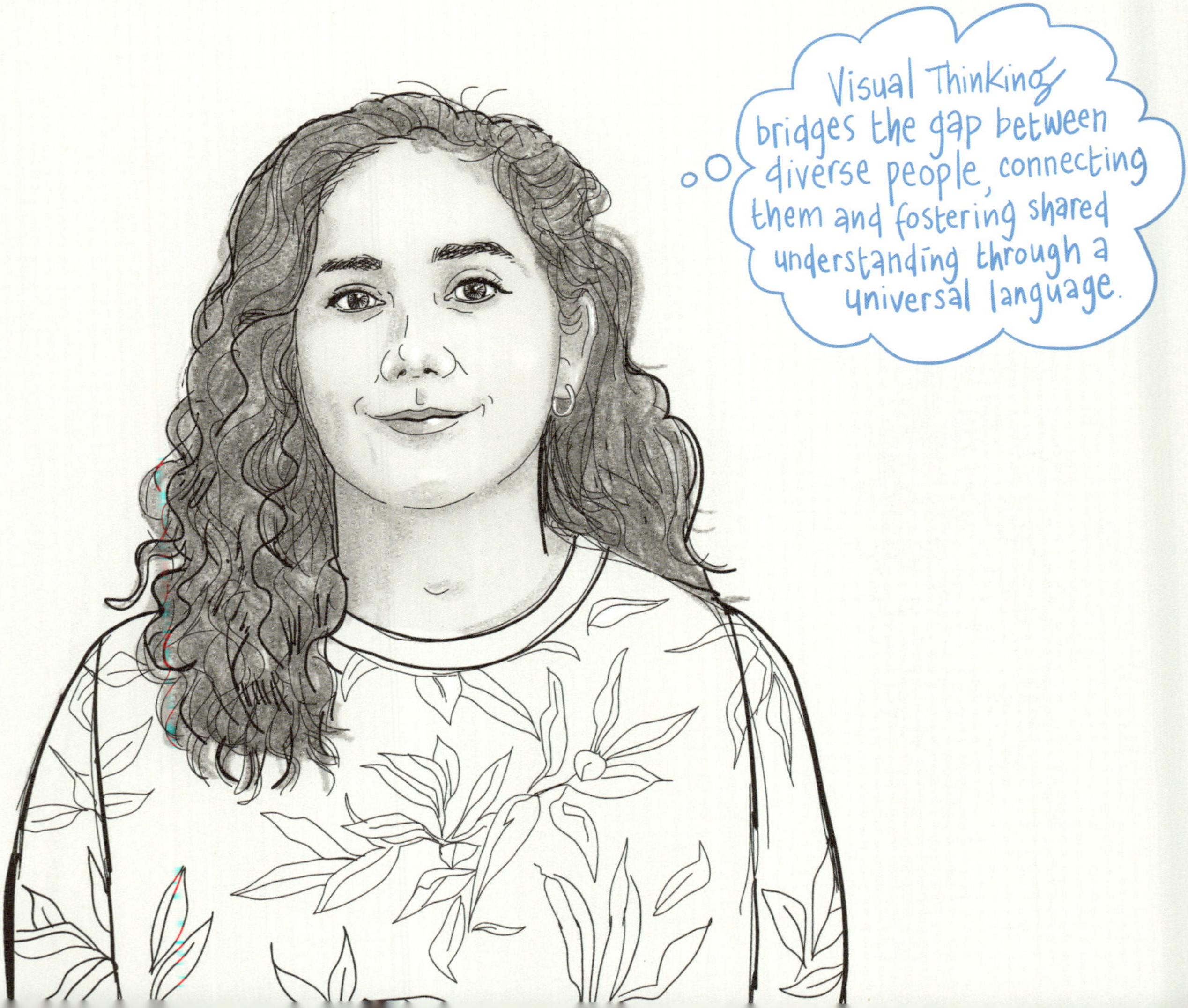

HOW WE MADE THIS BOOK

The creation of this book could not have been possible without the help of so many people! A special thank you to all our Buro BRAND colleagues for the support, inspiration and critical notes!

All illustrations in this book were done on a 12.9-inch iPad Pro with an Apple Pencil. We used the Adobe Fresco app, in combination with Adobe Illustrator on the desktop.

In addition to Willemien's own handwriting we used the following fonts:

Montserrat
Open Sans
American typewriter
buroBRANDhandwriting

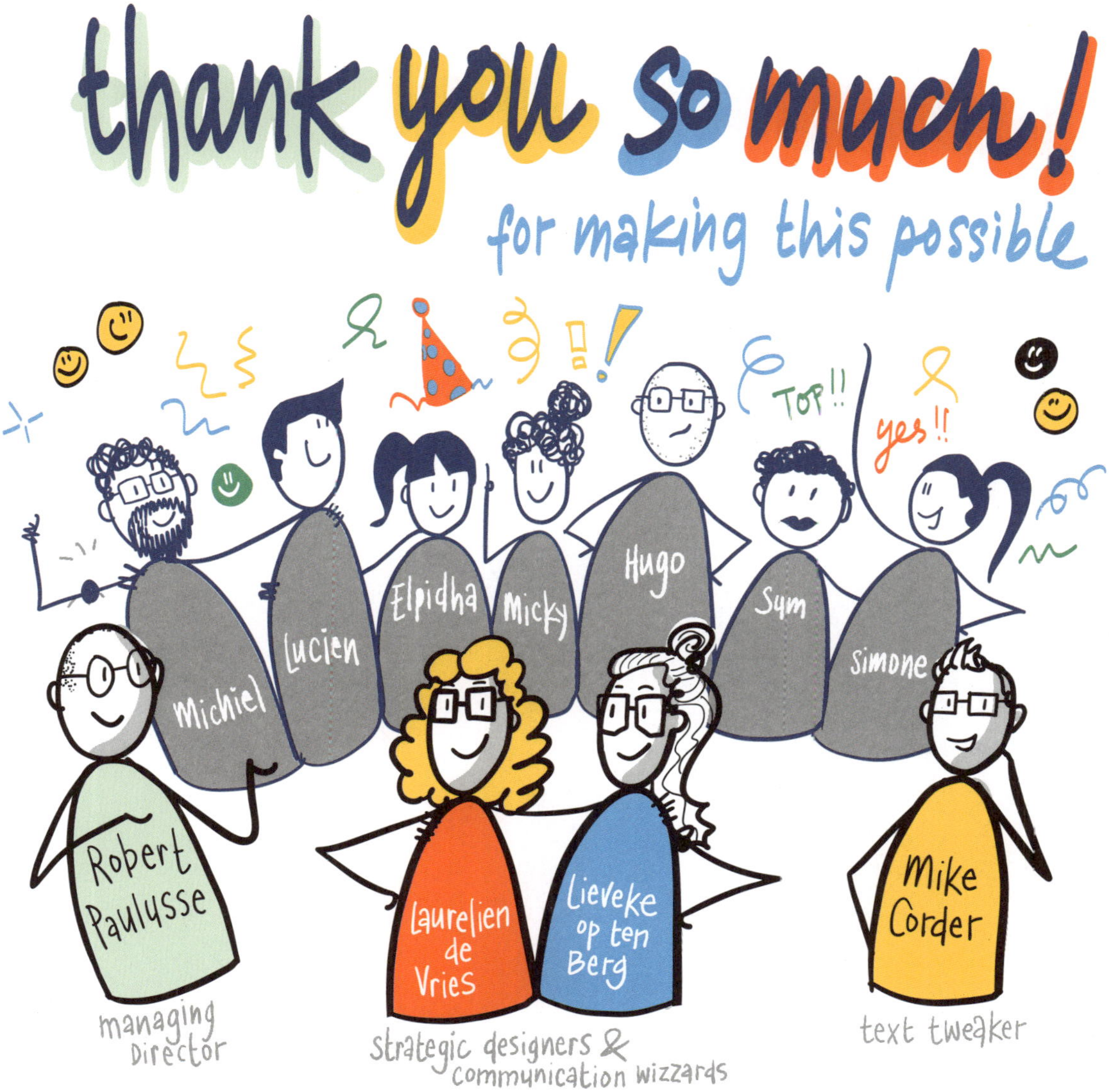

OUR OTHER BOOKS

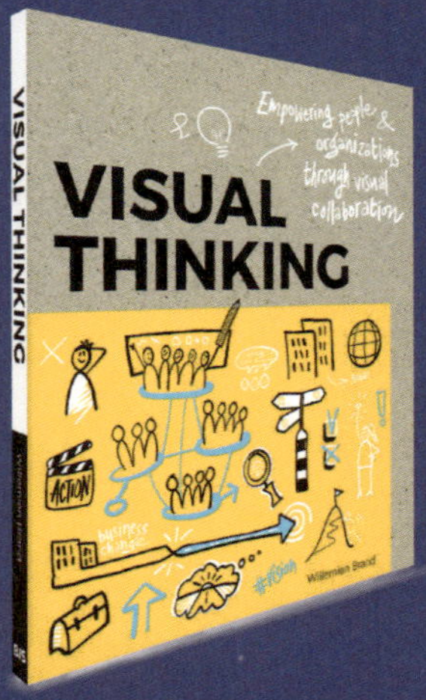

Visualization is a crucial part of the journey for companies seeking to boost enterprise agility, break down silos and increase employee and customer engagement.

Visual Thinking will help brush aside misconceptions that may have prevented you using these techniques in your workplace. From learning basic drawing skills to proven tools and models visually executed.

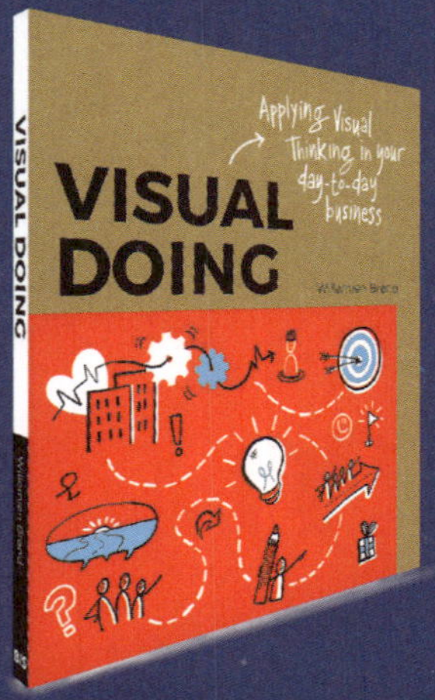

Companies are changing and in order to adapt and keep up they need to be flexible and fast. This calls for new tools and a visual culture within your organization.

Visual Doing leads you through a new range of exercises, techniques and subjects which will help you to tell your own visual story by looking at these subjects from different perspectives: 'me as an individual', 'we as a team' and 'us as a company.'

My Icon Library is an essential collection of impactful drawings that will empower you to embark on your own journey of visual thinking and storytelling.

My Icon Library is a source of inspiration and a go-to reference for whenever you need a visual that's a tad too complicated for your imagination or a Google Images search.